ALSO BY HENRY ALFORD

Would It Kill You to Stop Doing That?: A Modern Guide to Manners

How to Live: A Search for Wisdom from Old People
(While They Are Still on This Earth)

Out There: One Man's Search for the Funniest Person on the Internet

Big Kiss: One Actor's Desperate Attempt to Claw His Way to the Top

Municipal Bondage

AND THEN WE DANCED

A VOYAGE INTO THE GROOVE

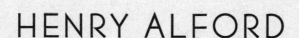

HENRY ALFORD

Simon & Schuster

New York   London   Toronto   Sydney   New Delhi

Simon & Schuster
1230 Avenue of the Americas
New York, NY 10020

First Simon & Schuster hardcover edition June 2018

SIMON & SCHUSTER and colophon are registered trademarks
of Simon & Schuster, Inc.

For information about special discounts for bulk purchases,
please contact Simon & Schuster Special Sales at 1-866-506-1949 or
business@simonandschuster.com.

The Simon & Schuster Speakers Bureau can bring authors to your
live event. For more information or to book an event, contact the
Simon & Schuster Speakers Bureau at 1-866-248-3049 or
visit our website at www.simonspeakers.com.

Interior design by Carly Loman

Manufactured in the United States of America

10 9 8 7 6 5 4 3 2 1

Library of Congress Cataloging-in-Publication Data

Names: Alford, Henry, 1962– author.
Title: And then we danced / Henry Alford.
Description: First Simon & Schuster hardcover edition. | New York : Simon &
    Schuster, 2018.
Identifiers: LCCN 2017044367| ISBN 9781501122255 (hardcover) |
    ISBN 9781501122262 (trade paper) | ISBN 9781501122279 (ebook)
Subjects: LCSH: Dance—Social aspects. | Dance—Humor. | Dancers—
    Biography. | Alford, Henry, 1962– —Humor.
Classification: LCC GV1588.6 .A44 2018 | DDC 792.8—dc23
LC record available at https://lccn.loc.gov/2017044367

ISBN 978-1-5011-2225-5
ISBN 978-1-5011-2227-9 (ebook)

CONTENTS

INTRODUCTION

Can you remember the first time you ever danced? Most of us cannot.

I mean, it's entirely possible that you or I boogied down while we were still in the womb, as Isadora Duncan claimed she did, maybe gently roiling our mother's amniotic fluid with a tiny, Fosse-esque shoulder isolation.

Or maybe it was more high-minded. Maybe, like Fred Astaire, we speculatively put on a pair of ballet slippers at age four to kill time while waiting for our irritatingly talented older sister to finish her dance class.

Or maybe we used a gardening implement to stun a small visitor—as Twyla Tharp did a rattlesnake at eleven or so, creating what she considers her first "dance"—and thus yielded a densely layered critique of man's effort to achieve dominance in the face of unnecessary slithering.

But it's all a little hazy.

However, I can remember the first time that I actively *enjoyed* dancing. Come with me now to suburban Worcester, Massachusetts, to a sunshiny Saturday afternoon in 1975. Behold my thirteen-year-old self, all boyish enthusiasm and buckteeth as I whiz past you on the street; savor the utter awesomeness of my bright orange Schwinn and its Naugahyde banana seat. That single bead of sweat on my brow? It may not be purely the result of strenuous bicycling. You see, I'm going to a girl's house and, anxious to convince myself that I'm heterosexual, have seemingly rendered my stomach a breeding ground for gossip-dispensing hummingbirds. Indeed, I had recently trimmed the plastic tassels hanging down from my bike's handlebars from five inches to two: a bold attempt to advertise my startling masculinity.

My classmate Carolyn had just bought the groovetastic Earth, Wind & Fire single "Shining Star," and she and our mutual friend Dorothy had invited me over to listen to it.

On arrival, I was surprised to learn that, while listening to the song, the girls had been practicing something I'd never heard of, a "line dance." Lion dance? Lyin' dance? My head teemed with possibilities, all of them potentially injurious to my air of short-tasseled machismo.

What alien forces allowed me to enjoy this session with Carolyn and Dorothy in a way that I'd not enjoyed previous dancing? I'm not 100 percent certain; I'm still working my murder board. But I've got two suspects. First, here was dancing proposed by a peer, not by a parent or teacher. Second, here was irresistible music.

The opening of "Shining Star" is an inviting tangle of what some would call "wet" bass notes: they're so reverberant and fuzzed that you can almost see them twist out of your speakers like a strand of DNA. This exciting jumble is followed by a sudden jagged rock face of horns. Then, before the lyrics proper begin, we get a string of invocations and greetings ("Yeah! Heyyy? Huh!"), the effect of which is to make the listener feel like he or she has arrived at the most honey-soaked, superfunkadelic part of the universe.

The line dance that Carolyn and Dorothy taught me was that conglomeration of mid-seventies grapevining and hand clapping, the Bus Stop—an assembly line of fun that features less flapping than the Funky Chicken but more dignity than the Bump.

It did not look like anything *I* had ever seen at a bus stop. Also, it felt like a shit-ton of choreography to me. But the fact that we stood shoulder to shoulder while dancing meant that we didn't have to look at one another, which hugely reduced the potential embarrassment. Dance is often a form of sexual sublimation, particularly if you are thirteen and in the darkish basement of a cute person whose hair smells like strawberries.

Moreover, the part of the Bus Stop where you tap your heels together twice was hilarious to us: it was so dorky and awkward-looking that any thoughts we might have developed about looking good were quickly siphoned off into a beaker called Comedy. Months later, when we ran into one another in the hallway at school, we'd each do the heel tap in the manner of a secret handshake. Like the signature move from the Hustle that John Travolta would immortalize in *Saturday Night Fever* two years later (point right index finger to left of left foot, then point same as far up and to the right of your head as possible), the heel-tapping was the part of the dance that you could really make a meal of. It was the part through which you could let the world know that your orientation was primarily ironic. If you crooked your elbows while tapping heels, you rendered your body particularly poultry-like, as if your feathers had been plucked and now your margarine-yellow carcass was dangling from some car's rearview mirror.

Yes, please.

I bring all this up not because I'm interested in smothered teenage sexuality (well, maybe a little), but rather because I'm intrigued in an anthropological sense by how the function of our Bus Stopping shifted. While boogying in Carolyn's basement, our movement was a way for the three of us to mediate in an unthreatening way the tangle of hormones swirling through our bodies: dance moves as flirtation. But at school when we three—and, gradually, three or four other classmates joined us in this—did the heel tap and the poultry arms, we were forming a group or private club: dance moves as insiderism. Then, thirdly, I remember later sitting on a bench at school one afternoon for a top-secret consultation with a classmate, and him signaling to me the oncoming presence of our teacher by tapping his heels together: dance moves as baby cam.

Of all the arts, dance is the most porous and adaptable. If words are the way that humans pinpoint and define experience, then it makes a certain kind of anti-sense that pure, wordless movement is a universal language. With the exception of certain gestures that some cultures find impolite or wanton, most physical movement is readable around the world: if, while standing in a busy intersection in Boston or Beijing or Abu Dhabi, you put your hands up in the air and start shimmying your shoulders and clapping rhythmically, most bystanders can figure out that you're not having trouble hailing a taxi.

Even better, though, is the fact that this universal language has crazy range: dance can relax you or whip you into a frenzy; it can be wholly instinctive or utterly self-conscious, fancy or down-and-dirty, mild or strenuous, communal or private. For some people, it's a spaceship: "To dance is to be out of yourself. Larger, more beautiful, more powerful," wrote Agnes de Mille, who changed American concert dance with her "cowboy ballet," *Rodeo*, in 1942 and who changed musical theater with her choreography for *Oklahoma!* a year later. For others, dance is a battle cry. As Gillian Lynne, the British ballerina who went on to choreograph *Cats* and *Phantom of the Opera*, puts it, "Nipples firing!"

Sometimes dance is a few different things at the same time. Consider the viral Running Man Challenge videos of 2016. Started by two New Jersey teenagers and then made popular by a pair of University of Maryland basketball players, the Challenge saw groups of people filming themselves doing variations of the street dance the Running Man to the song "My Boo" by Ghost Town DJ's. The meme spread to the NFL and the NBA, where it proved a winningly madcap way for groups to bond with one another, and maybe also to flex their collective muscles so as to psyche out the competition.

But when the Challenge then spread to police departments—who, at the time, were under fire for their treatment of minorities, with several controversial killings being much discussed in the media—the dance was working on a political level, too. "Yes, we're occasionally malignant, possibly racist defenders of justice," you could almost hear these uniformed officers telling us, "but we're not immune to the charms of precision choreography!"

"Dance is less easily pigeonholed than the other arts," Richard Powers, the Stanford University dance historian, told me in September 2016. I was sitting at his dining room table, high on a hill about ten minutes north of Palo Alto, and the boyishly handsome Powers had grown reflective. He told me, "But I don't think we can afford to sit in an ivory tower and talk about abstract ideals of the art form when we have such pressing problems and such a high degree of intolerance in the world right now."

We were two months away from the presidential election, and it was not uncommon to fall into conversation with strangers about police brutality or Donald Trump's proposed ban of Muslims.

I asked Powers to explain his comment.

Powers, who has taught historic and contemporary social dancing for forty years all over the world, started telling me that he sometimes lures potential dancers into the fold by emphasizing to them how social dance can make its participants succeed in the marketplace. "It's a good entry point," he told me. "They think, Okay, this is something I need."

In his book, *Waltzing*, cowritten with Nick Enge, Powers cites a

2010 scientific study which showed that NBA players who touch one another more in the early season subsequently score more baskets than players who touch less. Testing for causation, the authors of the study concluded that physical touch leads to cooperation and bonding.

Powers told me that to gracefully pull off one of the waltzes or polkas he specializes in, dancers need certain things. "They need to have respect for others on the team—they need to want their dance partner to win. Also, deep listening. And quick adaptability. All three of those are key in *social* social dancing, not competitive social dancing. And all three build empathy. Then, after practicing for weeks and weeks, all this stuff starts to become second nature to you. Dancers start to value one another's differences—they find difference and think, This is good, I can learn from this."

I tried to imagine Donald Trump looking at a dance partner's chador and thinking, Modesty. The only quality missing from my quiver of charms is modesty.

Powers looked out his living room window at a low-flying bird.

When he returned his gaze to me, he unpinned his grenade: "This is what our future leaders can take out into the world to defuse aggressive intolerance."

There's that ever-shifting nature of dance again: an unsuspecting Stanford student enrolls in one of Mr. Powers's classes, perhaps hoping to become more graceful or to find a mate or to learn what in hell a "progressive twinkle" is, and then, months later, Powers sends that student off into the world, a silent warrior with an invisible lightsaber that defuses aggressive intolerance.

What's going on here? Not to go all grandpa on you, but it's tempting, if admittedly a little far-fetched, to note that dance is one of the oldest arts, and thus to surmise that maybe all those extra years of existence have somehow enabled dance to become increasingly porous, to take on more meanings. But maybe a more fruitful tack to take here is to acknowledge that dance, and the reasons that we dance, are usually a reflection of the environment we're situated in. At your neighbor's eighty-fifth birthday, you might do some delicate touch-dancing, perhaps prompted by a desire to celebrate a life or by a desire to work off some cake-derived calories. But when you shimmy at a rock concert, you're more likely a slave to the rhythm, or someone looking to reap the maximum amount of fun from a $100 concert ticket.

The dynamic is even more pronounced with professional dancers. Take, for instance, Katherine Dunham, the dancer-choreographer and anthropologist who's been called "the matriarch and queen mother of black dance." In 1924, when she was growing up in the suburbs of Chicago, for her Methodist church Dunham organized a cabaret, complete with dance numbers, as a fundraiser: dance as community-building. A few years later, while a student at the academically rigorous University of Chicago, she decided to major in anthropology and focus on the dances of the African diaspora: dance as intellectual endeavor. In the 1940s and '50s, while touring with her eponymous dance company, she had frequent run-ins with racial discrimination which prompted her to become an outspoken activist: dance as political prism.

Or look at Louis van Amstel, the Dutch ballroom champion and *Dancing with the Stars* regular. "Dance has meant so many different things to me in the course of my career," he once told a fitness magazine. "At first, all dance meant to me was nothing, because my grandparents wanted me to dance. It wasn't my choice." Then, another color: "After doing my first competition a while later it lit up a fire for me which made me see dance as a sport. It became about winning." A third: "Because of my growing up with alcohol abuse from my parents and their unhappy marriage, I used dance as therapy. I could express my feeling through dance, but didn't have to share my personal feelings with anyone. If it weren't for dance I probably would have ended up becoming an addict myself."

In the upcoming pages, I'm hoping to canvass some of the more compelling roles that dance plays in this country. There are dozens that I won't be able to tackle, but rather than try to pick the functions that are the most representative, I'm going to concentrate on those I find the most interesting.

I'm intrigued, and maybe spurred on, by the fact that all the versatility and utility that I'm ascribing to dance flies in the face of some people's view of the art. Many scholars relegate dance to second-class status among the arts. They usually do this because they think it's a kind of theater, or because it often relies on music (indeed, dance and music are so intertwined for sub-Saharan Africans that many of the region's indigenous languages don't have separate terms for them, though they have a variety of ways to describe specific techniques or styles). This condescension is passed on to generation after generation via cultural osmosis: when I was little, I thought ballet dancers walked on their tippytoes so they wouldn't wake the audience.

I'm also partly fueled by the idea that dance, unless it's filmed, is "the art that vanishes." We tend to overlook this fact today: 2005 saw not only the debut of YouTube, but also of *Dancing with the Stars* and *So You Think You Can Dance*. But many dances created before the advent of film or video are lost to us because dance is so notoriously difficult to notate. Which makes me wonder if maybe all the versatility I'm seeing is a hedge against ephemerality. I mean, if you had owned your own indie coffee shop in the mid-nineties and seen glimmers of the Starbucks behemoth on the horizon, your instinct to diversify in the face of opposition might have led you to the thoughts "lending library" or "something really interesting with the bathroom."

Dance performs another kind of vanishing act, too. Every few decades, tap dancing seems to fade from the national scene; as comedian Louis C.K. says in one of his routines about his nine-year-old daughter, "She takes tap-dancing class. We started her with tap dancing because we figure, by the time she grows up, it'll be the 1930s again. She'll have this thing that she can do. That nobody enjoys watching." When the American appetite for swing dancing started to evanesce at the beginning of the 1960s, the spectacular dancer and teacher Frankie Manning, one of the inventors of the Lindy Hop, was forced to take a job at the post office, where he stayed for more than thirty years until the idiom was revived.

Or look at Jennifer Homans's *Apollo's Angels*. Considered the definitive history of ballet, the 2010 book bodies forth some 550 pages of inspiring and beautifully orchestrated coverage of the classical art before Homans inches her proverbial Ford Thunderbird up to the edge of the cliff for this big finish: "After years of trying to convince myself otherwise, I now feel sure that ballet is dying." Today's dancers, she writes, "seem crushed and confused by [ballet's] iconoclasm and grandeur, unable to build on its foundation yet unwilling to throw it off in favor of a vision of their own."

Thud. Tiny cloud of dust at canyon's bottom.

I should admit that I have a horse in this race. As a writer who specializes in participatory journalism, I'm often paid to enter new worlds, to live briefly in them, and then to type up a clear-eyed dispatch chronicling how a fish breathes out of water. So I'm pretty sure that anyone who is at all familiar with my work, on hearing that I've written a book about my experiences among the bendy, will think of the expression "To a man with a hammer, everything looks like a nail."

But let me recount a conversation that I had one afternoon in the summer of 2012. A friend asked me if any of the walks of life that I'd written about as a participatory journalist had ever subsequently taken root in my real life. I had to think about this. Then I admitted sheepishly, "One of them has."

Was it the story for which I'd made an entire dinner for friends using only items bought at a 99-cent store? Was it the one where Greg and I had traveled to Laos so I could ride and swim with a baby elephant? The one where an officious New York City health inspector had visited our kitchen and given me a failing sanitation grade?

No, the story that took root was one about Zumba. Six months after I'd written about taking Zumba classes, I was waking up at six-thirty two days a week so that I could hustle up to 14th Street to shake it shake it shake it like a Polaroid.

Whugh?

Granted, I had just turned 50, which in gay years is 350. This Giselle was dancing to his death not because a noble disguised as a peasant had betrayed him, but because he worried that his love handles were so shelf-like as to offer suitable support to a collection of decorative thimbles.

But was there something else going on, too?

One way to find out, I realized, was to embed myself by taking classes. Taking classes is a great way to see the functions and versatility of dance writ large, because one generation is handing the torch to the next, consciously or unconsciously offering up answers to the question "Why dance?" So, in the course of my investigations here, I try to partake in as many of the major kinds of dancing as possible. I enter this obstacle course with only a smattering of ballroom and square dancing and a lot of freestyle, rock and roll–type dancing to my name. I am 55 as I write these words, so prepare yourselves for many, many fascinating thoughts about back pain up ahead.

How did dancing—an activity that held no interest for me as a child and that hugely intimidated me as a young adolescent—come to happily occupy a lot of my thoughts and actions in later life?

Maybe if I investigate why *other* people dance, I'll better understand why I do.

Einstein said that the world's most powerful telescope would allow its user to see the back of his own head.

The next dance iteration I turned to after my Zumba sojourn was an effort to reduce stress. Part of its appeal was—and continues to be—that it did not necessitate me leaving the house. You see, I'm a living room dancer. I love to boogie down in my own home, snapping my fingers and spinning in circles just inches away from my coffee table and bookshelves, or to stumble-step to Stevie Wonder on the shag and the sisal. (Not only do I believe that anyone can dance, but I encourage this Anyone to dance wherever the hell he wants to.)

It started in the summer of 2012. I remember clearing the table after Greg and I had finished dinner. I'd written a story for the *New York Times* for which I'd spent five days undercover in Wolfeboro, New Hampshire, the lakeside town where then presidential candidate Mitt Romney vacations. When you write an article for a magazine, you generally are assigned a fact-checker who double-checks everything in your article, but at the paper of record, the writer is responsible for his own work. This is not calming. The potential wrongness of each of the Wolfeboro article's seventy or so facts throbbed gently in my head. The gin and tonic I'd swilled while making dinner hadn't helped. I needed something more galvanizing, more full-body. What to do? I'd already put away the clean laundry I'd brought home from the Laundromat, and Greg didn't need help with the dishes.

So I wandered into our living room, put on some Beyoncé, and started grooving on the white shag rug in front of our bookshelves. It felt immediately soothing. I got my hips swaying with a little Cuban motion, or some approximation thereof, and then I started rolling each of my shoulders backwards like I was trying to beckon a small fawn to scamper away from the forest fire. I became vaguely aware that our living room has no curtains, and thus that neighbors could potentially see me, so I turned off the lights. Even better.

I kept grooving like this following that night, almost always after dinner, usually by myself. An early favorite here was Funkadelic's gospel-tinged funk classic "Can You Get to That," a song which encapsulates the 1960s woolly avowal that intention or thought is a kind of transportation, a trope further evidenced by 1970's "I'll Be There," 1972's "I'll Take You There," and 1973's "Let Me Be There," but which, by the mid-nineties, had soured into the catchphrase "Don't go there."

Did I feel slightly pathetic at this point, trying to "get there" by myself in my living room? Yes, but it subsided. The awkwardness tended to be a reflection of poor music choice. I just needed a stronger beat.

Once I'd determined that I *could*, to the best of my abilities, get there, I then tried to get to other "theres" as described by Aretha Franklin, the Jackson Five, War, Parliament, Rihanna, the Bee Gees, Al Green, Arcade Fire, Hot Chip, and Daft Punk. On days when I hadn't had a chance to go swimming, I made an effort to make the dancing more athletic—I'd fold at the waist, eventually being able to put both palms on the floor, or I'd try to reach as far as possible behind me while standing, as if buffeted by a 7,000 mph wind.

Eventually, Greg started joining in. Then our friend Silvana, who had joined us dancing with Silvana's husband, Craig, one night, gave me a disco ball. It now hangs over the shag rug: a club is born. One night the dance floor even went tributewards. A week after David Bowie died, in January 2016, four of us slightly drunken revelers boogied down to a suite of Bowie songs, culminating in a ring dance to "Heroes."

All this gyrating and bumping into the furniture puts me in mind of a certain expression. Often when a speaker or writer wants to reference an occasion when proceedings reached an emotional peak that is beyond the powers of words, he or she will say, ". . . And then we danced." Prior to this hallowed phrase, the speaker will have offered up a full and highly detailed description of the meal before the dancing; or of the particular kind of half-light seeping through the bar's grubby, faded, cotton curtains; or of the complicated exchange of barbs and deprecations among a group of people that unexpectedly and gradually morphed into consensus and then celebration. But once "And then we danced" is broken out, a cone of silent acknowledgment descends over the conversation, and we all nod our heads knowingly.

We spend our lives trying to describe for one another various incidents and their subtle emotional underpinnings and repercussions, yet when it comes time to cite a moment of huge emotional scope, we rely on a shorthand that describes a wordless activity.

But isn't there more to the story?

DANCE AS SOCIAL ENTRÉE

1.

THE INSTRUCTOR, AN ATTRACTIVE, WELL-DRESSED WOMAN OF a certain age named Jean Carden, looks out at a group of forty boys and girls aged nine to fourteen. We're at the Gathering Place, a large, antiques-dappled catering hall in a sleepy town in North Carolina called Roxboro (pop. 8,632), and the kids are all dolled up: the boys are in blue blazers, neckties, and khakis, and the girls are in party dresses and white gloves. The young folks' collective mood is a study in agitated boredom—imagine a DMV for people who still drink juice out of boxes.

In her honeyed Southern drawl, Carden asks the group, "Do you all recall how to sit pretty? Who's going to sit pretty for me?"

An intrepid eleven-year-old boy raises his hand, and then, given the go-ahead by Carden, awkwardly motions to his partner to take her seat. As the boy lowers himself into the chair beside hers, he remembers to unbutton the top button of his jacket, as instructed.

Carden commends him warmly and then asks the group, "Now, who would like to demonstrate escort position?"

* * *

This is a cotillion, as offered by the National League of Junior Co-tillions, an organization established in 1989 with the purpose of teaching young folk how "to act and learn to treat others with honor, dignity and respect for better relationships with family, friends and associates and to learn and practice ballroom dance." There are now some three hundred cotillion chapters in over thirty states.

Of all the functions of dance that I'll write about, Social Entrée (along with the possible inclusion of Religion) would seem at first blush to be the most rarefied. But that's because, when people think of dance as a vehicle for social advancement, their brains alight first on fancy balls, an admittedly infrequent event in any mortal's life. But once you factor in the cool points or prestige to be earned from going to nightclubs or certain other dances, or to any kind of concert dance, especially ballet, the map for advancement gets decidedly bigger.

The Social Entrée function is usually a form of connoisseur-ship. Typically, man's dignity is linked to thought—the less prac-tical the thought, the more esteem we give it—but who says that ornamental movement and gesture can't occasionally yield re-spect, too? Moreover, as with poetry and opera, dance and its mysteries, not to mention its occasional extravagances, can elicit rolled eyeballs from the stoics and the uninitiated in the crowd—which, in a reverse-psychological way, can strengthen the resolve or exaltation of any individual hip enough to "get it." Membership may, as the advertising world tells us, have its privileges; but rar-efied membership has privileges *and* a vague sense of superiority or resolve.

The session of cotillion I'm watching is number two; after a third class, in a month's time, the kids will attend a ball at a country club in Durham, some forty minutes away. During the ninety-minute class, Carden intersperses the five dances that she teaches—these include the waltz, the electric slide, and the shag—with manners drills. The drill that reoccurs the most—four times—is introducing yourself to others in the room. Carden repeatedly sings the praises of eye contact and a strong speaking voice.

Sometimes the vibe of Bygone Era in the room gives way to heavy irony, usually as prompted by the music played for each assigned activity. When doing a box-step waltz, for instance, many of the kids' affect of grim penitence stands in dramatic contrast to a musical accompaniment the lyrics of which urge them twelve times to "let it go." At another point Carden tells the kids to stand at one end of the room and then to approach her one at a time and introduce themselves. But when she cues the music, the hall fills not with the slinky samba or light processional music that you'd expect, but rather with a heartrending and poundingly operatic version of "Ave Maria." It's a synod with the Pope.

Toward the end of the session, Carden tells the boys to escort the girls to the refreshment table and to avail themselves of lemonade and cookies. Seldom do you see a level of concentration like the one displayed by a nine-year-old boy, under the watchful eyes of a chaperone, a dance instructor, and thirty-nine hungry colleagues, using delicate silver tongs to wrangle a large, floppy, soft-baked cookie. It feels like brain surgery for an audience of cannibals.

Then, once the kids are all seated and nibbling, Carden tells them about their homework. They are to practice rising from a chair five times; to introduce themselves to a new acquaintance; to introduce someone younger to someone older, and someone with an honorific to someone without one; and to give two compliments to family members and two to friends.

When the class is over, I chat up a group of kids, including a shy, ten-year-old boy who spends a lot of our conversation staring at the floor. I ask him if he had fun during the last ninety minutes of his life, and he robotically answers yes. Then I ask him if he thinks having taken cotillion classes for a year has helped him at all. He stares at the maple floorboards beneath us and says, "I like to know what to do when maybe I'm in a restaurant and there are five hundred forks."

I hear ya, kid. My mother sent me to ballroom dancing classes when I was in the fifth grade. "It's what you did then," she told me recently, referencing the way a generalized feeling imparted by the media and acquaintances you meet in the produce section of your grocery store starts to simmer and simmer, finally bubbling over into an act of indeterminate purpose and questionable worth.

Previously, my mother had sent my three siblings to ballroom classes, too. When I asked my brother, Fred, what he thought had prompted her, he wrote me, "I think it was driven by her desire both to inoculate us with good manners and to establish or maintain social position amongst 'the attractive people.' Those urges must have been some mixture of insecurity, wanting to be admired by others, and a pre-digested sense of the proper order of the universe."

The twining of dance and social advancement, of course, has a long history reaching back to the Renaissance, when dance manuals were full of tips about comportment and posture, as if to remind us that "illuminati" rhymes with "snotty." Louis XIV's great achievement in the history of ballet was in the 1660s to lead the idiom away from military arts like horse riding and fencing, where it had been couched, and to push it toward etiquette and decorum.

Because physical touch comes with an implicit set of guidelines and precautions, the successful deployment of same bespeaks sensitivity and self-restraint. As the motto of the dance academy where Ginger Rogers's character works in *Swing Time* puts it, "To know how to dance is to know how to control oneself." Or, as an etiquette guide popular in colonial America coached, "Put not thy hand in the presence of others to any part of thy body not ordinarily discovered."

To this end, dancing, particularly ballroom and ballet, is often linked to the tropes of initiation and entrée—e.g., the first dance at weddings, or the first waltz at quinceañeras, wherein the father of the quinceañera dances with his daughter and then hands her off to her community. Once a dancer has been road-tested, she can be delivered to the new world she has chosen, thereupon to roar off into the night.

For professional dancers, the markers of social advancement are more aligned with quantities such as accreditation and celebrity. The flight path often runs: (1) Train till you bleed. (2) Join a company and distinguish yourself. (3) Write a memoir heavy on bonking. The prestige here is couched in steps 2 and 3, as the world marvels at what company you joined and what roles you danced. But there are lovely exceptions. In 1997 when the tap dancer Kaz Kumagai moved to New York from Sendai, Japan, at age nineteen, one of his early teachers, Derick K. Grant, was so impressed by Kumagai's immersion into and respect for African-American culture—an understandably large part of the tap world—that Grant and other black dancers gave Kumagai the honorary "black" nickname Kenyon. Respect.

Regardless of whether you're a social dancer or a professional one, all this weight can yield confusion and awkwardness. My ballroom classes took place in downtown Worcester, Massachusetts, in the basement of an imposing building that felt like the architectural equivalent of sclerosis. Once a week after school, twelve or so of us would gather and be indoctrinated in the rudimentary outlines of the fox-trot and the waltz. Chest up, shoulders down—how can you be upwardly mobile if you don't have an erect spine?

I enjoyed spending time with my friends: two of the twelve were Carolyn and Dorothy, with whom I'd later do the Bus Stop. They lived in my neighborhood, and were among my closest friends. There was a lot of willed awkwardness about the dancing itself—if you made it look too easy or too fun, then you'd be curbing the amount of time you got to exploit the hallmarks of the adolescent experience, manufactured pain and squirming.

The lesson on offer didn't seem to be about towing the line of being cool, or about dancing, but, rather, about interacting with members of the opposite sex. That a woman's upper torso, save for her shoulders, was out of bounds was not news to me: I had two older sisters and thus knew that breasts and their environs were a no-go area. That sweaty hands were something to be avoided was a more novel idea to me, but certainly brushing my dewy palm against my hip before offering it to my dance partner was not difficult to master. I can wipe.

No, oddly, the biggest challenge of these lessons, it appeared to my then tender mind, had to do with table manners, or should I say, get-to-the-table manners. At these lessons, it turned out, dinner was served: a sturdy Crock-Pot full of gooey, fricasseed mystery awaited us at the end of each class. Each of us was to approach the food table, plop a big spoonful of rice and Crock-Potted goo onto our paper plate, and then tread very, very carefully the twenty or so feet to the dining table.

Not for us the sturdy reinforced cardboard that goes by the name Chinet. No, ours were the bendy, gossamer-thin paper plates which, if picked up by their edges, would immediately taco on you. Which same action caused a dribble of goop to cascade onto your bell-bottoms.

So my first true exposure to dance was, at heart, less kinesthetic than dry-cleanological.

Right around this same time in my life—this is the early 1970s—I'd had my first exposure to modern dance performed live. I was a second grader at the Bancroft School in Worcester, and at assembly one morning in the school's auditorium, a woman danced for us. A zaftig, twenty-something gal in a tie-dyed leotard, she ambled out onto the stage and proceeded to thrash around to some percussive, conga-infused music, her body's rolls of adipose tissue rippling and inadvertently bringing the neon blossoms of her bodysuit to life in the manner of a human lava lamp.

My schoolmates and I could not stop laughing. Why was she moving like that? I wondered. Why the tie-dyed leotard? At this point in my life, I'd become enamored of Carol Burnett and Lucille Ball, and I thought, Surely this pageant of flesh before my eyes is meant to be appreciated in the same light as Ms. Burnett and Ms. Ball's work?

But, no. My homeroom teacher tapped me on the shoulder and looked at me crossly. Later that afternoon, our class was given a special admonitory lecture on art appreciation. We do not laugh at art, we were told. We admire it, we study it. We flat-line our gaping mouths and then cast over the remainder of our face a look of slightly dazed serenity. Later in our lives, we will resurrect this facial expression for run-ins with religious zealots, salespeople, art made from cat hair.

Whether you're watching someone get jiggy with it, or you yourself are the jiggy-getter, you need to cultivate a sensitivity about the flesh on parade. This can be particularly acute for the jiggy-getters. In the late seventeenth and early eighteenth centuries, the most popular form of dancing, the minuet, took the idea that dance is a builder of character and ran with it. In having each couple dance alone with each other while all the other couples watched them, the minuet became a forum for judgment and tut-tutting that lacked only *Dancing with the Stars*–style score paddles: not only were the dancers currently in motion being silently judged on their technique, bearing, and posture, but, as Jack Anderson reminds us in *Ballet & Modern Dance*, their flaws in dancing were viewed as flaws in character, too. As Sarah, the duchess of Marlborough, said of one dancer who endured the gaze of the duchess's gimlet eyes, "I think Sir S. Garth is the most honest and compassionate, but after the minuets which I have seen him dance . . . I can't help thinking that he may sometimes be in the wrong."

What's interesting to me here is the grounds on which the dancer is being criticized: though the history of dance provides countless examples of people damning dance on the basis of wantonness and the ability of this particular branch of the arts to cause certain body parts to flap or rotate with an excessive vividness, the duchess and her criticism are decidedly bigger picture—she's set her sights on honesty, compassion. We can almost see how, in the duchess's eyes, Sir S. Garth is the type of dude who'll step on a lot of toes, lie to the other dancers, and then ride home in his landau to not feed his kitten.

Other dancers, though, harness the moral gravitas they find in dance and use it to power a kind of sea change. Consider Jerome Robbins, who choreographed both for the ballet (*Fancy Free, Afternoon of a Faun, Dances at a Gathering*) and the theater (*On the Town, Peter Pan, West Side Story*). Robbins struggled for decades with his Judaism, at age thirteen chasing away schoolmates who peered into the Robbins family living room windows in Weehawken, New Jersey—they'd made faces while young Jerry Rabinowitz and a holy man from the local synagogue practiced reading the Torah. For the shame-filled young Robbins, ballet would have what he called a "civilizationizing" effect on his ancestral-tribal identity. "I affect a discipline over my body, and take on another language," Robbins would write, "the language of court and Christianity—church and state—a completely artificial convention of movement—one that deforms and reforms the body and imposes a set of artificial conventions of beauty—a language *not* universal."

One of the times that dance was a vehicle of entrée in my life, the idiom in question was neither ballroom nor ballet. In my junior year at the boarding school Hotchkiss, through the ministrations of a kindhearted high school pal, I was invited to the Gold and Silver Ball. Started in 1956, this New York City charity ball kicks off the winter breaks of teenage public and private schoolers in the Northeast, giving them an opportunity to swap stories about their parents' divorce proceedings and to practice smuggling liquor into a non-stadium setting.

Back then the ball was held at the Plaza Hotel or the Waldorf Astoria, and featured the dulcet musical stylings of a society band like Lester Lanin's, but in 1985 the ball moved downtown to the Ritz and later the Palladium, either because (according to the ball's organizers) the Waldorf had become too expensive or because (according to high schoolers) a sofa had "slipped" out one of the Waldorf's upstairs windows.

I remember how flattered I felt by the invitation. At my previous school, I'd been a storefront of overachievement, and, as a result, had had a series of nicknames leveled at me: Prez, Brain, Brownie, T.P. (for teacher's pet), Toilet Paper. So when I got to Hotchkiss, I was anxious to be considered cool and not overly directed.

Also, at age sixteen, I was just starting to notice my attraction to men, but was embarrassed by same. My slightly desperate need to fit in lay at the heart of one of my more shameful acts from this period. A shy and soft-spoken guy who lived down the hall from me in my dorm—a social outlier, who was not in my clique—asked me one night if I wanted to get high. I said sure.

We followed the prescribed route for discreet pot-smoking: he'd rolled up one bath towel lengthwise and put it at the base of his door to prevent smoke from seeping into the hall, and he'd rolled one towel width-wise for us to exhale our hits into. He'd blasted the room with Ozium air sanitizer, and had put fresh water in his bong lest spilling stale water necessitate the ritualistic slaughter of an area rug.

But after we smoked up, he did something unexpected: he put his hand on my knee.

I immediately stood, mumbled thanks, and ran-walked to my room. My heart thudded like a stuffed animal being quickly dragged down a staircase; it seemed like the walls of the hallway engorged and contracted slightly with each hurried step I took.

Thereafter it took me three months to acknowledge this guy in public again, and sustained eye contact remained an impossibility for the rest of the year.

So, the invitation to the Gold and Silver. Given that many of Hotchkiss's slightly intimidating coolios would be present at the ball, I thought, Why not? If I wanted to be cool myself, then I needed to log hours living amongst exemplars of that ethos; a burst of popularity, I thought, would smooth some of the tattered edges of my homophobia. The cost of the ball (more than $100) seemed exorbitant, and, moreover, I'd have to find a tuxedo somewhere, but: sure.

Back at my mom's in Worcester over Thanksgiving break, I found an affordable tuxedo in a thrift shop. The jacket fit well, but the crotch of the pants sagged mid-distance between my knees and my fruit-and-veg. Only a haberdasher for dachshunds could imagine a world in which one's genitals should fly so close to the sidewalk. I've never been noticeably well dressed—a WASPy wariness about caring too much about clothes runs in my family, and dovetailed nicely with my anxiety about appearing gay—but this was a new, uh, low. Once I'd brought my budget treasure back home, Mom laughingly pointed out that the waistband was a tad generous, too, so she nipped off an inch or so of it with her sewing machine. At last the pants made meaningful contact with my person.

Back at school, a month before the Gold and Silver, I had lots of time to feed my anxiety about mingling with my glittery friends while wearing pants that from certain angles still said "crotch goiter." My classmates' anxiety, meanwhile, was focused on where to drink before the ball—God forbid you should show up at the function not teetering on the brink of projectile vomiting. My high school memories are full of examples of trying to make the most of some tiny amount of some illegal substance; one Saturday we resorted to spiking a watermelon with half a bottle of dry vermouth. It's a nice buzz, if you're an ant.

Came the day of the ball. Let us summon up a cloud cover of empathy and indulgence over the next paragraph, as the author's memories are, due to the ravages of alcohol and experiential fervor, somewhat impressionistic.

I don't remember where I pre-gamed. I don't remember where the ball was held. I do remember that the ball had a two-part construction: in one room, a society band played while girls in taffeta gowns and cocktail dresses touch-danced with their willing partners; in another room, rock boomed out of speakers. I gravitated, naturally, toward the latter.

The hours evanesced. No one mentioned my pants. I befriended no dachshunds.

But then, a few hours later that same night, something staggeringly, epically, supersonically groovy happened. Nine or so of us had ended up at our classmate Carl Sprague's parents' house for a nightcap. We were standing in the Spragues' living room when someone informed me that we were all going to try to get into Studio 54. I laughed. My drunk had worn off by now, but, still: funny. We'd all heard about the illustrious nightclub—mostly stories about how impossible it was to get into. Each night a big crowd of people would mass in front of the velvet ropes in a pageant of ritual humiliation; over time, the people turned down by the bouncer would include Mick Jagger, Frank Sinatra, Warren Beatty, and Diane Keaton.

So my first reaction, on hearing the plan, was, Why bother? But then, given the jolliness of the evening, my second reaction was, What the hell?

I idly asked the group how many cabs we thought we'd need, and as my friends' excited chirrups dissolved into more mundane mutterings related to coat retrieval and taxi logistics, I heard Carl say, "No, we don't need cabs. I got a limo."

That no one questioned or remarked upon this plot point—the surprise limo—says something about whimsical Carl, who had a bust of Byron in his dorm room and would grow up to be a production designer who'd work for Wes Anderson and Woody Allen.

Sure, I thought on hearing about the limo, we'll be ignored or rejected by the bouncer, but the stretch will whisk us away in a glamorous storm cloud of slightly singed entitlement.

We piled into the vehicle.

After a drive across the gridded isle, the limo sidled up to the curb outside the club, where some sixty hopefuls were huddled on the sidewalk. As the nine of us tumbled out of the vehicle, I glanced at our group as if from the bouncer's point of view: a knot of fifteen- and sixteen-year-olds in formal wear, their leader (Carl), six-foot-one and blond. We looked like the Norwegian cast of *The Sound of Music.*

Our bodies were somewhat smooshed together: it was cold, and we seemed to be unintentionally duplicating the crowded seating of the limo ride. The slick bottoms of my awful patent leather shoes were a slippery hell on the sidewalk; when I looked down, though, I noticed that no one else's party shoes were faring much better.

Are you familiar with the Bob Fosse formation known as an amoeba? That's when a very densely packed huddle of dancers moves cloud-like as one across the stage. Fosse got the idea from those people in Hieronymus Bosch paintings who are hatched from eggs and have multiple arms and legs.

Imagine a Fosse amoeba, but drunker, preppier.

The bouncer took one look at us, and waved us on in.

* * *

I'm intrigued that disco, a dance phenomenon originally promulgated in this country by minorities (blacks, Latins, gay men), partly in reaction to the dominance of rock and roll, would become so oppressively exclusive. Slightly antithetical, no? But I guess that when you build a shimmering island paradise out of body glitter and pairs of assless chaps, you can either say to the rest of the world "Come on in" or "You better be as decorative as we are."

Studio 54 decidedly went with the latter, reordering the hierarchy by allowing admission only to those people fabulous enough not to be cowed by the club's ninety-foot ceilings, its ceiling-suspended sculpture of a moon that snorted cocaine, the balcony bleachers covered with waterproof fabric that was hosed down daily. It was a bold clientele, a clientele unafraid to express itself via police whistle. (After President Carter's mother, Lillian, went to Studio 54, she reported, "I'm not sure if it was heaven or hell. But it was wonderful.") Outside on the sidewalk, co-owner Steve Rubell would stand on a fire hydrant to surveil the crowd of people trying to gain admission. "People would wait for hours in the freezing cold, knowing it was hopeless," Johnny Morgan writes in *Disco: The Music, the Times, the Era.* "Sometimes someone would be allowed in if they took off their shirt, others if they stripped naked. [Doorman Marc Benecke] let in the male half of a honeymoon couple but not the wife. Limo drivers were let in, their hires not. Two girls arrived with a horse. Benecke had them strip naked, then said only the horse would be allowed in." Donald Trump was a 54 regular, but would rarely dance; as one patron put it, Trump was there to cut the deal while others cut the coke.

For many of those admitted, the net effect of this stringent door policy was to make us fixate on the clubgoers. I managed to wiggle into Studio 54 three times over the years, and indeed, each time, people-watching was the draw. You might see the ectoplasmic Andy Warhol or the über-fabulous Grace Jones; you might see the transvestite roller skater in a wedding dress with the button that read

"How Dare You Presume I'm Heterosexual"; you might see enough age-disparate male couples to suggest that the evening's theme was Father-Son.

America.

2.

Implicit to the trope of social entrée is the trope of personal trans-formation: by entering a new milieu, you are made new—or, at least, can choose to present yourself as someone new. According to the American Dream, life in our nation should be rich and fruity for all people regardless of their class or the circumstances of their birth. "Homeless to Harvard" is not just the name of a turgid movie on Lifetime, it's a national ethos that bespeaks our dynamic, if some-times crippling, fascination with destiny and self-transformation. Fueled by the popularity of Benjamin Franklin and his rags-to-riches trajectory, Americans have long clung to the belief that, with enough hard work, no one need ever learn that your birth name is James Gatz.

Which puts me in mind of a certain dance pioneer. Since the late 1950s, my family has been friends with Phyllis McDowell and her family, who lived about a mile away from us in New Haven, where we lived before we moved to Worcester. Phyllis McDowell is one of Arthur Murray's twin daughters.

At mid-century, Arthur Murray's name was synonymous with ballroom. A dance instructor turned entrepreneur, he had several hundred dance studios bearing his name, many of which still exist; it's been estimated that over 5 million people have learned to dance because of these studios. His students over time would come to in-clude Eleanor Roosevelt, John D. Rockefeller, the Duke of Windsor, Margaret Bourke-White, Enrico Caruso, Elizabeth Arden, Cornelius

Vanderbilt Whitney, and Jack Dempsey. In the movie *Dirty Dancing*, Patrick Swayze plays an Arthur Murray instructor.

Though I never met Mr. Murray or his wife, Murray's name was invoked often in our household because of our friendship with the McDowells. My parents met Arthur and Kathryn Murray—"Once at the McDowells' house. Phyllis and Teddy used to have us over to watch the show," my mother told me, referring to *The Arthur Murray Party*, a dance show that ran from 1950 to 1960 and was hosted by Kathryn. "TV was pretty new then so you'd all get together to watch stuff."

At the time, I was wholly uninterested in the fact that Phyllis and her four foxy daughters were the progeny of famous people. It simply didn't compute. However, two facts about the McDowells made the clan fascinating to me: (1) their house had a bomb shelter, and (2) Mr. McDowell was rumored to have a knife inside his car in case he ever needed to cut himself out of his seat belt. This was a period of my life when I was devoting a lot of time thinking about rocket jet packs, so you can imagine the swank that a bomb shelter and a concealed weapon held for me; at some deep level of consciousness I must have realized that the McDowells were as close as I was ever going to get to the James Bond lifestyle.

Indeed, as if these two spectacularly cool items weren't freighted enough with danger and excitement, there was yet a heightener: Phyllis's twin sister, Jane, had married the man who invented the Heimlich maneuver. Yes, *Mrs*. Maneuver.

The level of emergency preparation in this family practically caused my young brain to explode; you imagined that if you bumped your head or skinned your knee at the McDowells', chopper blades would signal the airborne arrival of cat-suited Coast Guard ninjas.

Born Moses Teichman in 1895 to poor, Jewish, Austrian-born parents who ran a bakery in New York City's Harlem, Arthur Murray was, as he would later say, a "tall, gawky, and extremely shy" child. At

Morris High School in the Bronx, he would add, "my bashfulness and diffidence had become pernicious habits." He stuttered; his mother belittled her children and told them they'd never succeed.

Murray dropped out of school and struggled to keep various jobs, but after receiving dancing instruction from two sources—a female friend and a settlement house called the Education Alliance—he returned to school, which he now found easier because the dancing had given him a modicum of poise.

A serious student of architecture, Murray would find his fortune in the dancing craze of the 1910s (as the new century dawned, many Americans had grown tired of dancing to their grandparents' music and had started dancing in huge numbers to ragtime instead). By day Murray worked in an architect's office, and by night he frequented various New York City dance halls, where the raging popularity of animal dances like the turkey trot (dancers took four hopping steps sideways, with their feet apart) and the grizzly bear (dancers would stagger from side to side in emulation of a dancing bear, sometimes helpfully yelling, "It's a bear!") was slowly being supplanted by the calmer one-step (with their weight on their toes, dancers would travel across a room taking one step for each beat).

"Arthur first turned to social dancing as a means of meeting girls and becoming more popular," his wife, Kathryn, would write in her book, *My Husband, Arthur Murray*, cowritten with Betty Hannah Hoffman. "To practice dancing, Arthur used to crash wedding receptions which were held in public halls."

Murray left his architecture job and took classes with instructors Irene and Vernon Castle. The most famous dancers of their day, the Castles helped "tame" the wildness of the animal dances and made social dancing respectable. The Castles soon hired Murray to work at their school, Castle House. Then, after a sojourn teaching at a hotel in North Carolina for an instructor named the Baroness de Kuttleston, Murray opened the first Arthur Murray dance studio, located in the Georgian Terrace Hotel in Atlanta. By the time Murray stepped down from the presidency of his company in 1964, his three hundred franchised studios were grossing over $25 million a year.

What I love about Arthur Murray is his notion that dancing is a kind of conversation set to music. In his book *How to Become a Good Dancer*, he writes about how a foreigner who has not learned English has difficulty making himself understood. "He is so busy trying to think of the right words that he stammers and hesitates. And so it is with dancing. . . . To be a good dancer you must be able to dance without having to concentrate on the steps."

The metaphor of dance-as-conversation also nods to the ever-escalating, back-and-forth nature of what is called a "challenge dance," a feature of many dance idioms (e.g., tap dancing has the hoofer's line, hip-hop has battles). In *Top Hat*, for instance, when Fred Astaire and Ginger Rogers dance on the bandstand to "Isn't This a Lovely Day (to Be Caught in the Rain)?," Fred does a step, Ginger copies it; Fred does another step, Ginger copies it but adds a little zing, etc.

But Murray's story is equally interesting to me when seen in light of two themes that reoccur throughout the history of dance: humiliation and snobbery. Many dancers—Bob Fosse and Twyla Tharp among them—spend a part of their lives hiding from their friends and family and colleagues the fact that they dance. To admit that you're a practitioner of the leaping arts is to open yourself to inspection on the fronts of economic status, carnality, taste, self-involvement, and body mass. For men, of course, the tendency to waft one's person through space, be it for monetary gain or simply for enjoyment, is especially psychologically tender. Though typically the forces of antagonism here are bound up in notions of masculinity, sometimes they are more class-based: when in 1924 Kathryn introduced Arthur to her father on their first date, the father asked the young suitor what he did for a living. Murray chose not to mention that he had already put away $10,000 in the bank or that he drove a Rolls-Royce, but instead simply said that he danced. Kathryn's father responded, "I do, too, but what do you do for a living?"

Whenever insecurity is much in evidence in a particular arena of activity—I'm looking at you, fashion, royal courts, glossy magazines, high-end restaurants—that arena's denizens will, in an effort to ease anxiety, create or pay heed to easily recognizable protocols and brand names; e.g., your friend didn't just spend $900 on shoes, she spent $900 on *Manolo Blahniks*. Murray's uncanny talent as a salesman saw him both combating and employing this humiliation/snobbery axis. On the former front, he had great success selling mail-order dance instruction: customers could buy paper "footprints" that you'd put on the floor and step on. The footprints had markings that corresponded to directions in a booklet. His book *How to Become a Good Dancer* had you trace your own shoes onto paper, and then make five copies of your "feet." Murray encouraged you to dance alone at first, until you got up and running. Imagine the relief that a pathologically shy, aspiring dancer would feel, knowing that he wouldn't have to go to a studio and endure the gaze of others.

More tellingly yet, Murray the advertiser was not above speaking to a potential customer's insecurities. "Most people lack confidence," he told his wife. "Subconsciously, they would like to have more friends and be more popular, but they don't openly recognize this desire." When writing ad copy for his dance studios, Murray and his wife—one waggish line of criticism against Murray runs that, since Kathryn did most of the writing, Murray made his fortune "by the sweat of his frau"—sometimes mined Murray's own travails from adolescence. An awkward evening he'd spent as a sixteen-year-old turned into an ad titled "How I Became Popular Overnight." The ad's copy ran, "Girls used to avoid me when I asked for a dance. Even the poorest dancers preferred to sit against the wall rather than dance with me. But I didn't wake up until a partner left me alone standing in the middle of the floor. . . . As a social success I was a first-class failure."

As Mrs. Murray writes in her book, "Arthur found that no man wanted to admit that he was learning to dance, but he didn't mind saying that he was learning the rumba. It was something like the difference between saying your feet hurt and your foot hurts. We ran smart-looking ads that now sound corny, but they appealed in those days to businessmen who read New York's leading newspapers and business journals: 'Does your dancing say "New York" or "small town"? Where do the fastidious satisfy their craving for the up-to-the-minute dance steps and instruction? A secret? On the contrary, they happily pass the word about Arthur Murray's delightfully modern studios where chic meet chic.' " This ad was rigged out with pictures of attractive women; the pictures' captions extolled these women's good social backgrounds.

In its heyday, ballroom and its attendant glamour could take you places. Fred Astaire and Ginger Rogers both came from modest backgrounds, but went on to become icons of sophistication and elegance; ditto Astaire's idols, Vernon and Irene Castle. In Murray's case, ballroom's power to raise one's station in life was noticeable not only in who Murray became in his success but also in who worked for him. In the wake of the Bolshevik Revolution, the fall of the Hapsburgs, and the upheavals of the Depression, impoverished European aristocrats were happy to take jobs as instructors at Arthur Murray studios: at one point Murray's work staff included a baroness, several countesses, and a White Russian prince.

Pinkies: they're for extending.

It occurred to me that I had a good opportunity to witness up close the aftermath of Murray's work and life: I could talk to his daughter Phyllis McDowell. So, one balmy August day, I visited her at her summer house in Fenwick, an old-money enclave on the Connecticut shore where she's been going for more than fifty years.

Phyllis, now eighty-nine, was all accommodation and bemusement and warmth. Barefoot, nut brown from tanning, and wearing a bright yellow Izod shirt and a Lilly Pulitzer skirt that set off her beautiful legs (she danced weekly until a few years ago), she invited me to sit on her porch and drink ice water with slices of lemon in it. Her silvery-white hair was held in place by a barrette. She has a sly smile and wonderfully warm, welcoming eyes that seem perpetually to be responding to faint music from another room.

I asked about the bomb shelter. ("Ted had some funny ideas," she told me.) I asked about the footprints. ("It was a very architectural approach to dancing. If men were ever embarrassed about dancing, this mechanical approach made it much more palatable.")

But what I really wondered was, What was it like to be the daughter of someone whose orientation—both to dance, and to life—was so aspirational? Phyllis told me, "Nothing escaped my father's attention—like if the lightbulbs were dirty or there was dust anywhere. He was very fussy about grammar. He was intolerant of any indulgences—especially alcohol, which was my mother's nemesis. He'd make you unpack a suitcase if you packed too much. No wonder I'm a Quaker now."

Arthur and Kathryn Murray didn't tell young Phyllis and Jane that the family was Jewish; when, as a teenager, Jane read about the traditional Jewish meal the seder, she thought it was a kind of wood. At age sixteen, Phyllis and Jane were taken to a plastic surgeon for nose jobs. The twin girls started attending Vassar, but when their father visited the campus one day he found the student body to be unkempt, so he convinced the girls to transfer to Sarah Lawrence.

In Phyllis and her sister's youth, an instructor would come to their house each week to give them dance lessons (like her father, young Phyllis stuttered). After college, the two sisters spent a summer working as Arthur Murray instructors, during which time Phyllis fell in love with and married a fellow instructor, Mr. McDowell.

"Have you come across the story," Phyllis asked me, chuckling, "where my father tells my mother, 'We're going to have a TV show! I want you to host it,' and my mother says, 'I don't know anything about acting or singing,' and my father tells her, 'Don't worry. The screens are so small that nobody will notice'?"

"I did see that," I said. "I also liked in your mom's book when she talked about doing acrobatics on the show in her ball gown, or roller-skating on the show, all of which caused you to ask her, 'Mother, do you think the things you do are really appropriate?' "

"We were such little snobs. Parents can't do anything right. Here my parents were, adventurous enough to have their own TV show at a time when no one else except Milton Berle did. They were fun and funny. Mother would call me after every show from Sardi's. It was exciting."

As the afternoon wore on, Phyllis's and my conversation gradually drifted toward her father's demise in 1991. He and Kathryn were living in Honolulu at the time. Phyllis told me, "I remember just before he passed, he was lying out on the lanai. The last words I remember him saying were 'We were so poor, we had to use newspaper as toilet paper.' Isn't that a peculiar thing to say? Why would you dwell on that?"

I tried, "Maybe it was a statement of appreciation? Like, life was so bad back in the day, but then he managed to make it a whole lot better?"

"That's a nice way to look at it."

I looked over Phyllis's shoulder at the sparkly Connecticut Sound, only a block away. I had about an hour before my train back to New York, and Phyllis said she was going to lie down for a few minutes before driving me to the station. I said that I'd brought my bathing suit and was hoping to take a quick swim.

Phyllis, whose spirits had started visibly to flag, suddenly brightened. "That's a great idea," she said. "Take our golf cart!"

DANCE AS POLITICS

1.

THE BALLROOM DANCING LESSONS OF MY CHILDHOOD WEREN'T my first exposure to dance instruction. In third grade I'd made the acquaintance of a charmer by the name of Dough-See-Dough.

In the early 1970s at my elementary school in Worcester, Massachusetts, teachers would sometimes of an afternoon foist square dances on us. The renewed interest in folk dancing during the 1960s and '70s mirrored the utopian idealism of the earlier of those two decades, and blossomed amid an uptick of folk singing and ethnomusicology; it was a time when men with beards were using the word "community" a lot.

The dance I remember best here is the Virginia Reel: the group forms two lines of an equal number of dancers, who face each other, boys on one side, girls on the other. The couple at the top of the line, while skipping or bouncing on the balls of their feet, hook arms and twirl around each other, and then each hook and twirl with every member of the opposite line (boys with girls, girls with boys), always returning to their partner for a hook-and-twirl after each "away game."

You'd think that any break from multiplication tables or the causes of the American Revolution would have been welcome diversion, but most of us kiddies trudged through these dances in a zombie-like state of grim obligation. I didn't mind standing in the non-leadership part of the line: the effort expenditure was minimal, and no one was focusing on you for long. But to be the lead couple was to be saddled with responsibility. The lead couple had to remember always to return to each other, and had to remember with whom they'd just danced. Also: you were skipping, and let's all just silently agree that this particular brand of bounciness is a good look only for the heartier leprechauns. The combined demand on my memory and motor skills was a lot to ask of someone who had difficulty fitting a pillow into a pillowcase and who was convinced that Saran Wrap's campaign of self-adherence was a conspiracy to discredit children.

The Virginia Reel's salvation was the thrill of centrifugal force as you whirled your partner to the next post. All the clunking around seemed worthwhile once you were rewarded with a brief blast of the dizzies. My classmates and I could also see the inherent appeal of do-si-doing (or, as we thought of it, Dough-See-Doughing), which we did when dancing square dances: the potential for delightful body-crashing loomed large here.

But I'm going to guess that there was probably something going on at a deeper, subconscious level, too. This was, after all, our first non-parental, non-televisual exposure to the war between the sexes. The script ran, I'm crossing my arms as if in disapproval or silent judgment, and then, while circling you, I'm gonna wash you down with a heaping dose of side-eye.

It was only in 2015 that I learned about the importance of square dancing to automobile titan Henry Ford (a name which, given its similarity to mine, was invoked in my presence throughout my childhood). As Megan Pugh points out in *America Dancing: From the Cake-*

walk to the Moonwalk, Ford was, in many ways, "the great modernizer: he invented the assembly line, mechanized labor, collapsed distances with his Model T, and sped up the pace of American life. But Ford wanted to slow things down, too." He championed square dancing in all its wholesomeness by throwing dance parties for friends and his employees, by publishing a 1926 manual of old-timey dances, and by successfully rallying to get square dancing into the phys ed curriculum of public schools in Dearborn and Detroit.

All good, no? Well, the problem lies in the "wholesomeness" part. An anti-Semite and isolationist, Ford thought that America's roots were, and should continue to be, white and Protestant. Much of his fervor for square dancing was a reaction to the wildness of jazz dancers like Lindy Hoppers. He thought dancers' bodies should not touch, and that dancers should put a handkerchief over their hands lest flesh touch flesh.

Ford told the *New York Times* in 1925 that square dancing could make its participants "less hurried and more neighborly. People lived further apart [previously], but knew each other better. They worked harder, but had more leisurely recreations. They weren't pushed by a mania for speed. There was a community of interest, of work, of pleasure. Farmers, folks who are supposed to be rough and ready people, had an innate gentleness of manner that is rare today. The square dances had much to do with that."

I find Ford's ideas about Jews repulsive. I'd like to rub him raw with Golda Meir's hankie. But the idea that he saw square dancing as the medium through which to create his straw-flecked utopia is fascinating to me.

Somehow, the inherent power of stepping and twirling and bouncing to music spoke to the industrialist. The man who had done more than any other individual to speed up America now wanted to slow it down.

"Perhaps progress means speed," Ford told the *Times*. "I don't think civilization does."

2.

When it is political, dance shares a lot of similarities with the other arts—e.g., the very act of dancing is, in some contexts or climes, political, just as expressing certain views while living under a dictatorship might be. Then, once you add touching or gyrating or same-sex partnering or revealing clothing, you only up the ante. To be gay and to dance in a club after the 2016 shooting in which forty-nine people were killed at the Pulse nightclub in Orlando is to experience powerful volts of ambient, free-floating solidarity; it would be difficult for this experience *not* to feel political.

When compared with the other arts, concert dancing (as opposed to social dancing) gets a special citation here. Politically charged performing arts usually require more bravery from their enactors than politically charged non-performing arts like literature, because these enactors are probably in the same room with their audience during the performance. Us writers tend to savor the shock waves from the sanctuary of the pub.

Admittedly, putting the words "politics" and "dance" in the same sentence feels a little dubious. Two things come immediately to mind. The first is those lame attempts made by actual politicians—typically, former politicians, or aspiring ones—to boogie publicly in an effort to appear likable. Behold 2016 presidential candidate Donald Trump sashaying awkwardly in a black church in Detroit just months before the election. *Dancing with the Stars* gives its contestants a huge canvas to paint on here—former House majority leader Tom DeLay showed us what happens when a blocky middle-aged white dude unleashes his cha-cha–fueled "Wild Thing"; former Texas governor Rick Perry began one of his routines on the show with that most exalted of choreographic tropes, a visit to a corn dog stand.

Sometimes a politician's deployment of dance is more notional. Just two weeks before the 2016 presidential election, candidate Hillary Clinton, who'd gotten a lot of attention for a shoulder shimmy she did during one of the debates, told listeners of the radio show *The Breakfast Club*, "I keep telling people I want to close the deficit, and one of the deficits I want to close is the fun deficit. We gotta close the fun deficit. I'm sick of all this meanness—why don't these people that support my opponent go out dancing? I think we need a big national dance."

The second thing that comes to mind when contemplating the politics/dance axis is equally tinged with need or desperation. Cue the Saturday night in college when you trudged to a dank basement space to see a leotard-clad friend and her troupe crawl across a spray of dirt and pottery shards while keening their offering's title, *Diaspora and the Ravages of Civil War: An Evening*.

I'm not saying that political dance is inherently inferior to other kinds of dance. Rather, overtly political dance, like all overtly political art, confounds its audience: its viewers don't know whether they're applauding the work or the cause. When comedians do jokes solely to make audiences agree or applaud rather than laugh, the audience responds with what is known among comedians as clapter. Other forms of political art generally elicit from their audience a Mona Lisa smile and an ambiguous "You're *so brave.*" Moreover, political dance pieces—with occasional exceptions like Savion Glover's *Bring in 'da Noise, Bring in 'da Funk* or Kurt Jooss's ballet *The Green Table* or maybe Busby Berkeley's "Remember My Forgotten Man" from *Gold Diggers of 1933*—are rarely considered a choreographer's best work.

In the case of one Broadway show, dance was used to soften the blow of politics. In the middle of *Fela!*, Bill T. Jones's terrific 2008 show about the Nigerian musician and human rights activist Fela Kuti, the Fela character encouraged us all to stand up and shake our *nyansh* (booty): "Let's just get everybody to participate in moving their *nyansh*. And, in this way, they can look at the *nyansh* of these women [dancers] and appreciate it—not just from a voyeuristic, you know, pornographic standpoint, but really appreciate the craftsmanship." Which, indeed, seemed to be a part of the experience of dancing while standing in front of our seats; Greg and our friend Liz and I got all artisanal with our *nyanshes.*

But Jones has also talked about how this audience participation eased us audience members into what was, for some Broadwaygoers, a fairly tough sell: not only were Fela and the musical form he pioneered (Afrobeat) largely unknown on these shores, but the man was a cocky, raunchy, fire-breathing revolutionary who roundly applauded the virtues of marijuana and polygamy. He married twenty-seven women on one day in 1978. He was arrested more than two hundred times during his life. One Fela song from the show is called "Expensive Shit," and it is not metaphorical. The show ends with coffins being laid on the stage to protest injustices suffered by Nigerians and other Africans.

So, a little communal motion-making is a nice way to take the edge off such extremes. As Sahr Ngaujah, one of the actors who played Fela, has put it, "Why not give people candy, if that's what you want? They don't have to know that it's full of vitamins and minerals, you know what I mean? If it's sweet, they're gonna eat it anyway."

Indeed, American dance has a longish history of being an equalizer or intermingler, as evidenced by what many dance historians see as our first national dance, the cakewalk. Originally devised as a way for slaves to mock their masters—the cakewalk has you puff up your chest and kick your legs high in the air, exaggeratedly strutting in a circle or line like a very fancy sparkle pony—the dance became by the 1880s, a period when more than one hundred black people in the U.S. were lynched each year, a national craze wherein the races intermingled. Plantation owners would watch slaves imitate them, and former slaves would watch plantation owners imitate slaves imitating plantation owners. As they say at Disney: the circle of life.

* * *

More typically, however, it's the works that were created during politically charged times, as opposed to works that are themselves overtly political, that are the keepers. Alvin Ailey's beautiful *Revelations*, created at the height of the civil rights struggle in 1960, charts African-American tenacity from slavery to emancipation. It's powerful not because it's a condemnation of human bondage, but because it celebrates steadfastness and faith.

Or consider ballet after World War II. Given that ballet's roots are in French and Italian court life during the Renaissance, the idiom would seem not to be a great fit for America, a country which, as discussed in the last chapter, is sometimes in love with its own egalitarianism. But in the first half of the twentieth century, ballet started to seep into American culture, mostly via either the vaudeville circuit or Sergei Diaghilev's Ballets Russes, which first toured North America in 1915. (Some credit Diaghilev, who nurtured the careers of five of the most important choreographers of the twentieth century—Nijinsky, Massine, Fokine, Nijinska, Balanchine—with making ballet a modern art. All this from a man whose white-streaked hair earned him the nickname Chinchilla.)

In 1942, Agnes de Mille choreographed her "cowboy ballet" *Rodeo* for the Ballet Russe de Monte Carlo. Set on a ranch out West, this ballet, along with its contemporaries *Billy the Kid* (choreographed by Eugene Loring) and *Filling Station* (Lew Christensen), helped make the point that ballet was not solely the province of effete, hand-kissing Europeans and their rarefied concerns—a view held by some of the more fanatical modern dancers of the time. Ballet could be about ranch hands. There could be dust.

But the real ballet explosion on these shores occurred after the war, when arts leaders, many of them with ties to a now-ravaged Europe, decided to install on our economically robust shores some of the cultural riches that were now rubble-covered or in abeyance overseas. The companies that would become American Ballet Theatre and New York City Ballet were launched in 1939 and 1948 respectively.

When the Iron Curtain fell between the United States and Russia after the war, many Americans saw the need, in the face of the Communist Party and its secret police, to flex our democratic and cultural muscles. U.S. government-sponsored organizations that promoted American arts started springing up—Radio Free Europe took to the airwaves in 1949; in 1958, President Eisenhower signed into law an act that would result in the building of the Kennedy Center.

(Speaking of Kennedy—First Lady Jacqueline Kennedy got in on the act, too. Her first guest at the White House was George Balanchine. When the first lady served the great choreographer tea, he asked, "You don't have anything stronger?" He later told the press, "She looks like a pussycat"—high praise from a man who taught his cat Mourka to do *jetés*. On another occasion, when the first lady invited Rudolf Nureyev and Margot Fonteyn to visit with her, she transported them to the nation's capital via White House jet.)

By the mid-sixties, ballet was a decidedly non-hazy feature on the American cultural landscape—the $7.7 million that the Ford Foundation threw at the art in 1963 didn't hurt—and would continue to thrive during the dance boom of the 1970s and early 1980s. Nipples firing.

As you may have noticed, I like political dance best when the politics are covert or ancillary or unintentional. I have trouble rallying enthusiasm or the ticket price for any dance piece featuring soldiers' dog tags or the narrated transcripts of dead children. But I'm very curious about the small-bore intrigue of who in his orbit a dancer will confess having an injury to (the dancer who inflicted it? the person who might recommend the injured dancer for a gig?), or about how all the soreness that my dancing in the last six years has visited upon my body has caused me to triple my consumption of hot water.

It's also intriguing to see how the political climes under which a dancer or choreographer grew up affect the work he later creates. Take, for instance, George Balanchine, whose *Nutcracker* has introduced millions to the joy to be found at the intersection of the Marzipan Shepherdess and fifty pounds of fake snow. Born in St. Petersburg in 1904, Balanchine would study at that city's Imperial Ballet School; dance and choreograph for the Mariinsky Ballet; and move to Europe and join Sergei Diaghilev's Ballets Russes before coming to the U.S. to cofound two of ballet's most important institutions, New York City Ballet and the School of American Ballet.

But I'm more interested here in another part of Balanchine's legacy: he is the leading exponent of the plotless ballet.

Born to a musician father and a social climber mother, young Georgi Balanchivadze loved playing the piano but hated dancing. His parents were itinerant, and sometimes lived separately from their children. Young Georgi was aware that they—especially his mother, whom he'd later call "the queen of the glaciers"—favored his siblings over him.

At age nine, against his will, Balanchine was entered into St. Petersburg's Imperial Ballet School. He kicked and screamed; he'd later say that he felt like "a dog that has just been taken out and abandoned." (He'd be abandoned again five years later, when his mother and his siblings joined Balanchine's father in the Georgian Republic, where Mr. Balanchivadze had been appointed the minister of culture. Balanchine never saw his parents or sister again.)

The school was supported by the Russian court—indeed, students were considered to be members of the czar's own household—and was a bastion of hierarchy and discipline. Yes, the school's servants picked up after the children and made their beds for them, but the students had to wear severe military uniforms and were regularly made to take cold showers. It was only after years of strenuous barre work and floor exercises that the students were allowed to perform. Georgi had bruises on his body from the teacher who would rap students with his knuckles while wearing heavy rings.

Young Balanchine was solitary and spookily self-confident. Possessed of a high, reedy, nasal voice, he had a tic of twitching his nose and sniffing that would earn him the nickname "Rat." Arts patron Lincoln Kirstein, who would bring the young choreographer to the States in 1933, once said of him, "He's Georgian. Stalin's type. He seems soft as silk, but he's like steel. He's really rather sinister."

How did Georgi view the decadent aristocracy that ruled Russia? In his book *George Balanchine: Ballet Master*, Richard Buckle writes, "Georgi was for the most part unaware of the political situation—politics meant little to the enclosed community of Theater Street. . . . [The students] had probably heard that Nicholas II had himself taken over the supreme command of the armed forces, but they could not have realized that as a result political power had been passed to the empress's ineffectual favorites, and the country was disintegrating. They must however surely have heard of Rasputin's murder in December 1916 and the czar's abdication the following March."

Came the revolution—or, should we say, revolutions. Ballet had been supported by the court, so it would be easy to imagine that the Bolshevik revolutions of February and October 1917 might have spelled the demise of crinkly tulle and of fictional characters who can't help themselves from turning into puppets or falling in love with nymphs. But a high-powered arts enthusiast—Anatole Lunacharsky, the Bolshevik commissar for education—persuaded Vladimir Lenin that ballet and opera were not counterrevolutionary.

Now that Russia's dysfunctional monarchy had been interred, the prevailing mood of Balanchine's city was joyous. As was that of Balanchine and his fellow students: "They'd put up with ancient humiliations from haughty caretakers and senior students because that was the order of things," writes Elizabeth Kendall in *Balanchine and the Lost Muse*. "They'd been passive pawns, not just of their education but of school rituals designed to remind them of their 'place.' Now this arbitrary arrangement had ended, and something more human was on the horizon."

This more human something, alas, was no box of chocolates, either. Due to shortages and deprivation, learning and performing ballet at the school was never easy. To begin with, food was scarce in St. Petersburg after the revolution; residents would make "cutlets" out of coffee grounds, or, worse, as Balanchine would later say, "Sometimes we catch rat and we kill and eat rat." (How his nickname must have stung.) One day Georgi saw a skeletal-looking horse collapse on the street, whereupon a swarm of the street's residents flew out their doors wielding knives and proceeded to hack the horse up for food. Meanwhile at the school, heat and costumes and makeup were not in abundance. You could see your breath in the studios, and students would sometimes make dresses out of umbrellas or coats out of the seats of railway carriages.

Which brings us, of course, to the fact that many of the stunning masterworks that Balanchine would go on to create—*Serenade* (1934), *Concerto Barocco* (1941), *Jewels* (1967), to name just three—feature simple costumes and minimal décor. The choreography is the star here, not the spectacle or the storytelling. "Many of these ballets showed up best when danced in practice clothes against a simple cyclorama," biographer Bernard Taper wrote of a practice that Balanchine started with the young New York City Ballet in 1951. The less you have, the more you have to make of it. As Balanchine put it, "Our poverty is what saved us."

Back in Russia's capital in the 1920s, the very fact that Balanchine would gain the experience he needed to become one of the city's most sought-after choreographers owes something to political reality, too. When introduced in 1921, Lenin's New Economic Policy, which promoted "state capitalism," saw the opening of a huge number of dance venues in the capital. Here, in cabarets and on more traditional stages, Balanchine would start to hone some of the choreographic hallmarks he would become known for. He liked to get the corps dancing (years later, criticized for the lack of uniformity in the NYCB corps' dancing, he'd comment that the aesthetic he was aiming for was that of an unclipped garden). He loved dazzling footwork, few or no *demi-pliés*, high *arabesques*, and long leaps. He strove for dancing that was precise but natural-looking—"Serve a glass of champagne on your heel" he'd tell one dancer; when another's work looked forced, Balanchine said, "You look like you're coming from the toilet."

For many of us ballet-goers, the high point of the Balanchine canon is the magisterial and stirring *Serenade*, a lushly romantic work in four movements that is set to Tchaikovsky's *Serenade for Strings*. It's possible, as I did the first time seeing it, to gasp at both the opening tableau (seventeen ballerinas in pale blue tulle, outstretching their arms skyward) and the ballet's moment of surprise (a ballerina takes down her hair and then falls on the ground), and then to tear up at the work's conclusion.

But the acme of Balanchine's ability to make music visible—and more important, the ability to make movement shorn of story or flesh-and-blood characters elicit an emotional response from viewers—is probably the moment, fifteen minutes in, of *Concerto Barocco*. Set to Bach's Double Violin Concerto in D Minor, the work is mostly a piece in which two female soloists each take on the life of one of the violins. But *Concerto Barocco* bursts into Technicolor amazingness when the two soloists flit off, leaving behind the corps of eight women.

The audience is staring down the barrel of the dancers—they're arranged in two columns of four. The dancers are all hopping on their toes with their arms *en haut*—sproing! sproing! Then it happens: half of the dancers start down-casting their arms on a count of three, and half of them on a count of four. It feels like you're beholding the world's most elegant threshing machine, or a Swiss clock that's made entirely of wrists and elbows. It's weirdly pleasing: in the early 1970s, a young Mark Morris, arguably the heir to Balanchine's exquisite musicality, saw *Concerto Barocco* for the first time and was so thrilled by this moment that he burst out laughing.

But you can't consider Balanchine as an artist without also considering women. He lionized them. When Kirstein first broached the idea of Balanchine coming to the U.S., Balanchine said he would love to live in any country that could produce so splendid an entity as Ginger Rogers. One of the most famous utterances of Mr. B (as his dancers would come to call him) was "Ballet is woman." It's entirely possible that, had Mr. B not existed, the long list of women he choreographed for—Alexandra Danilova, Tamara Toumanova, Marie-Jeanne, Mary Ellen Moylan, Maria Tallchief, Tanaquil Le Clercq, Melissa Hayden, Diana Adams, Allegra Kent, Suzanne Farrell, Violette Verdy, Patricia McBride, Merrill Ashley, Gelsey Kirkland, Heather Watts, Darci Kistler—would have come to our attention anyway. But it's also possible to say that, for most of these women, he was their greatest influence.

He was fascinated by women's inherent complexity: "Put 16 women on the stage, and it's everybody—it's the world," he once said. "Put 16 men on, and it's always nobody." But if the New Economic Policy's approach toward women had been ambivalent—while Russian women were meant to work shoulder to shoulder alongside their male compatriots, they were also needed to be hungry consumers of the influx of new consumer goods—so, too, was Mr. B's. Some critics, like Ann Daly in her 1987 essay "The Balanchine Woman," argue that Balanchine objectified women (Daly called ballet "one of our culture's most powerful models of patriarchal ceremony").

I suppose that you can find fuel for this argument in Balanchine's personal life, too. The man who married four dancers during his lifetime and made women the exalted focal point of many of his works also thought that a dancer's bearing children was a treacherous betrayal of both ballet and him. ("Now, Allegra, no more babies," he once told Allegra Kent. "Babies are for Puerto Ricans.") For a ballerina to be singled out by Mr. B was both a blessing and a curse: Suzanne Farrell was one of a number of young ballerinas Balanchine would fall in love with, idolize, and be crushed by when their affection waned. When Farrell married a fellow New York City Ballet dancer named Paul Mejia, Mr. B snubbed her and withheld roles from Mejia, causing the two dancers to retire from the company.

A cynic might view Balanchine's approach to ballet as a kind of power grab: to make ballets that have no plots is to make the choreographer the author of the show. Ambitious theater directors like to mount the classics rather than new plays because then if the show is a hit, the attention goes to the director not the playwright; it would be possible to see Balanchine through this lens. But this interpretation is undermined by Balanchine's devotion to music (he thought, "Music is the floor that dancers dance on," and considered composer Igor Stravinsky his mentor), not to mention his disinterest in money or titles and his belief that his work was perishable ("Ballets are like butterflies. Who wants to see last season's butterflies?"). Moreover, during the 1930s and '40s he worked regularly in two highly collaborative arenas, Broadway and film (his vampy ballet "Slaughter on Tenth Avenue" from the 1936 production of *On Your Toes* is canonical), and yet was not thought to be uncollaborative or an egoist. Too, his commitment to his dancers' growth as artists was so deep that he would sometimes choreograph in order to improve them—e.g., he liked to give Suzanne Farrell lots of *pas de bourrées* because hers needed practice.

In the end, he emerges a snuffly, sympathetic despot with a spectacular legacy. At New York City Ballet, Kendall writes, "he reproduced the apparatus of the Imperial Mariinsky, but without the monarchy and the protectors, balletomanes and higher-ups courting ballerinas. It was just him. He was ballet master and teacher to his ballerinas—and tsar and suitor and balletomane and mischievous companion, all at the same time."

The tsar in charge—sounds like a lot of dance studio owners, no?

3.

Have you ever made a political decision—drawn a line in the sand, or voiced an opinion—that had unexpectedly long-lasting repercussions? I did the first time I undertook ballet seriously.

I'd read about teacher Kat Wildish on the Gibney Dance website. Unusual for having danced for both of New York City's preeminent companies—she was handpicked by Balanchine at New York City Ballet to dance in one of his last works, *Adagio Lamentoso*, and at ABT Sir Kenneth MacMillan created the role of the knitting lady in his *Sleeping Beauty* for her—Wildish, now in her late fifties, teaches a very popular and challenging class for beginners.

On a balmy evening in August 2016, I walked into a huge, mirror-lined studio on the fifth floor of 890 Broadway. Formerly owned by choreographer Michael Bennett (*A Chorus Line*, *Dreamgirls*), 890 Broadway is a building where ABT and a lot of Broadway shows rehearse; while walking down its dark, slightly ominous hallways it's easy to convince yourself that you're at the epicenter of the dance world.

I took a deep breath, prepared to clutch onto a barre for dear life. Yes, I'd taken three ballet classes before, but everything I'd read about Wildish's class led me to believe that, when it came to Absolute Beginner ballet classes, this was Mount Everest. The Gibney website used the term "devilishly tricky."

In walked Wildish—petite, blond, and brimming with energy. She was wearing pearl earrings, and her shoulder-length hair was pulled back and scrunchied. Eyeing the group of us who were stretching out and staring into space, she sauntered over to me, introduced herself, and said, "We're having a *pas de deux* workshop after class, up at City Center, if you'd like to come. I always invite the men because we usually don't get enough of them."

I thanked her, and expressed mild anxiety about the current class, let alone the more challenging-sounding workshop.

"I understand completely," she said. "See how you feel after class, yeah?"

She explained that the *pas de deux* students would perform at a student-faculty showcase in a month's time. This struck me as exciting—there aren't many opportunities for ballet students, let alone beginner ones, to perform. It also seemed like a wonderful pedagogical goad. Carrot, stick.

The barre portion of Wildish's class is longer than most teachers', about an hour. We *tendued*, we *arabesqued*. So committed is Wildish to the concept of alignment—she talks a lot about how your inner ear should always be just in front of your ankles—that, half an hour into class, I decided that she should call her autobiography *Ears Over Ankles*. Throughout the barre, Wildish would walk up to various students, sometimes asking questions ("How's the leg?" "How was your trip?") that bespoke her sharp memory and stellar social skills. Most charmingly, she sometimes walks up to you and, instead of offering a correction or appraisal, simply widens her eyes in sympathy and says "I *know*."

The most challenging barre exercise saw us putting the ankle of one straightened leg up on the barre and then, leg still up there, turning 180 degrees, folding at the waist and putting first our palms and then our forearms on the floor. It's like you've jumped out a window and, mid-jump, decided to do a push-up. Equally difficult: go into *passé* by making a number 4 of your legs, then *relevé* on the foot that's on the floor while putting your arms elegantly over your head *en couronne*, and then hoooooold it. I wouldrai if I couldrai.

As students around her thrashed and flailed, Wildish remained upbeat and delightfully loopy: Carole Lombard serving cocktails on the deck of the *Titanic*.

We dragged the barres aside for the "center" portion of class.

Wildish told us about a trip to Costa Rica she'd taken during which a two-toed sloth had approached her tour bus. She then led us on an adagio variation—she called out to the pianist, "Something slow, Benjamin! Painfully slow!"—during which she told us to extend our index and middle fingers as if we were that same sloth approaching a tour bus. A second variation, which did *not* have us reenacting part of Wildish's vacation, ran *glissade* R-*glissade* L-*glissade* R-*pas de bourrée* L-*arabesque*-turn 90 degrees in *arabesque*-repeat, which is about as Absolute Beginner as Greece is Turkey. During a third variation I remembered that *jeter* means "throw" not "jump," which seemed like a more accurate description of my untrained body's grim and stolid lurching. Jeté-braham Lincoln.

In the last fifteen minutes of class, we twenty-two students— mostly women in their twenties—huddled in a corner of the studio while Wildish rattled off complicated variations that we would perform three at a time as we ran diagonally across the room. "Men first!" she said, in a reversal of almost every ballet class in the world. She explained, "It's not fair that the men always get to go last, because seeing other people doing the variation really helps."

It would also help, I would conclude some ninety seconds later, if the two other men in the class were absolute beginners. But, as it turned out, on that particular evening, one was a professional dancer who was rehabilitating an injury, and the other was a flawless Asian man whose name was pronounced *hero*.

Given that I'd been able to pull off only about 60 percent of the choreography, I felt that it was only fair to give Wildish the opportunity to rescind her invitation to the *pas de deux* workshop if she chose. So, at the end of class, I walked over to her and said, "As you can see, I'm working with a modest skill set. But I'd love to join you if you still need men."

"Great!"

"Let me ask you, though—is there a lot of choreography?"

"I can't really answer that," she said, fiddling with her bag. "You should probably just come and see?"

"Okay. But I wouldn't want to make you guys look bad, so please feel free to tell me if I don't cut it."

"That's entirely up to you. I shouldn't make that decision, you should."

Oh, the tyranny of a laissez-faire government. It's one thing for a highly trained, omniscient authority to take you aside and gently counsel you, "You're not there yet, hon." But it's another to leave this question up to the hon himself, thus giving the hon the opportunity to prove himself both unready *and* deluded.

As we would do for the next four Mondays, Wildish and three other students and I left the Gibney class together and took the subway fifteen minutes up to City Center for her private *pas* class. On the first of these nights, walking down Broadway toward the F train, Wildish told me that she had just taught in Italy and then spent two weeks lying in the sun in Sardinia.

"All that sun!" she said. "I'm going to look so old. But you know what? I don't care."

"You're beloved," I said. "When you're beloved, you get to make the rules."

Wildish smiled modestly.

This seemed like the moment to tell her that I was fifty-four.

"I'm older than that," she said unfazed. "And I've had two hip replacements."

"You still move beautifully."

"Thank you. I danced into my forties."

"Lots of older folks dance," I said, savoring the fact that professional dancers are thought only to have about a decade's worth of good dancing in them.

"Right? Look at Alessandra Ferri, who just danced Juliet for ABT at fifty-three."

"Or John Selya, who just toured with Twyla Tharp at forty-six. Or Margot Fonteyn, who danced into her sixties."

"It can be done," Wildish said.

"If you sell it, they'll buy it."

The *pas* classes were held in a large studio in midtown, and were mostly being conducted not by Wildish but by her colleague Jon Drake, a sly, good-looking dude in his thirties who has danced for Oregon Ballet Theatre and was in the national tour of *Dirty Dancing*.

"You'll like Jon, he's Southern," Wildish whispered to me as we exited the elevator and approached the studio. I said, "Oh, you mean he has nice manners?" Wildish shook her head and said, "Even better: he has sarcasm."

Once in the studio, Wildish introduced me to Drake with "Jon, this is Henry With Four Classes."

Drake drawled, "Hi, Henry With Four Classes."

Over the next three Mondays, an ever-shifting group of sixteen or so of us dancers in the workshop rehearsed a ninety-second-long routine. In it, the man rotated the woman 360 degrees while she was *en pointe*; then he'd hold her in *arabesque*, outstretching his leg behind him; then they'd do a series of elegant steps taking them closer to the audience, the man twice holding the woman around the waist so she could do a series of *pirouettes*.

The women had the much harder work here. Yes, in between some of these moves, us fellas were meant quickly to put our arms *en haut*, but that ain't all that. No, the much more difficult part for me was holding my *en-pointe* partner around the waist so that she was perfectly upright.

Throughout the workshop, we'd switch partners every fifteen minutes or so; Wildish announced at one point that we wouldn't know with whom we'd be dancing at the presentation, so we should get used to working with everyone.

The first three *en-pointe* women I worked with exhibited a tendency, under my unsure administration, to topple. I couldn't figure out when a partner was perfectly upright. Should I look in the mirror? Look at her neckline? Nothing seemed to help.

On seeing my frustration, Wildish padded over to me in her pointe shoes. She dismissed my third partner and stood *en pointe* in front of me. I clutched onto her waist.

"No, you're grabbing," she said.

I readjusted.

Better.

"But I'm not on," she said. "You've got me leaning to the left."

I guided her rightward.

"Nope, still not on!" she said.

I tried again. She grimace-smiled.

She came down to the floor and said, "You try. Show me your *sous-sus.*"

Uh, *sous-sus?* Have we not established that I am Henry With Four Classes? A *sous-sus* has you go into fifth (right foot in front of left, but pointing in opposite directions), then *demi-plié*, then *relevé* while you put your arms *en haut*.

Wildish saw me flail and suggested, "Okay, try going into *arabesque* instead."

I did, to the best of my ability. Whereupon she deftly wrapped her hands around my waist with the amount of pressure you'd exert if you were pushing an elderly woman out of the way of an incoming bus but were anxious you were going to pierce her papery skin.

Ah. Got it.

I think.

I soldiered on. Shortly into the second *pas* class, I realized that the more my partner's body resembled my own, the better I was able to gauge her verticality when *en pointe*. But whenever I worked with a tiny ballerina, or a willowy one: Topple City.

"It's really not fair that you got stuck with me again," I told a petite redhead when we were partnered up for the third time in two classes.

"No, no, it's fine," she countered. "Plus, it helps me to know what I need."

Indeed, to a one, the ballerinas were all kind to and indulgent of me. Unlike the men, the women had all had to audition for the class, and many of them had been dancing since they were children, yet I detected none of the hauteur that we associate with the bunhead.

I was now taking Wildish's Monday and Wednesday classes in addition to the *pas* workshop. Having thrown out my back three months earlier, I was surprised not to be experiencing any lumbar soreness or exhaustion as a result of all this ballet. My modest aching was confined to my feet, which throbbed gently—a lovely accompaniment to the more generalized bodily dread that my anxiety about the performance was visiting upon me.

"Don't think of the presentation as a performance, it's more like a lecture-demo," Wildish announced at the second *pas* class. Nevertheless, was I crazy to think that I should be practicing a classical art in front of a paying audience after what would be only twelve lessons? I spent most of the second *pas* class waiting for Wildish to take me aside and gently give me the slip. The performance was to be one of eight or so six-minute-long presentations at the Peridance Capezio Center in the East Village, where Wildish also teaches, and presumably was meant to entice uninitiated students to take her class. But who in his right mind would look at my herky-jerky fumbling and think, I wanna dance just like *that guy*? I was the dancer equivalent of typos.

At the end of the third of my Absolute Beginners classes at Gibney, Wildish joked with a few of us, "Ballet is an addiction and I'm your dealer. I'm open 24/7." Then she looked at me—at this point I'd taken seven of her classes in three weeks—and said, "Henry's an addict now."

"It's true," I said, nodding my head. "As Anna Pavlova said on her deathbed, 'Prepare my swan costume.'"

Wildish cocked her head unsurely, as if she'd taken a bite of an omelette and encountered a raisin.

Then she smiled and enthused, "All right."

A half hour later, at my third *pas* class, I told my partner that I was still having trouble determining the point at which a ballerina was perfectly vertical. I'd had a small amount of success in the second class, with a partner who was wearing dangly earrings; if the earrings weren't oscillating, then I knew we were solid. But surely I couldn't ask all the women to accessorize like Stevie Nicks for the performance.

Increasingly anxious about exposing my raw talent to strangers who had paid $20, I told one of the women, "I don't care about looking like an ass at Peridance, but I wouldn't want to make a partner look bad."

"You won't," she said. "Kat won't let you."

"When I signed up for this class, I told Kat to tell me if I didn't cut it, and she said, 'You be the judge of that,' which is slightly terrifying. That's why I'm taking her Monday *and* Wednesday classes now—to be fair to you ladies. What's that Thomas Jefferson quote about how a strong democracy relies on a well-informed electorate? I'm trying to be a well-informed electorate."

"That's great," my partner said. "We're all constantly improving."

It was also during this third *pas* class that a fellow dancer referenced a group e-mail that Wildish's assistant had sent out to all the *pas* performers. I'd not received it. My e-mail had been acting up that week, so I wasn't sure if not having received the e-mail was a technical glitch, or whether it had been intentional. Maybe Wildish and Drake were sending me a message by not sending me a message? So I walked over to Wildish's assistant and said, "I didn't get that e-mail. If this is benign neglect, I totally understand."

No, no, she assured me, and, whipping out her phone, proceeded to resend the e-mail, which I received. It explained that the last *pas* class would be our dress rehearsal, and was to be held in the space at Peridance where we'd be performing. Also: there was an optional but encouraged tech rehearsal on Friday night. And: the performances were Saturday and Sunday.

Two performances? Good God, I thought—I'm not only supposed to perform in front of a paying audience, but then I'm supposed to do it again? I remembered that, in the electric chair, Ethel Rosenberg required two zaps.

The next week, some thirty minutes before the rehearsal, five of us—three other students, Wildish, and I—went to get a bite to eat at one of those make-your-own-salad places near Peridance.

I'd been wanting to ask Wildish something. I looked at her as she tucked into her turkey salad and said, "A possibly ignorant question."

"No question is ignorant."

"How come, if ballerinas can *pirouette* and spin all on their own— if *Swan Lake*'s Odile can do thirty-two *fouettés* all on her own—then why does it get harder once you add a dude to the equation?"

Wildish grinned as she put down her plastic fork.

"Well, it depends who the dude is. He makes it easier for her if he's not grabbing her. It's like any relationship."

"Huh. Right. I don't know why I'm still finding it so difficult."

"Ballet is hard, yeah?" Wildish cooed.

"It is." I jested: "Maybe my homosexuality is getting in the way."

"It has nothing to do with sexuality! Rather, it has everything to do with sexuality and . . ."

". . . And nothing to do with orientation?" I offered.

"Exactly. For instance, all us ballerinas loved Marcelo Gomes as a partner," she said, referring to the openly gay ABT former principal. "He's like"—here she outstretched her arms elegantly—" 'Here is my shiny, new refrigerator!' "

Shiny new refrigerator: I liked that. Food for thought. Food storage for thought.

I had assumed that at the last rehearsal we would be running the ninety-second routine over and over so that muscle memory would kick in. I'm a slightly nervous performer even with activities I've done for years and am good at, so I think you'll understand me when I say that my current abdominal swirling seemed especially jangly, eel-like. The best antidote would be rote repetition. Yes, I'd practiced by myself in my office and at home (while thinking 'Shiny new refrigerator!,' which had helped), but running the routine at least several times in the space where it was to be performed would be highly reassuring to me.

So you can imagine my surprise when, at this last rehearsal, it turned out that we spent only ten minutes on the routine. Instead, we worked first on entering briskly with a partner in that synchronized clippity-clop clippity-clop that motors ballet dancers out from the wings; seldom have I felt more like a sexy centaur. Then we practiced a move in which the ballerina goes up *en pointe* and the man holds her at twenty-degree angles to the left, right, and back. Shiny new refrigerator, with a tendency to lean.

As for the routine, it was gradually becoming clear to me that during the presentation, we might or might not actually run it, just as we might or might not do some of these new moves that we'd just learned. Add this to the fact that we might or might not dance with the people we like to dance with, and you get a giant neon sign in your head that reads, "Be prepared . . . to improvise!"

Then came the bombshell. In the last seven minutes of the rehearsal, Drake taught us the most difficult move yet, a "fish." A feature of many *pas de deux*, a fish dive sees the man wrapping his arms around his partner's legs so he can hold her up in the air while she's in *arabesque*, and then tilting her floorward (in an even more challenging version, the man holds her in this position above his head).

"Jesus Christ! I can't believe he's teaching us this now!" I said with a huff to my partner, who smiled at me with the vague sympathy of a fellow shopper staring at an empty Power Rangers shelf the night before Christmas. She and I proceeded to do three fishes, each of which came out a little less accomplished than its predecessor. This led me to believe that I better tell Wildish and Drake that I had pulled my back out three months earlier, and thus was probably not a reliable fisherman.

I found Wildish over in the corner of the studio, fiddling with her camera. I told her about my back, and said I wasn't sure I could be relied on to pull off a fish.

"That's fine! You don't have to do it," she said, and then, responding to another student's question, she flitted off.

You don't have to do it. Meaning, "Please don't"? Meaning, "Please don't make me have to tell you not to show up on Saturday"? Meaning, "When the rest of the class does a fish, please go into a Monty Python routine and slap your partner with a haddock"?

I wasn't sure. So I walked over to Wildish again and said, "So should I still come on Saturday if I can't do a fish?"

Wildish turned to Drake, who was standing next to her, and said, "Jon, we have an injury here, so we just won't have him do the fish, okay?"

"That's fine," Drake said. "Not everyone has to do every move."

Ah.

When anything goes, anything goes.

I knew that, of all the dancers, I was the one who most needed the precious extra practice time that Friday's optional tech rehearsal would offer. Yet, bewildered by the somewhat loosey-goosey approach to the whole proceedings, not to mention Drake's having saved the most technically challenging move for the last seven minutes of rehearsal, I now decided to abstain from the tech rehearsal. As a political act. As a vote of no confidence in myself. Granted, this was hardly the stuff of Nureyev defecting from the Motherland, nor of a Rockette announcing that she didn't want to dance at the Trump inauguration. And yet. Also: since Drake had thrown a bunch of new moves at us in the last rehearsal, who knew that he wouldn't do it again at the tech?

My decision spelled my demise. Because, had I gone to the tech rehearsal, which was held at the strange hour of 10 p.m., I'm quite sure that the next morning I would have woken up groggy and out of sorts, as I do whenever I'm up past midnight.

But instead, on the morning of the performance, I woke up at my usual 7 a.m. and, registering the fact that it was a sunny Saturday morning, acted on my feelings of amorousness by rolling over onto Greg and proceeding to make love to him.

At which point I threw my back out again.

An hour later, I wrote a plaintive e-mail to Wildish's assistant explaining that I was hunched over and radiating with pain and wouldn't be able to make the performances. I asked, "Will this keep one of the women from being able to perform? If so, I'd love to buy that person flowers." The assistant wrote back promptly, saying, "No need to worry, everyone will go on, no need for flowers."

That night I hobbled over to Peridance. A fifteen-minute walk took me forty-five minutes. On arrival at the school, I was brimming with shame—not because of *how* I'd thrown my back out, but that I'd done it all, and that I'd seen fit to do so twelve hours before curtain. This Uncle Drosselmeyer had no Christmas gifts to dispense because he was using the nutcracker as his walker.

In Peridance's lobby, I noticed one of my *pas* classmates walk by, whereupon I instinctively ducked around a corner so she wouldn't see me. I stood at the back of the theater to watch the show (sitting was hugely uncomfortable, as it would be for three weeks). But then I got nervous that Wildish might notice me and maybe even acknowledge me in front of the crowd, so, for the *pas* presentation (which was lovely, if much looser than the other classes' offerings), I sat. I scooted out immediately after the show, opting to send my congratulations to Wildish via e-mail.

The next three weeks were a slightly challenging and self-questioning time for me. I felt like I'd broken a contract. All creative endeavors that you take on with other people, dance included, are bets that require a leap of faith: I'll believe that you can muster up some innovative choreography if you believe that I can artfully configure my person into that choreography's demands. But as soon as one of you calls the other's bluff, you endanger the implied contract, and you hold it up to the harsh sunlight and start fixating on the fine print. In no way did I feel like Drake or Wildish were responsible for my back. But I'd foundered on the brink of my grasp exceeding my reach.

It took three weeks for me to be able fully to sit without soreness or pain. I stopped going to any dance classes. I visited a chiropractor, an accupuncturist, two massage therapists. I spent a lot of time lying in bed or, even better, on the floor. I developed three ugly blisters from hot compresses. Once I could swim again, I swam many, many laps with a delicacy befitting bomb-dismantling.

It took six weeks for me to start going back to Wildish's Absolute

Beginners class. Two weeks into my reentry, I was having lunch one day with my friend Jenny, who asked me how my ballet dancing was going. Alluding to the varying types of ballet dancers—from *danseur noble* to *demi-caractère*, all the way down to *grotesque*—I mused, "I'm not a *danseur noble* anymore. My *noble* has left the building." Jenny clucked sympathetically. And then I uttered the statement that older dancers throughout the centuries, while peering over elegant, porcelain demitasses, have unbosomed to their confidantes: "I'm trying to go a little more *demi-caractère* with my barre work."

With time, I got back up to speed. When I ran into an acquaintance on the street one day, I told her that over the summer I'd started taking ballet but had thrown my back out. She asked what ballet move I'd been doing when it had happened.

"It wasn't during a class," I said. "It was while I was doing something very intimate to my boyfriend."

Her eyes widened, and she started to gasp.

I reacted instinctively. "Not a blow job!" I said with a huff. "I wasn't giving a blow job!"

You see, I may not be the best refrigerator salesman in town. I may exhibit tentative *pliés*, an impressionistic grasp of choreography, and the stamina of a six-week-old infant with the flu.

But I have my pride.

DANCE AS REBELLION

1.

IN HIGH SCHOOL—THIS IS AROUND THE SAME TIME AS I WENT
to the Gold and Silver and to Studio 54—I finally started enjoying
going to school dances. The ones I'd been to previous to this, when
I was thirteen or fourteen years old, had been a squeamish agony.
The pain of trying to look like I was enjoying myself on the dance
floor was second only to the fear that my classmates would think I
was lonely if I stood too much on the sidelines. I remember once,
while lurking on the edge of the cafeteria at a school dance in sixth
grade, anxiously removing my shoe and shaking it as if there were
a pebble in it, simply to look busy.

But at boarding school a few years later, where we'd bop around
to the Rolling Stones and KC and the Sunshine Band, I was glad to
pierce the awkward sexual tension of adolescence and to dull the
daily throb of homesickness with aerobic activity. Yes, the anxiety
I'd felt about looking lonely still persisted here in high school, but
the venue for this discomfort had changed from the dance floor
to the dining room. Lest I look like a loner when I walked into the
dining hall for dinner at Hotchkiss, I'd started lurking outside the
door of the hall and then glomming onto any group that entered;

or I'd enter the hall at the very end of the allotted dining hours, when most people had already eaten and cleared out; or I'd just skip dinner altogether. Hotchkiss didn't have a prom, but I was able to harness all of the anxieties that such an event might foster, and then to wallpaper these anxieties over the course of an entire school year, solely through the medium of dining hall arrival.

But at Hotchkiss dances, the lonely/popular axis seemed easier to negotiate than it had at middle school because the crowds were larger and the lights dimmer. Also, there was, compared to the folks who'd showed up to my earlier dances, a higher incidence of nonconformists to rally around. I always tried to dance with my classmate Heidi, a particularly free spirit on the dance floor; in motion, her hair looked like the Static Electricity Ball photo in a science museum brochure. I longed to be as uninhibited as her, both on the dance floor and off.

When I went off to New York University in 1981, my opportunities to dance, usually at discos or in bars, doubled or even tripled. To a quavering young person who was trying to smother his homosexual impulses because he thought to do so would make his life easier, what I saw in New York's discos and bars was both ammunition and incoming gunfire.

On the negative side: beholding a sinuous dancer sinuously and unabashedly boogying with his or her sinuous same-sex partner could, depending on my mood, strike me as hedonistic or wanton. I'd been kicked out of boarding school my junior year for smoking pot and drinking, and now felt burned by my fun-seeking ways. I certainly hadn't, as a result of my expulsion, turned prudish about partying or getting my freak on, but I was keen to find examples of alternative culture that were orderly and unthreatening. There's a particular disco move that made me uncomfortable: closing your eyes and rocking your head with an opened O-mouth, you rub your hands up and down the sides of your head as if trying to force the nut butters stored in your cheeks to ooze out of your ears. The look is one of pure abandon, and it struck me as overripe—a dog with worms who rubs his anal glands against unsuspecting surfaces.

But there was a positive side, too. If the motivator that goes by the name "keep the party going on" is an excuse to engage in a lot of numbing, ultimately unhelpful behavior, this same movement toward uninhibitedness can open your eyes to things you heretofore hadn't appreciated. Sometimes when I walked down the street in New York, good-looking dudes would stare at me. I'd look down at the sidewalk. I knew that these stares were invitations, and/but they unsettled me.

But at discos, in the half-light, my internal monologue got drowned out by the eddies of movement and sound, and my body became host to a free-floating sneer of delight. The dance floor clearly wasn't the real world, and thus my actions thereon would bear no consequences. One night at the disco Xenon, having closed my eyes for twenty seconds while boogying, I opened them and noticed that a handsome male dancer ten feet away was staring in my direction. He smiled at me.

By 1982, I had started frequenting a large, beer-smelling gay bar in the East Village called Boy Bar, where I liked to dance. I met Mark, one of my first serious boyfriends, there. I met a magazine editor to whom I sold my first article.

I had started to smile back.

2.

Because the use of dance as a mechanism of rebellion is an act of defiance, the Rebellion function shares a lot of similarities with the Political one. However, this rebelliousness may or may not have a mandate or desired outcome—it may simply be a spontaneous reaction that bears no message or intent. In many instances, the vividness and wildness of dance-as-rebellion is possibly rooted in the fact that so many of us experience body shame early in our lives, and later find ourselves casting off this taint via bodily thrashing: there's nothing subtle about twerking or the Electric Daisy Carnival and its three hundred thousand arm-pumping party makers.

Indeed, neither I nor twerkers nor Electric Daisy–goers—nor Rosie Perez ferociously popping and shadowboxing to Public Enemy's "Fight the Power" in the opening credits of *Do the Right Thing*—were the first young twentieth-century Americans to deploy social dancing as a mechanism of rebellion. Consider, for instance, teens in the teens.

"During the pre-war Ragtime Era," Richard Powers, the Stanford dance historian, has written, "many young Americans had been chastised by their elders for a number of violations against decency, including using slang, dancing low-class dances, and enjoying synco-pated music with African-American influences. Progressive women were especially criticized, for abandoning the corset, wearing shorter skirts that exposed their ankles, cutting their hair short, and leaving the 'separate sphere' of their domestic domain to be socially and politically active in the public arena."

So, in the 1920s, young people responded to these criticisms by upping their ante with even wilder dancing and slang, not to men-tion shorter hair and clothing. They started dancing the shimmy, the bunny hug, the black bottom. But the dance most associated with flappers, of course, was the Charleston, which gained huge popularity when it was performed to James P. Johnson's song "The Charleston" in the 1923 Broadway musical *Runnin' Wild*.

That a woman who dances the Charleston engages in a lot of provocative flashing of her bare knees says a lot about women at that moment in American history. In 1918, World War I had ended, leaving in its wake a lot of widows and women inured to waiting for the men to return. That same year, the country was invaded by the Spanish flu epidemic. These twin engines of mortality impressed upon many women the idea that life is short. Two years later, women had won the right to vote, giving credence to the long-burgeoning belief that the fairer sex should be able to behave just as freely as the menfolk did. Women started initiating dates with men in greater numbers. Stir into this pot many young women's contempt for Prohibition and the temperance movement, as well as fashion's response to the economic boom (the increase in leisure activities like golf and tennis required looser clothing), *et voilà*: who *wouldn't* want to stoop slightly at the waist in order to dazzle with her patellae?

"But the peak of rebellion in social dancing was really amongst American teens of the 1950s," Powers told me. "That was one of the few times when a whole generation of adults has presented a unified condemnation of a youth culture."

It is the defining hallmark of the teenager to feel both marginalized and choked by rules. But for 1950s teenagers such feelings were particularly acute. The threat of nuclear war and the Communist menace had inspired in the older generation an almost parodic interest in the virtues of raising families in calm, orderly environments, which in turn prompted them to draft a lot of rules about hair length and appropriate language. At the time, there were no TV or radio shows addressed specifically to teens, so when teens started to hear music about young love and moonlight and fatal car crashes, it was like the hand of God descending from the sky.

Most of the dancing that American teens did in the 1950s was swing-based. Each community or region would develop its own variation or style—both because it was fun to play with the form, and because kids didn't want to dance the way that their parents did. In one high school the dancing might be low and smooth, Powers told me, and in another it might be angular and wild. The demise of this micro-artisinalism was spelled, though, on August 5, 1957, when Dick Clark convinced ABC to broadcast *American Bandstand* nationally, at which point young dancers across the country started taking their cues from the same source.

When the older generation saw how galvanizing all this music and dancing was to teens, they lashed back, particularly when the source of the swinging was African-derived. Rock-and-roll records were banned, students were kicked out of schools, dances were shut down.

Perhaps you've seen the chilling documentary *Hairspray*.

3.

With social dancing, the catalyst for rebellion would seem always to be repression. Against a backdrop of police brutality toward black citizens in the 2010s, other young dancers launched into the crotch-thrusting Whip and the Nae Nae; faced with the economic recession of the 1970s, some bold young folk rose from their bar stools and hurled themselves into the punk idioms of pogo dancing and moshing (come 2017, though, some punk bands, in response to requests from women and minorities, started abandoning mosh pits at their shows and introducing "safe spaces" instead: angry but sensitive!).

With concert dancing, a certain amount of repression is an effective catalyst of rebellion, too. But my research suggests that it might also help to have a name like Isadora, Martha, or Twyla.

To most contemporary minds, the name Isadora Duncan (1877–1927) conjures up two things—long, flowy movement enhanced by long, flowy garments; and a long, flowy garment (her hand-painted silk scarf) getting inextricably caught in the spokes of a car wheel. (It was an Amilcar, not a Bugatti as is commonly thought.) But the woman who made bare feet the symbol of modern dance was a whole lot more.

In the nineteenth century, female dancers had been occasionally idolized and almost always suspected of loose morals, but Duncan, who rejected the tight-fitting clothing of her day, helped smash those stereotypes by inventing her own way of moving and pronouncing herself a full-blown artist. Identifying herself as "an Enemy of the Ballet," she tackled the artistic establishment and did so without credentials or institutional backing or family money. Indeed, she even had the audacity to lecture the wealthy about the evils of money while hitting them up for donations.

Born in San Francisco, she dropped out of school at age ten because she found traditional education stifling. She would go on to endure much personal tragedy in her life—in 1913, when she was thirty-six, her two young children would drown when their runaway car plunged into the Seine, and she'd lose a third child in childbirth a year later—but she emerged resolute and mission-bound. Scorning scenery and costumes and popular music, she was the first dancer, or among the first, to dance to "important" music that had not been written expressly for dancing (e.g., Chopin, Beethoven), which shocked the art world. She vowed never to marry (this didn't quite pan out) and had hundreds of lovers. She danced while pregnant and unwed. When she moved to Moscow in 1921—she was passionate about the tumult that led to the creation of the Soviet Union, and wanted to start a school there—she choreographed dances full of fury at social injustice, and declared, "Yes, I am a revolutionist. All true artists are revolutionists."

Her own dancing was polarizing. She danced barefoot during a time, the Belle Epoque, when piano legs were often covered so they wouldn't excite men. She did not have a dancer's body (all the drinking couldn't have helped: her nickname was Isadorable Drunken). Balanchine thought she looked like "a drunk fat woman who for hours was rolling around like a pig." But for a more nuanced view, here's what choreographer Frederick Ashton told TV interviewer Dick Cavett about seeing Duncan perform in London around 1920: "There was a lot of galumphing, and she was getting quite stout in a way, but nevertheless there was some extraordinary force of personality, and a system of dancing which was to me absolutely fascinating. She had a wonderful sense of repose and stillness which was, you know, incredible, and I mean, really, she'd stand still for a very long time, and you thought, 'Well, when on earth is she going to move?' and suddenly she would just put out a hand and it was magic."

Though she may not have been as free-spirited as her reputation suggests—the writer Peter Kurth has pointed out that she took lessons when she was a dance hall performer, and that she was a "chaste nymph" until twenty-five—she nevertheless emerges an avatar of free will. An atheist and a bisexual and a Communist sympathizer who had all three of her children out of wedlock, she was not afraid, even in the middle of performances, to weigh in on the topics of the day. Her thoughts about dance were particularly fiery: she thought ballet called for a "deformed skeleton" and "sterile movements." She thought the Charleston looked like a series of "tottering, ape-like convulsions," and that jazz rhythm should remain the province of "the South African savage."

You might call Isadora racist, but you wouldn't call her shy. In *My Life*, her perfumed and at times hilariously melodramatic memoir, she writes about how, in 1896, at age nineteen, she stood outside a Chicago theater and pestered a stage manager into introducing her to director and promoter Augustin Daly, to whom she would gush, "I have discovered the dance. I have discovered the art which has been lost for two thousand years." Later, after Daly had cast her in unsatisfyingly small parts in some of his shows, Duncan asked him, "What's the good of having me here, with my genius, when you make no use of me?"

To proclaim oneself possessed of genius is to vault over the barriers of modesty and decorum that so many of us others struggle with. But Duncan kept vaulting. Her force of will has been an inspiration for countless others, even if this inspiration has at times been a mixed blessing: Agnes de Mille maintained that the publication of *My Life* "proved dreadfully unnerving to the young. Several virgins of my acquaintance went conscientiously astray in the hope of becoming great dancers."

Impassioned, willful, unashamed. Isadora Duncan made the world safe for talking about yourself in the third person while smoking a clove cigarette.

Duncan shares some characteristics with another important dance pioneer. Martha Graham (1894–1991), too, was highly opinionated and anxious to plant her flag in opposition to ballet. Her work, too, unsettled audiences. Her work, too, condemned intolerance. Like Duncan, she hailed from California (though she'd been raised in Pennsylvania). She shared with Duncan the paradox of having a personality big enough for drag queens of future generations to emulate, while simultaneously (and ironically) disliking being filmed. And, as with Duncan, she's sometimes called the Mother of Modern Dance.

But if Duncan's work was billowy and attenuated and partly improvised, Graham's was spikey and angular and set. While ballet typically conceals effort, Graham's choreography, built on the principles of "contraction" and "release," often highlighted it, because Graham thought dance should mirror life, which is full of effort. As she once put it, "Life today is nervous, sharp, and zig-zag. This is what I aim for in my dances." She wanted to dance like a Kandinsky painting. Think bent arms with weirdly crooked fingers, or dancers collapsing to the floor behind them. In her most celebrated work, *Lamentation,* a seated dancer, wrapped in jersey such that only her hands, face, and feet are visible, writhes and undulates for four minutes: Graham was seventy years ahead of the rest of the world in seeing the potential horror of being trapped in a Slanket.

Graham's parents, strict Presbyterians, didn't want her to become a dancer. She studied at the Denishawn School, started in Los Angeles by modern dancers Ruth St. Denis and Ted Shawn, and then joined the Denishawn Dancers. She started her own company in 1926; early company members included Merce Cunningham, Paul Taylor, and Anna Sokolow, who would choreograph for Broadway and cofound the Actors Studio. (Given that these three then went on themselves to rear a younger generation of dancers and choreographers, maybe Graham is better called the grandmother of modern dance.) She gave prominent roles to dancers of color during a time when such dancers were under-utilized because they were considered "exotics."

Graham drew from a wide variety of sources for inspiration for her choreography—classical mythology, Noh, Kabuki, Chinese opera—but the net result is less universal than deeply personal: she considered her dances to be "a graph of the heart." She used spastic movements, falls, and trembling to chart themes that she thought dance usually neglected. Some of the work is explicitly sexual; audiences were sometimes shocked to see Medea or Jocasta or Phaedra or Clytemnestra venting their libido. To prepare dancers for such heights, Graham was not afraid to give her female dancers the correction "You are simply not moving your vagina." Paul Taylor wrote, "Sometimes I think she views us men onstage as giant dildos." She once said, "I won't have virgins in my company"; another time she told her company, "By the time you have left, I will know everything about your sex lives." Her school became known among dancers as the House of the Pelvic Truth.

Over the course of her career, she would clash with both the NEA and Congress. You need only glance at the titles of some of Graham's works to get the sense that she wasn't afraid of the proverbial dark: *Revolt, Deaths and Entrances, Lucifer, Immediate Tragedy, Heretic.* In *Cave of the Heart* (1946), one of Graham's many modern adaptations of Greek myth, a rageaholic Medea eats her own entrails. In her uncompromising study of sexual exploitation *Phaedra's*

Dream, Hippolytus's explicit homoerotic duet gave a new reason for his romantic rejection of his stepmother.

In person, Graham had titanic charisma—even when she wasn't in the room, she was in the room. A vegetarian who would eat "placid fish" like sole but not "valiant" ones like salmon, she lived with dancer Erick Hawkins for nine years before marrying him.

She was not without a temper. As she once told dancer Robert Cohan, "I'm a tiger and I love to use my claws." To this end, she had a number of wonderfully vivid expressions in her arsenal, chief among them "I am just frantic, absolutely a boiled owl!" and "I'm being nibbled to death by ducks!" She critiqued one dancer with "Oh, Sophie, you are so agricultural"; one of Sophie's colleagues was told, "I am thankful for just one thing about you. That you are not twins." After seeing her friend Agnes de Mille's performance of *Three Virgins and a Devil* at Ballet Theatre in the early 1940s, Graham delivered what is among the best damning-with-faint-praise compliments ever uttered: "In a small, in a tiny obscure way, this is a classic of its kind."

Loath to relinquish roles that she had created for herself, Graham—who liked to tell students, "Remember, one day you will all die"—danced well into her seventies, long after her Kabuki looks and high dudgeon had devolved into unwitting camp. This attests to the highly personal nature of her work. "It wasn't until years after I had relinquished a ballet that I could watch someone else dance it," she writes in her memoir, *Blood Memory*. "I believe in never looking back, never indulging in nostalgia, or reminiscing. Yet how can you avoid it when you look on stage and see a dancer made up to look as you did 30 years ago, dancing a ballet you created with someone you were then deeply in love with, your husband? I think that is a circle of hell Dante omitted."

Even her ideas about talent seem to fly in the face of conventional wisdom. In her gold-standard memoir *Dance to the Piper*, Agnes de Mille writes about going to see a latter-day production of her own cowboy ballet *Rodeo* and being hugely disappointed in it: "There was no way of ensuring lasting beauty." Outside of Schrafft's restaurant, she runs into her pal Graham, who, speaking "from a life's effort," counsels de Mille: "There is a vitality, a life force, an energy, a quickening that is translated through you into action, and because there is only one of you in all of time, this expression is unique. And if you block it, it will never exist through any other medium and it will be lost. The world will not have it. It is not your business to determine how good it is . . . it is your business to keep it yours clearly and directly, to keep the channel open. You do not even have to believe in yourself or your work. You have to keep yourself open and aware directly to the urges that motivate you. . . . No artist is pleased. [There is] no satisfaction whatever at any time. There is only a queer divine dissatisfaction, a blessed unrest that keeps us marching and makes us more alive than the others. And at times I think I could kick you until you can't stand."

Isadora Duncan and Martha Graham paved the way for yet a third troublemaker.

At this point in my choreo-investigation, I reached out to Twyla Tharp. I'd just finished reading her memoir, *Push Comes to Shove*, a juicy account of how a dancer and choreographer who started out in the kooky, experimental avant-garde in New York in the 1960s (in her first work, *Tank Dive*, she wore bedroom slippers and put a yo-yo to sleep) figured out a way to parlay her dazzling eccentricity into mainstream popularity.

Fifty years is a really long time for a choreographer to remain active and relevant. Twyla has created more than 160 dances for her own company as well as New York City Ballet, Paris Opera Ballet, and London's Royal Ballet, among others; an enviable number of her works are now included in the classical repertory (*In the Upper Room*, *Bach Partita*, and *Nine Sinatra Songs* among them).

In Tharp's hands, rebellion is mostly about rubbing up against, and abrading, the canon. She created the first crossover work to mix modern and classical dance (1973's *Deuce Coupe*, commissioned by the Joffrey Ballet and set to the music of the Beach Boys). Three years later she made what some consider the best-ever example of the crossover ballet, *Push Comes to Shove*, a high-energy vaudevillian romp which starred Mikhail Baryshnikov. These works fanned the flames of the animosity that ballet purists feel toward modern dance, an antagonism maybe best captured by Russian ballet reformer Michel Fokine's comment, "Ugly mother standing in wings watching ugly daughter perform ugly movements on stage as ugly son makes ugly sounds on drum, is modern dance." (True to form, Twyla's critics contend that her sometimes intentionally awkward choreography doesn't mix well with pointe work.)

You see her rebelliousness in how she conducts herself, too. A shrewd and sometimes ruthless businesswoman—in 1985 she was one of the first choreographers ever to stoop to making dancers pay to audition—Twyla is unusual in the dance world for having seized the reins of commerce by presenting some of her works in Broadway theaters: the first was 1980's *When We Were Very Young*, followed by her 1981 collaboration with David Byrne, *The Catherine Wheel*. Her other Broadway offerings have seen her interpreting Frank Sinatra (*Come Fly Away*), Billy Joel (*Movin' Out*), and Bob Dylan (*The Times They Are A-Changin'*).

I met her work via film. The movie *Hair* came out just as I was falling in love with New York City. I saw it at the soaring and cavernous Ziegfeld with a friend. When we came out of the theater at the end, elated, I spun in a circle with my arms outstretched and then simulated my favorite part of the film, the cop-mounted horses sashaying sideways. (The horses are Lipizanners. Twyla taught the horses' moves to the dancers, not the other way around.) To see horses dance like that was to be confronted head-on with the strange charm of surprise; I felt like I'd found a new room in my house.

But now, thirty-six years later, I find myself fascinated by the explicit way Twyla wrote in her memoir about the various motivations that wafted her along her flight path. In the back of my copy of the book I wrote in pencil nine of those she specified: to understand life through movement; to unite jazz, modern, and ballet; to continue a tradition of women dance pioneers (Twyla's first company, like Martha Graham's, started out all-female); to find music's equivalent in movement; to see dancing recognized as part of one's everyday life; to demystify the elitist, museum-quality of dance; to investigate the boundaries of classical technique; to achieve financial independence; to revenge and repair the past.

I sent her office an e-mail. Alas, Twyla's assistant wrote me back to say that, what with writing her fourth book and teaching at Barnard and readying a tour to celebrate her fiftieth anniversary in the field, Twyla was too busy to sit down with the likes of me. However, they suggested I join them in an upcoming performance of Twyla's 1970 community dance piece *The One Hundreds*.

A product of her avant-garde beginnings, when Twyla was still unearthing beauty from bedroom slippers and yo-yos, *The One Hundreds* was inspired by baseball. She'd been living in the woods one summer and watching a lot of the all-American pastime when she realized that most baseball plays last about eleven seconds. So she made a dance in which two people simultaneously perform the same one hundred sporty movement sequences, each of which lasts just that long; then five dancers each simultaneously perform twenty of the sequences; then one hundred volunteers who are not professional dancers—this is where I was to come in—each simultaneously perform one of the eleven-second-long sequences. The new performance was to take place on a Saturday night, in lower Manhattan's Rockefeller Park.

After blithely writing the assistant back to say I'd love to join, I went online and watched a few clips of the piece being performed. I was bowled over by how much choreography can be fit into eleven seconds. Only a few of *The One Hundreds*'s movements are baseball-specific; there are allusions to cheerleading, boxing, golf, rock and roll, and ballet. Some of the sequences are majestic (one is an homage to *La Sylphide*), some are hilarious and awkward (while running in place, the dancer repeatedly slaps her underarms). Unexpectedly, *The One Hundreds* is not the Twyla dance in which the dancers start casually to spit: that distinction belongs to *The Bach Duet*, her romantic *pas de deux*.

Anthropologists sometimes divide dances into three types: those done for the gods, those done for other people, and those done for oneself. It was not lost on me that, in my newfound interest in dance, all of my dancing had fallen into the third category, as it will when (a) you're not especially interested in having people watch you dance and (b) all of your former experiences with following specific choreography have led you to believe that you're more Isadora than you thought you were.

By the same token, however, it occurred to me that by avoiding choreographic routines, maybe I was denying myself some larger and more extroverted form of satisfaction or sublimity. When the Rockettes all hit their mark in unison, they produce a collective sigh.

Would I ever know such a feeling?

Aware that on the day of the performance I'd be randomly assigned a sequence, I was anxious to see how quickly I could pick up Twyla's alternately slinky and jerky moves. So, standing at my desk in my office one day while watching a YouTube clip of five Dance Chicago dancers, I tried to pull off one of the bits: you outstretch your arms downward and bring them up over your head while lifting your right leg up and then slowly pushing the leg down to the ground. You do this three more times; then, arms straight down at your sides, you tilt forward and kick each of your legs backwards four times. Now the same thing, only you're leaning backwards and kicking your legs forward; next make a big circle with your right leg, hop side to side from one leg to the other, swing your arms sideways and then up and to the front.

If you get it right, the effect is that of a stork with a trick knee trying to take flight.

On my first outing, I achieved only a 20 percent mastery. All trick knees. My stork could flap, but he was in no hurry to get airborne.

I kept flapping, working through the sequence five or six more times, gradually getting my mastery up to 60 percent.

The stork could fly, but only about three inches off the ground.

Meanwhile, during the six weeks before the performance, I did more Tharp research. In the script of a videotape called *Scrapbook* that she made in 1982, Twyla says, "*The One Hundreds* shows deterioration almost as a scientific matter. First, the highly trained, disciplined and rehearsed dancer performs a series of movements approaching an absolute in clarity. Passed down to dancers less well-rehearsed, the movement declines until, when executed by completely untrained bodies, the same movement is seen with no detail and little definition." She concludes, "Thus, the original *One Hundreds* was an investigation of physical rigor and its deterioration."

What a relief. Elaborate swan-simulating choreography, even in an eleven-second burst, is just far enough out of my grasp to rattle me.

But deterioration I can do.

With just days to go before the big day when I'd be assigned my sequence and given a few hours to hone it, I decided to visit the retired dancer and Tharp alumnus Jamie Bishton. Jamie is a longtime friend I've known, sort of, for twenty-five years. He lives in Los Angeles with his husband and two children.

Naturally, I was curious to know how he'd come to dance. A child gymnast in LA during the 1970s, Jamie broke his arm at age fourteen, thus ending his gymnastics career. His orthopedic surgeon, seeing that his patient had fallen into a depression, encouraged Jamie to take a dance class as a way to start getting more endorphins back into his system. Jamie, whose appreciation of dance at the time was, as he said, "nonexistent," signed up for a jazz class. And loved it. He then studied with Donald Byrd at UC Santa Cruz, went on to CalArts, and danced briefly for Bella Lewitzky. These achievements under his belt, he saw it was time to do what everyone had been encouraging him to do for a few years: go east, young man.

When his father learned that his son had bought a $99, one-way ticket to New York on People Express, the Greyhound Bus of air travel, Bishton senior "freaked out. He said, 'I'm not gonna let this happen.' He bought me a round-trip ticket on United. He said, 'This round-trip ticket is open-ended, so whenever you need to come home, if it doesn't work out, you have a ticket to come back.'"

Telling me this, Jamie—one of the more humble luminaries, in any field, that you could hope to meet—looked down at the ground. We were sitting on the back porch of his cozy, beautifully appointed house on a quiet street in LA, a slightly eerie silence having pervaded the backyard once Jamie's husband had spirited off his and Jamie's two kids to the grocery store.

Jamie looked up and finished the story: "Because my dad made me feel like it was okay to fail, I didn't. I stayed in New York for twenty-five years."

Jamie danced for Lar Lubovitch and, from 1985 to 1988, Twyla. He followed Twyla to American Ballet Theatre, and stayed there for two years, whereupon Mikhail Baryshnikov, who would become a mentor to Jamie, invited him to join the White Oak Dance Project, a company that Baryshnikov and Mark Morris formed in 1990.

After eight years with White Oak, Bishton returned to Twyla's fold in 1998 to perform for her again, and to be her assistant and the director of her dancers.

I asked Jamie how dancing Twyla's work was different from performing other choreographers'.

"She allows you to be yourself," he said. "Other choreographers want things a very certain way, and your challenge is to meet what they want. I worked with Mark Morris a lot and, not that he didn't want my interpretation of his work, but countless times in the studio, Twyla would choreograph something on me and she'd be sitting in her chair and would say, 'Okay, you're gonna start from the corner, come in and run, and then jump, and as you're jumping you're gonna go into *arabesque,* and then bring your legs together and then you're gonna land on one leg and come down into an *arabesque.*' And then she would mold it to my body."

I said to Jamie, "She does a lot with a shrug. Does she say stuff like 'Throw it away'?"

"Not so much 'Throw it away,' more about release. Aggressive: yes. There's an attack to her work."

"She's said in interviews that she asks for 'insane commitment' from her dancers."

"And you want to give her that. Because she's going to pull out of me as an artist what I didn't even know existed. But she's hard. Working with her is very hard. The hardest part is, when she's done with you, she's done. She severs relationships and communications. It's because of the intense relationship with her in the studio. It becomes a kind of divorce. I'm one of the few dancers who left on a good note. But at the airport, when we'd finished the last performance of the work we were doing at the time, *Diabelli* at the Hancher Auditorium in Iowa, she said goodbye, and that was one of the last times I've ever seen her. I thought, Oh, there'll be another project, something else will come down the line. But no, that was it."

I'm reminded here of the weirdest line in Twyla's memoir. It comes toward the end, after she's chronicled a number of her romantic relationships with men, most of whom she worked with— painter Peter Young, artist Bob Huot, Baryshnikov, rock promoter Bill Graham, David Byrne.

Twyla writes, "Like primitive peoples eating the hearts of lions to consume bravery, I seemed to mate to acquire talents."

Jamie is unusual in the world of Tharp dancers not only because when he rejoined her he served for a time as director of her dancers and her assistant, but because in 1991, while the company did a residency at the Ohio State University, Twyla had Jamie do half of *The One Hundreds* as a solo.

"It was a one-off," he said. "And no one hundred volunteers."

I asked, "Is it harder to learn a bunch of random movement sequences rather than something with narrative?"

"It requires a different memory chip. It requires mnemonics. I would think, This is the shaking hands one, this is Scratch My Foot."

"This is Heidi Gets on a Plane to Scotland," I said, remembering having read about the title another Tharp dancer had given to one of the moves.

"Exactly. It's that children's game, 'I'm going to the market and buying apples and bananas and . . .' It starts as a brain exercise but then physical memory kicks in."

We talked more about the upcoming performance. I confessed, "For a nonprofessional like me, who's a little daunted by the task, the saving graces are that (a) it's about deterioration, and (b) Hermione Gingold did it at age eighty."

At various times that *The One Hundreds* has been performed, celebrities like Dick Cavett, Estelle Parsons, Miloš Forman, and singer and pianist Bobby Short have been among the one hundred, as was Gingold, the British actress with the absurdly ribbitty voice who played the grandmother in the movie *Gigi* and the mayor's haughty wife in *The Music Man.*

Jamie smiled at the mention of Gingold. He said, "You're gonna be a star! When you get there, just make sure you have enough room to dance in. Everyone's gonna be jostling for position."

"I'll get my elbows going."

"Yes. And have a good time! What makes it a unique experience is that you'll be doing it with ninety-nine other people. I mean, when do one hundred people ever agree to do anything for even *one* second, let alone eleven?"

I asked Jamie what he made of Twyla's interest in deterioration, and he suggested that *all* dances suffer it. Referring to one of Tharp's most beloved dances, he said, "That's what I saw over the course of *In the Upper Room,* from being in the original company to various pick-up companies and to ABT: not that it got lost in translation, but in each new version there was deterioration away from what the dance originally was."

"You mean that the dancers' moves get looser in each new production?"

"Things get lost. It depends on who's setting the dance, and what they remember, and what their understanding of the physicality is. It might be the right steps but not have the right intent."

In the Upper Room feels like a masterpiece. Twyla has called it a "secular mass." Set to a pulsating, soaring Philip Glass score that seems to burst through the rafters, the dance sees thirteen dancers, thanks to wonderfully spectral lighting from Jennifer Tipton, alternately materializing onto and disappearing from a fog-drenched stage. The dancers are in two groups: the three men and three women who are writhing and thrashing while wearing sneakers are known by the company as "the stompers," while the other seven, including four women in fire engine–red pointe shoes, have a more slicing and shearing quality, and are referred to by the company as "the bomb squad." Are we in Heaven? If so, this is the most aerobicized view of the hereafter on record; you'll be able to eat *anything* here because the workout is so hardcore. It's the *Oresteia* of leaping and wriggling. But maybe the more apt way to view this tour de force—it's the one dance of Twyla's that is invariably met with a standing ovation—is as a battle between the towering, sky-directed classicism of ballet and the dirt-born, shrugging unpredictability of modern. Here is the ultimate smackdown between earth and air.

But, in the end, what's so galvanizing about *In the Upper Room* is its sense of urgency. The dance shares two qualities with the best suspense films: the stakes are high from the get-go, and the movement of the piece is one of constant escalation. It starts at 10 and builds to 17.

Back in New York, I kept trying out various *One Hundreds* moves that I found on YouTube. I could imagine a world in which Twyla's shrugging and aggressive nonchalance were within my scope of bodily capability, but some of her sudden shifts of tempo, not to mention a lot of the ballet moves, were entities I'd have to resign myself to watching, not doing.

Part of me wondered if the three-and-a-half hours of rehearsal that us volunteers would get on the day of the performance would be enough to settle my mounting nerves. Another part of me thought, There'll be ninety-nine other people dancing at the same time, so why worry?

But mostly I wondered what the dance as a whole would seem like. I couldn't find a video of the whole twenty-two-minute-or-so thing, only parts thereof. Dance critic Marcia B. Siegel, who wrote a book about Twyla called *Howling Near Heaven*, once described *The One Hundreds* as "conceptual, boring, fascinating, spectacular," which sounded about right.

Then, the day before the event, in a *New York Times* story, Gia Kourlas called *The One Hundreds* "glorious."

From my office, I sent Greg a link to the *Times* story, and titled the e-mail "Pressure mounting!"

That night at home, we started talking about the event and Greg said, "I can't wait."

I said, "It should be really cool. I just read about another high-concept piece that Twyla did around the same time, though. When her company performed it in Paris, one French critic lamented having to endure quote-unquote 'this hairy and untidy outburst.'"

Greg said, "By which he meant the 1960s."

The meeting place for the event, which was part of the Lower Manhattan Cultural Council's River to River Festival, was a one-thousand-square-foot-or-so, ground-floor space right next to Rockefeller Park: a sparsely furnished glass box that might otherwise have been a Citibank or Foot Locker.

I gave my name to one of the smiley young folk manning the table in the space's entryway. She said, "I'm gonna assign Savannah as your teacher." Savannah Lowery, the New York City Ballet soloist who would be missing that company's fall season to dance with Twyla.

I had arrived in both senses of the word.

About thirty people milled around the space, many of them standing and chatting, some of them sitting on the floor, some of them stretching. There'd been no wardrobe requirements in either of the two e-mails we volunteers had received; the cumulative dress code on display suggested a Lululemon store that was hemorrhaging harem pants.

Gazing at the room, I was surprised to see Twyla herself, sitting on the windowsill. Silver-haired, she's tiny and birdlike, and was dressed in jeans and grubby white New Balance sneakers. She was talking to her assistant.

Because there'd been no acknowledgment of my being a member of the press when I checked in, I took it that Twyla didn't know I was in attendance. I also figured that there were probably a bunch of other press people taking part in the event. (I would later meet Claudia Roth Pierpont, who was participating, and writing up the experience for the *New Yorker*.)

Given that Twyla looked neither busy nor beset by admirers, I decided to walk up to her and try to say something that would make an impression. Though, in the moment, I was not trying to be rebellious, I would later come to think of it as so. In the moment, my brain went immediately to the time that Twyla herself performed half of *The One Hundreds* as a solo. While Jamie Bishton had done *Half the One Hundreds* to fill up a program of repertory, Twyla herself did it at the Spoleto Festival in Italy in 1975 in order, according to *Howling Near Heaven*, to show off to Baryshnikov, who Twyla knew would be in the audience, and with whom she was hoping to work. After her performance, she went to the after-party, where Baryshnikov, whom she had not really formally met yet, walked up to her and gave her a glass of champagne.

I'll let Twyla's memoir take over here: "The party was much too crowded. We became restless. Outside, the evening was clear, the air warm; the moon lit the winding streets that pitched steeply down from the palazzo to our hotel. Soon we were running barefoot down the town's ancient sidewalks, laughing at the pleasure of moving together. When we arrived at the hotel we paused. We were both winded, speaking different languages; it seemed ridiculous even to ask. In my room, I found that the famous muscles I had only seen tensed in performance possessed an extraordinary softness. As we explored each other's bodies, the confidence we had as dancers let us invent transitions that flowed as smoothly as well-drafted duets. Afterward he fell asleep and I watched his body shake, throwing off the remaining tension from his incredible dance efforts. It was dawn before I closed my eyes and when I awoke he was gone."

So, taking a deep breath to calm myself, I walked up to Twyla on her windowsill perch and, without introducing myself, said, "Hi, Twyla, I just wanted to say what an honor it is to be doing this."

Her head tilted back slightly, she looked down her beaky nose and over the top of her horn-rims at me. ("I am so near-sighted," she has written, "that as a child, before I had glasses, I could not see into the mirror. So of course I understood that you play and dance by feel, not sight.")

Twyla's expression was pure deadpan, in the manner of a silent film comedian.

She reached out her hand to shake mine and said, "Thanks for doing this."

ME: I just read the part of your memoir where you did part of *The One Hundreds* at Spoleto. You had such terrific results! I only hope our results tonight will be as good.

Slight pause.

TWYLA: Well, all right.

As soon as I skulked away from Twyla and disappeared into the crowd, I thought, I am an asshole. Who in his right mind, on meeting a woman in her seventies, let alone one who's been nice enough to include you in one of her works, cuts right to her sex life?

Also, I had not expected this level of expressionlessness. Yes, when she accepted her Tony for *Movin' Out*, Twyla said she'd once auditioned for the Rockettes: "I got through the 64 *fouettés* and they said, 'That was all fine and good. Could you smile?'" Yes, the book *Howling Near Heaven* has dancer Sara Rudner, who worked with Twyla for two decades, saying that when Twyla watched rehearsals, "you could never tell what emotion she was feeling," and that "Twyla didn't come up to you and say, 'God, that was great.'

She would not say anything." (Rudner chalks up the blankness of Twyla's screen to a kind of puritanism that grew out of her Quaker background.)

In retrospect I interpret my comment as both rebellion and homage. See, when you read a lot about Twyla, or talk to people in her orbit, her most oft-mentioned characteristic—besides the tireless dedication and the thrumming inventiveness—is her brashness. This reputation is partly self-fanned—in her memoir, she describes herself as "obnoxious" twice and "blunt" once; of her meeting with Bob Joffrey of the Joffrey Ballet to discuss making *Deuce Coupe*, she writes, "I was my usual brash, no-bullshit, direct and rude person." In Paul Taylor's beautifully written memoir, *Private Domain*, Taylor refers to this former member of his company as a "wisecracking little mole-twerp." At the time, company member Twyla thought that Taylor had sold out as a choreographer; he'd assign her a phrase and she'd respond, "You're kidding," becoming, in her own words, "absolutely and intolerably obnoxious." When Twyla leaves Taylor's company, he writes, "Really didn't want to lose you, Twyla honey, but why can't you be less abrasive, less watch-spring tense? Because you're talented and insecure and driven, that's why. Like me."

Yes, she's famous for what she does with bodies, but that doesn't mean she can't deploy her mouth. There's a funny passage in *Howling Near Heaven* wherein Twyla and some of her dancers are doing a site-specific dance at the Metropolitan Museum in 1970 that starts to go slightly awry. When Twyla launches into a solo that the other dancers have not had a chance to see before, they hover on the edge of the performance space, unsure whether or not to enter. So Twyla dances over to them and yells, "Get the fuck back!"

A few years earlier, when a janitor at Judson Church stumbled onto a Tharp rehearsal and indignantly asked how people could be dancing on a Sunday, Tharp fired back, "How dare you disturb a bunch of women doing God's work!" (This churchly iconoclasm is immortalized in *Hair*, too: in the film's LSD sequence, Tharp plays the airborne eminence in the chapel who marries Claude and Sheila, and who can be seen standing on the altar and kicking off her shorts to reveal striped panties beneath her surplice.)

Members of the media, too, can be the target of Twyla's animus. "She hates being interviewed," Bishton told me. "She hates having her picture taken," Twyla's assistant told me. In 1996, when a *Los Angeles Times* reporter writing a feature about Twyla's new work—it was called *Tharp!*—asked her if the work marked a new direction for her, Twyla replied, "That's only mostly a stupid question."

Seen in this light, my comment made more sense to me. I must have been unconsciously trying to out-Twyla Twyla.

Some ten minutes after my brief interaction with Twyla, her assistant found me in the crowd and introduced me to her. I apologized for not having introduced myself earlier. Twyla asked that we talk off the record. I worried, of course, that she would bring up my earlier comment, but she did not. We talked for about ten minutes. I will say simply that it's no surprise she's a successful artist (she comes across as focused and direct, but anxious to talk about big concepts) or that she's written three books in the self-improvement genre (she asks a lot of questions about you you you).

When a few of my awkward stabs at wit were met with blank-facedness, I focused instead on talking about *The One Hundreds* and complimenting her on her work. I told her that I loved the part of her memoir where she said her first dance was stunning a rattlesnake with a hoe, and I told her that I admired her bravery in presenting some of her shows in Broadway theaters. I brought up our mutual interest in film, and it was only here that she let me know I had stumbled; when I suggested that film might save dance from being, as it is sometimes referred to, "the art that vanishes," she had a sarcastic response that made me wonder if I'd ever heard an interview subject respond in earnest to a question with "Doy" or "D'oh" or any of the faux-primitive d-words deployed to acknowledge an interviewer's apparent stupidity.

We split up into our groups. Savannah Lowery—a tall, warm, twenty-something who feels instantly like your fun-loving, jocky big sister—looked at the twelve of us in her group and asked, "Do we have any dancers, because I have two sequences with splits. One from a standing position." Three young women volunteered. "Great," Lowery said, "I want to get those harder ones out of the way first."

We moved over to the corner of the room, and Lowery started patiently explaining the first sequence—the standing splits one—to one of the women while the rest of us watched, some of us standing, some of us sitting on long conference tables.

Lowery spent about fifteen minutes with the first three dancers. The sequences were intimidatingly complicated. I tried to offset my tension by looking at the chaos surrounding me; it looked like the room was about to burst into a Diet Coke commercial. Off in the distance I saw Twyla twirling 180 degrees while taking an iPhone video of the cumulative welter. Then she sat on the floor to photograph a woman whose sequence involved somersaulting backwards.

Hearing Lowery say, "Okay, now I have one for one of my guys. This one is a football one." I snapped back to attention.

I looked at the only other male in our group—he was willowy, with misty, spaniel eyes and ringlets of hair down to his shoulders—and I thought, I got this. I raised my hand.

"Great!" Lowery enthused, and then proceeded to show me the sequence. You know those football drills where the players bend their knees slightly and hold their fists up in the air at chest height and then piston their legs while pushing a heavily weighted object (a tackling sled) across the field? Imagine doing that, but then, halfway through, suddenly realizing you need to grapevine like you've never needed to grapevine before.

Lowery made the sequence look extremely easy, but as soon as I tried to do it, the image in my head bore no relation to what my legs and arms did. She did the sequence for me ten or eleven times, slowing it down and breaking it into pieces, but I started to feel like I was taking up too much of her time, so I took an iPhone video of her doing the steps.

Lowery moved on to the other male dancer, and I started looking at my video. I had gotten through it twice when Twyla walked over to me. The second she started speaking, I knew how I had erred: I shouldn't have been learning the dance from the video, it's an intellectualized approach to what should be a purely kinesthetic experience. While talking to me, Twyla did her thing with me, her rock-on-the-balls-of-her-feet-while-staring thing. This was at once thrilling (I have the attention of the world's most accomplished living choreographer) and rattling (How has she gotten so far with such a limited repertoire of facial expressions?).

She didn't seem disappointed with me. No need for that. But I was disappointed in myself. Indeed, during our subsequent three-minute-long talk, I stashed my iPhone in my pocket and found myself reflexively brushing my fingertips against my pants as if to wipe off any iPhone-derived besmirchment.

During this three minutes, Twyla did a marvelous thing. At one point, out of the corner of my eye, I saw a dancer's hand fly into the air—have I stressed that there were more than a hundred people rehearsing in a space the size of an airport Cinnabon? Twyla must have seen it, too: she grabbed the front of my shirt at chest level, as if to choke me to death, and then, rotating me twenty-five degrees to my right, positioned me parallel with the bathroom wall, out of harm's way.

* * *

I went back to my group's huddle, hoping to find in their ministrations either inspiration or succor.

Lowery continued teaching them for another forty-five minutes or so. While instructing one woman in her forties to do a sequence that included a lot of shoulders and cross-stepping, Lowery said of Twyla and the move, "But she doesn't want it pretty, she wants it dirty." When another woman made a slightly bewildered face on being shown her sequence—the one where you run in place while slapping your armpits—Lowery neatly defused any tension by saying, "I know—weird, right?"

Meanwhile, over by the window, Twyla gave instruction to Pierpont, the *New Yorker* writer, who was there with her husband, a warm, rumpled man in his sixties who walked with a cane. "The cane is good," Twyla said to the husband. (In the past, *One Hundreds* volunteers have included paraplegics.)

Pierpont's husband went into his sequence for Twyla's inspection. Between counts six and eight, an arm thrust saw his cane lift up in the air like a sword, which caused him and his wife to grin.

He looked at Twyla as if to say, "Why not?"

Twyla stared at this unblinkingly and, five seconds later, ignored it by complimenting him for finishing the sequence on eleven.

Gradually seven of my group had wandered outside, where we were practicing our sequences in a courtyard while a family of four, eating in a Le Pain Quotidien that overlooked the courtyard, gazed at us disinterestedly.

Soon, Lowery joined us outside. We asked if she'd watch us do a run-through, and she said sure. She wondered if any of us still had any questions.

I asked, "How should I arrange my face?"

"You're grrrrrrrr," Lowery said, gritting her teeth fiercely. "Like when you play football."

"I don't."

"Well, like you've seen in movies."

Got it.

Lowery said that, in our first run-through, she would count the eleven out loud, so we'd know where we were supposed to end.

"Except for you," she said to me. "Because yours ends on eleven-*and.*"

What?! I'm not supposed to be in synch with everyone else at the end?

I gnawed on this bone for about fifteen seconds before realizing that it was too picayune a detail for me to worry about. No, I should focus on larger issues, such as the preceding eleven seconds of movement.

We ran through our sequences three times.

I got better.

We had almost three free hours before we were to return to the check-in site to "stage" the piece. I went out into Rockefeller Park and kept practicing my sequence for about half an hour, until my shoulders and thighs ached. My inspiration was Twyla—a workaholic, a practitioner and preacher of the gospels of discipline and routine. (Baryshnikov, after *Push Comes to Shove*: "Twyla takes it for granted that the choreographer and the dancer can do a single *enchaînement* three thousand times to get it right. I had never had the habit or discipline to do anything so many times and with such concentration of energy.") I wanted to get on this bus for her. I tried not to be bothered by the fact that I was doing my moves at about half the required speed.

At a certain point in my efforts, I noticed, out in the largest open part of the park, Twyla and her seven dancers rehearsing. I sat down on a park bench and watched them for a while. I was sort of hoping to see my football sequence; I didn't. But it didn't matter.

The dancers' work was gorgeous, full of weird, slinky surprises and bursts of muted elegance.

Over the years, Twyla has specified at least two motivations for *The One Hundreds*: to build community, and "trying to get the world to dance so that they'd understand us." As I sat on the bench, this second aspiration spoke to me. In the dancers' hands, or should I say bodies, Twyla's use of everyday gesture coexisted seamlessly with the more formal splits and *jetés* and *relevés*. In the past when I'd appreciated effortlessness in art, it had mostly been a notional matter: I could see the lack of strain, but I didn't know, and possibly couldn't even imagine, what this strain would actually look like. But having struggled with my tiny percentage of the choreography that the dancers were doing, I didn't simply know it, I could almost feel it.

Studies in neuroscience have borne this out: the neural mechanisms that are fired when you see movement are very close to the ones fired when you engage in that movement yourself. As neuroscientist Marcel Kinsbourne has written, "Perceived behavior gives a leg up to more of the same in the observer, who becomes a participant."

Which is to say, though I would have liked to have sat there and watched the dancers run through the whole dance, I could only watch for ten minutes or so: it was too exhausting.

It occurred to me that maybe my uptick of dancing in the previous four years was partly an attempt to make going to the ballet or going to see Michelle Dorrance or Pina Bausch's company even richer. Once you've been on the factory tour, you really start to taste the cinnamon.

Why hadn't this occurred to me earlier?

Duh.

Eager to work off some of my nerves, I walked home, took a shower, and lay on my bed for an hour.

I returned to Rockefeller Park a half hour before the call time, so I could check out the vibe of the field where the performance would be held, and practice a little. It had gotten overcast, and even rained a tiny bit, which had made all the green of the tree-dappled, mist-tinged park look lush and fecund. There was a brooding quality to the heavens and the Hudson River below; the boats that scuttled past the park looked worried. The grass was damp, and I appreciated the fact, like I have never appreciated the fact before, that I would not be doing splits from a standing position.

Over the next twenty minutes, I had great fun talking to four or five other volunteer dancers; knowing that you are backing up seven gorgeous, super-talented young dancers is a cross between going backstage at a Broadway show and hearing your name announced over the radio.

If there is a blatant manifestation of snobbery in the dance world, it is that nonprofessional dancers like me are not called nonprofessional dancers, but, rather, non-dancers. I felt instant camaraderie with all my fellow "non-dancers" and thought, Maybe what's missing in my life, particularly given that I work freelance, is acquaintanceship. I have my tiny handful of close, trusted friends, and I have the swarm of faceless thousands whenever I walk down the street, but sitting in an office by myself all day really curbs my mid-level intimacy.

I walked the two blocks back to the meeting space. Approaching it, I saw Twyla in the window. She winked at me. Had she seen me practicing like a demon? Had she seen me watching her rehearsal? I wasn't sure what the wink was celebrating, but I decided not to overthink it: on a cool winter night, ambiguity can warm you.

I went inside. I knew I needed to run my sequence a few more times, but Twyla was standing in a central location in the room, talking to Alex Brady, a rugged, preppy dancer in his forties who works for her. Part of me was desperate to have her see my sequence, but a larger part was afraid that she would. So, I, uh, punted: I walked thirty feet away from her to the north side of the room, putting a large pillar between us, and proceeded to run the sequence such that she could see only the part I did well (the middle), but not the parts that were a little shaky (the beginning and end).

She had the good grace not to come over to me. However, soon she addressed the crowd, saying, "It's easier for me to yell at you in here than out in the park." She explained that we would break into two groups; each group would run onto the stage at the conclusion of the five dancers' dancing, then we'd be given a count of four, and then go into our sequences.

The vibe in the room was one of restlessness, burgeoning excitement.

We started filtering out of the meeting space to go to the park, and I overheard one of the other dancers—a woman in her fifties— mention her "pregnancy."

"Oh, are you pregnant in this?" I asked.

"Yep," she said, putting her hands about three inches from her stomach, as if calming the fetus with Reiki.

"I'm a football player," I offered. "I probably knocked you up."

"Don't tell my husband."

Out in the park, we—all one hundred of us—rehearsed the volunteers' entrance, dance, exit, and curtain call three times.

Gradually an audience accumulated; it looked like about two hundred people.

The two initial dancers, dressed in white shorts, shirts, and sneakers, launched into their beautifully synched moves, which elicited many sighs and a few gasps and chuckles from the audience. After each eleven-second sequence, the dancers would walk back to their initial starting place, which gave the piece the pleasing quality of a hundred ocean waves.

Three-fourths of the way through the two dancers' part of the presentation, one of the one hundred tapped me on the shoulder and pointed at them: they were doing my sequence.

I had not recognized it because, in my mind, it happened at half the pace.

The next five Tharp dancers, all doing different sequences at the same time, were even more fun to watch: a tiny circus of gesture.

Then we, the one hundred, burst onto the scene, and blew the whole thing to smithereens.

Those eleven seconds are a bit of a blur to me, but I know this: I did not do all the steps. I did five of them and then, on noticing that everyone else was almost at the end of their sequence, I turned and stuck my landing. Eleven-*and*.

The audience had arranged itself in a long, skinny line, so when we hundred ran back onto the stage area of the lawn for our curtain call, we mirrored this long, skinny formation, but with tiny clumps of people at either end; from a bird's perspective, we must have looked like a toothless comb.

We bowed. Then the seven dancers emerged from behind us and Twyla from the audience, and they bowed.

In the group-huggy after-scrum, people said goodbye to one another. Twyla told me she hoped we'd see each other again, and Lowery said to get in touch if I ever came to New York City Ballet. I felt light-headed from the ether of working—albeit for eleven seconds—with these two huge talents.

Interestingly, all three of the reviews of the performance that I came into contact with during the next few days—one from Greg immediately after the performance, and ones in the *Financial Times* and *New York Times* a few days later—dwelled on the eleven seconds that my fellow volunteers and I had contributed.

Greg came up to me at the end of the performance and hugged me, saying, "That was cool!" Then: "It was an interesting confusion at the end. I never know with Twyla's work where to focus my attention, so with a hundred of you dancing at the same time, it was like 'Here is my problem as a choreographer.'"

In the *Financial Times*, conversely, Apollinaire Scherr extolled the multiplicity of movement ("Cunningham tilts, Broadway shuffles, Paul Taylor strides, a baseball pitch, Graham contractions, a golf swing, Gene Kelly gallops, ballet pantomime and hoofer patter") but landed squarely on the big group scene at the end, which she called "a beautiful egalitarian chaos."

Meanwhile, in the *Times*, Brian Seibert also took note of the diversity of gesture ("It's as if Ms. Tharp were cruising the supermarket of American dance, grabbing items from every aisle and filling up her cart"), but then saw the big crowd scene as an emblem of Twyla's career: "In 1970, she was saying goodbye to the avant-garde and hello to music, on the cusp of a brilliant decade of invention and fame. The ending of 'The One Hundreds,' so massive and yet so short, condensed and yet flung wide open, is like the Big Bang. Ms. Tharp has sometimes described the work as an artifact of its time, but it's really a portrait of her back then, exploding."

Pierpont's *New Yorker* article came out a week later. I was surprised to see myself mentioned ("a man named Henry, who wore a yellow shirt, announced that he was going home to take a shower: 'This is a lot of pressure.'"). I was thrilled, too, to see how she described our work's ending: "It looked as though the unmediated language of dance were taking over the world."

Reading that line again, I heard the curmudgeonly voice of Henry Ford moaning about neighborliness and community involvement.

Maybe we hadn't done it as he envisioned, but done it we had. Non-dancers, building bridges through the medium of non-dance.

DANCE AS EMOTION AND RELEASE

1.

THE MINUTE YOU BECOME AWARE OF YOUR UNDERPANTS DUR-
ing the day is the minute your day becomes hostage to underpants
management. I can be at the very top of my game, everything larky
and full speed ahead, when all of a sudden, blammo, the only
thought occupying my brain is an elasticized waistband's uncanny
ability to creep ever-northward.

But I can't let my mind wander down this particular ill-lit pathway
right this second because my contact improv teacher Chisa Hidaka,
a petite dancer with a mischievous grin, has just given me a task.
A daunting task.

We're standing in an old, funky studio in downtown Manhattan,
where she's told me she wants me to run toward her and the other
two students in our class—they're standing shoulder to shoulder
in a row, like conjoined triplets—and to jump up and into their
outstretched arms.

Um, okay.

I walk twelve feet away from the other dancers, for the purposes
of velocity and stalling. I turn and stare at them. Two of them are
women under five-foot-seven, one of whom is pushing fifty; the other

is a good-looking, patrician dude who does not scream "stevedore." It's like I've been asked to land a 747 in an airport's frequent flyers lounge.

I banish from my mind all thoughts of undergarment creep. But now I can't stop thinking about Nijinsky. Choreographer and ballet dancer Vaslav Nijinsky wowed early twentieth-century audiences with his *ballon*, or ability seemingly to hang in the air. His sister Bronislava's journals tell us that Nijinsky could, astoundingly, count to five while off the ground. Meanwhile, he was often doing those little back-and-forth foot flutters known as *entrechats*. Of which he could do twelve.

But I am not Nijinsky. Floating is not part of my, uh, m'oeuvre. So.

I take a deep breath, I try to relax my shoulders. I recall Nijinsky's own comment on his trademark talent—"Not difficult. You just have to go up and then pause a little up there." I think, Fuck you.

I start running.

I leap and twist, and as I do, every food overindulgence of the past two weeks flickers in my brain like a Vietnam flashback: the two gin and tonics I slurped down out of anxiety at a party two nights earlier, the three-fourths of a pint of Häagen-Dazs I recently ate with a tiny salt cellar spoon in an effort to appear dainty.

And: ker-*plunk!*

My shoulders and upper back land nicely in the arms of the sturdy woman on the left side of the triad: totally adequate. But somehow my lower torso never gets very high in the air, and winds up smooshed against the other two dancers' knees like a bone-in prosciutto that has tunneled out of prison only to be pinned against a chain-link fence by a powerful searchlight.

I recover my feet, withdraw, and look hopefully at my teacher.

Slightly awkward pause. Slightly awkward pause floating in the air Nijinsky-like.

"You're falling down," Chisa says, finally. "But you need to fall up."

(Author slaps own forehead with palm of hand.)

* * *

For some of us, dance's most compelling function is its ability to provide release. The tensions that we hold in our body—and sometimes the emotions held in abeyance by those tensions—get a nice little jiggle from strenuous movement. Unlike the Rebellion function, though, this kind of dancing is generally not a reaction against anything.

Too, this is the function of dance that has most made its mark in everyday speech, whether we be doing our "happy dance," or "waltzing through" some part of life obliviously, or triumphantly "dancing in the end zone." While most of these expressions are metaphors for joy, we occasionally see other emotions referred to also, via the language of dance—e.g., in the heat of a negotiation with a Realtor, you might "do a little tap dance," denoting frantic effort. Or: the intense resolve and magisterial elegance of both matadors and bulls have earned bullfighting the nickname "the ballet of death."

The Emotion and Release function can be fraught. The trick for us dancers is knowing when to jiggle and how much to jiggle. Crossing this line can bring accusations of arrogance or wantonness. The Carolina Panthers quarterback Cam Newton, for instance, took some heat in 2015 and 2016 for popularizing a dance move called dabbing. Devised originally by Atlanta-based rap group Migos, dabbing is a slightly more stylized version of sneezing into your armpit, but without the sneeze. As TweetBoogie, my hip-hop teacher at Alvin Ailey, explained to my class when she put dabbing into a routine she had choreographed for us in January 2017, "Dabbing is like an exclamation point. It's like"—here she raised her fist in the air sideways, not straight-on like a Black Power fist—" 'Yeah!' "

Newton popularized the move in October 2015 when his team was on a winning streak and he started doing it as part of his post-touchdown dancing in the end zone. The craze swept the Carolinas and trickled into other parts of the country, with elderly folks at retirement homes and young women at baby showers joining in on the faux-sneezy fun.

But some people saw Newton's dabbing as unsportsmanlike. Including a concerned mother who wrote to the *Charlotte Observer* on November 17, 2015: "I don't know about your family life, Mr. Newton, but I think I'm safe in saying thousands of kids watch you every week. You have amazing talent and an incredible platform to be a role model for them. Unfortunately, what you modeled for them today was egotism, arrogance and poor sportsmanship."

Come the next season, Newton, asked whether he would be dabbing again, replied, "I have to put that aside."

By that September, he'd already devised a new routine for celebrations: a rhythmic dusting-off of his hands, followed by a Superman pose.

I have the opposite of Newton's problem: I need to jiggle more. Why can I do stuff on the dance floor—particularly if I'm high or drunk—that I could never do off it?

Some background. I've always been able to say things to my cat that I'm too emotionally constipated to say to Greg. "I love you so much," I'll tell Linda. "I wish I could take you on the plane with me. When I get home, we will spend many hours lying on the couch and nuzzling."

It's not that I'm unable to say this stuff to Greg. It's simply that I don't. Or that I do it once every two years. I suppose I'm more apt to be baldly emotional and needy with Linda because she is mute and non-responding; she can't reflect back my candor and longing to scale, and thus I'm free of potential embarrassment. Linda's typical response to such endearments is to extend one of her paws toward me as if my face were a touch screen.

I bring this up because, given the details of my formative years that I've relayed so far, it occurs to me that you may be wondering if

I have a substance abuse problem, or if I'm unable to attend social events without a minder, or if I have a strangled relationship with my sexuality.

No to all of these. However, I'm more or less emotionally closed off. I'm generally unable or unwilling to tell others that I love them; and, outside of hugging family and close friends and family hello and goodbye, I'm a confirmed non-toucher.

"You're a WASP, yes?" I hear you ask. Indeed.

But the armchair psychologist in me sees most of these traits as more nuanced. Though, yes, anchored in my upbringing. If the person who's bankrolling your fancy education is homophobic, as my grandmother gave every indication of being, you learn to steel your more lavender impulses. Then, in eighth grade, when you're sent away to boarding school and you're intimidated by the experience, your steeliness only helps to shut out the unpredictable world of emotions. You put your nose to the grindstone. Surrounded by competitive and sometimes envious boys, you learn to downplay your achievements.

I remember another hip-hop class that I took from the young, fiery, and sarcastic TweetBoogie. I had grown curious about Tweetie, as she's called, because I'd seen her teaching in one of the clean, glassy, state-of-the-art Alvin Ailey studios while wearing her Timberland boots. A largish, metallic nameplate on her baseball cap read "BRONX." I knew she'd be fierce.

Indeed, at the first class I took with her, she mentioned five times the importance of emotion in dance. At one point she told us, "You don't have to look like a dead doll." When she saw me smiling at this comment, she asked me, "What is that look on your face?" She walked over to me—this was a biggish class, with about forty students—and told me to hold on to her while we did the routine together. I put my hand on her shoulder. "No, like you're my peoples," she said. I put my arm around her waist. We did the routine together, after which she nodded at me with slight resignation, as if to say "That did not cause me to vomit," and then reminded the class, "If you don't put any emotions behind the moves, people are gonna look at you like, Whaaaaaaaa?"

When you erect a protective barrier between yourself and the messy intrusions of others, you start to hear the whaaaaaaaas. Statements made to me over the years by friends and lovers have included "You're half Spock," "I only know you on the page," "Try to be a *little* more effusive than usual," and "I'm your boyfriend but I've never felt like you rely on me for anything."

2.

Over coffee with my friend Robin one day, I told her that I'd been home-dancing two or three times a week for the past year. She asked me, "Have you done 5Rhythms?" I had not, nor had I heard of it.

5Rhythms, a kind of ecstatic dancing, is a "movement meditation practice" that was created by Gabrielle Roth in the late 1970s. Obsessed as a child with Jesus and the saints, Roth at age seven begged her parents to send her to Catholic school, which they did. In college, she got pregnant the first time she made love; a subsequent abortion left her feeling ashamed and betrayed by her unsupportive boyfriend. Since adolescence, she'd loved the way that dancing in her bedroom to rock and roll had boosted her confidence and helped her escape the duties and obligations of being obedient; but now, according to her memoir, *Sweat Your Prayers*, "in my dance I began to forgive myself for a sin I couldn't name or remember committing." The more she danced, the more she came to believe that "thousands of years ago, some men got together and, in the name of God, separated all matters having to do with the spirit from the flesh. Flesh was denigrated and the body became the enemy."

How this worldview shakes out for us practitioners is as follows.

You enter the studio, which is usually lit with candles or a string of white Christmas lights lying on the floor. Simmering, mood-heavy, instrumental music is percolating—maybe a swirl of synthesizer is eddying around your ankles, or, off in the mid-distance, a scrum of pan flutes waxes increasingly breathy and pre-orgasmic. As you start to stretch out, a teacher's voice starts softly intoning over the PA system, urging you to relax, maybe addressing specific body parts. This gentle urging continues over the two hours, as the music starts to mirror the five essential rhythms that Roth—who passed away in 2012—thought we operate in: flowing, staccato, chaos, lyrical, and stillness. (Three adjectives and two nouns: you don't come to ecstatic dancing for the grammar.) Though 5Rhythms teachers occasionally call a partnered dance and offer specific tasks ("Say hello to your partner with your hips"), there's otherwise little to no specific choreography. The point is to listen to the music, and to keep breathing and moving.

Initially, I was besotted by the spaces that most of the 5Rhythms classes I go to are held in—one a largish studio at Joffrey Ballet that overlooks the handsome red brick, Venetian Gothic bell tower of a women's-prison-turned-library, the other a gorgeous and vast eleventh-floor space in the West Village that used to be Merce Cunningham's studio and now belongs to the Martha Graham School. When I walked into the latter—it's about the size of two tennis courts, and has sixteen-foot ceilings and lots of nine-foot-tall windows on two sides of the room that look majestically out over the city—the dramatically enflamed narrator who lives inside my head announced to me, "This is where I'll do my best work." To have this much space, let alone the fact that it's space drenched in dance history, is to want to move in a way as beautiful as the surroundings. On nights when I am the first dancer on the glossy, dove-gray floor at the Martha Graham space, I feel like a gold medal–winning figure skater for whom the entire world has been personally Zambonied. It would almost be impossible for me to act or be casual hereon; I have to match the exaltedness of the setting.

The people-watching at 5Rhythms events is fairly great, too, especially at the Tuesday night session at Joffrey, which can draw as many as a hundred dancers, thus rendering the dance floor much more like a nightclub than a yoga class on wheels. Here is a tall Caribbean man who, bending at the waist and stagger-walking forward, is dragging his dreadlocks across the floor as if to demonstrate a time-consuming new way to apply floor wax; here is a poignant-looking, possibly Levantine woman in her thirties who, no matter what else she does on the dance floor, will for two hours slowly swirl her clutch purse from its strap in perfect, gentle circles.

I will confess to tuning out, for the most part, the suggestions that come over the PA, difficult as they are to hear over the wash of world music and the occasional pop tune. Sometimes the teachers' directives are wonderfully on-point and helpful ("Dance faster than you can think," "Turn your body into a shape that mirrors your current emotional state," "Be aware of your impulse, but then don't necessarily act on that impulse"), but other times they go a little fortune cookie on you ("Find your movement medicine," "Let the mystery into your guesthouse," "Give permission to your armpits: 'This is who I am now'"). Fortunately, the most frequently spoken directive at 5Rhythms classes is the one that I probably need to hear the most: "Soften." But the instructors sometimes exhibit a tendency for creating word salads—a tendency that reached its acme for me at Joffrey one night when I heard over the speakers this bizarre directive: "Unreliable spine! Unreliable spine!" The young man dancing next to me straightened with a look of faint alarm, as if in receipt of an unanticipated bowel movement.

It's not uninteresting to see what becomes of people when they unbuckle themselves, as happens throughout the evening, particularly during the fast, noisome chaos songs. I've seen dancers take off their shirts and dance hungrily at their images in the studios' mirrors; I even had to witness one couple's tumbling to the ground and starting to finger each other. One night, a bearded, raw-boned, red-haired man with a Northern Europe accent howled and screamed into the dark corner of the Graham studio for several minutes: Vincent van Gogh with a gut wound. I tend to bust out a vaulting or helix-style move, as if planting a flag on a South Pacific island from which the emperor's troops have made a hasty withdrawal. Or I go all slo-mo, repeatedly opening my mouth in slo-mo, too, as if to slo-scream, "The bommmmmmmb is in the suuuuuuuuuuuuitcase!"

Early on in my 5Rhythms foray, I fell into conversation one night with a fellow dancer, an academic who teaches at a local university. She told me that each week she comes to class she tries to "bring a problem, and then dance the problem." On another occasion, I asked a young hippieish-looking dude if he was okay: he'd been lying on the floor and sobbing.

"I'm trying to dance through something," he told me.

"Does that work?"

"Totally."

Sold. In 2000, when I broke up with my then boyfriend of ten years, it took me a year to right myself emotionally. What helped the most was swimming; as I've put it to friends over the years, I "left my divorce" on the bottom of the NYU pool. Given this, I saw no reason why I couldn't effect a similar outcome via ecstatic dancing. So, on a couple occasions when I've been pissed off or hurt for some reason, I've brought this pain to 5Rhythms and thrashed it out. The smaller my hurt, the better it works. I can demonstrably thrash into oblivion an unthoughtful comment that a colleague made to me earlier in the day, but I'm less successful at altering a simmering, weeklong malaise.

In the same way that a blocked or preoccupied actor can be unlocked by being given a piece of "business" like ironing clothes or unloading groceries, so, too, can my internal monologue be drowned by a jumble of spins and leaps. "Movement never lies,"

Martha Graham famously exaggerated, overlooking the comic mugging and robot-dancing that we all do in high school or office settings, not to mention the splash-fabulous but heartless gyrations that professional dancers do when they start phoning it in. But in other instances, Graham is dead-on: the body is often pure subtext.

It's during the fast chaos songs that you're most likely to shake off a mood. When 5Rhythms dancers get going to this music, it looks like a dance floor freak-out. People are releasing their neck and letting their cranium wobble as if they've been semi-beheaded. Your arms might resemble lightning. Your hips might move to South America. During such paroxysms, it's simply impossible to obsess over a tiny matter such as your best friend's having not returned your e-mail in four days (which may explain why I'm able to put emotion into improvised dance but not into set choreography: choreography, for me, is an e-mail that takes me four days to respond to).

The inevitable tangent to entering into this kind of physical maelstrom, of course, is its opposite: I started to become increasingly interested in stillness and hesitation. Shortly into my 5Rhythms dancing, Greg and I re-watched *The Gay Divorcee*, whose "Night and Day" number is a fairly spectacular portrayal of reluctance. While the besotted Astaire sings the intro to the song ("Like the beat-beat-beat of the tom-tom") in a hotel room overlooking the sea, Rogers walks away from him (she's in the midst of trying to divorce her geologist husband), so he runs ahead of her and blocks her. They do this a few times, cat and mouse, cat and mouse. Finally, she walks away, only this time he spins backwards before grabbing her hand. She turns to him. He lets go of her hand, and does a few steps and a spin on his own. Then he grabs her hand and pulls her in close. They launch into a beautiful duet, all centrifugal force and airborne chiffon ruffles, at the conclusion of which he seats her on a couch and asks "Cigarette?" But Ginger—who, at age sixteen, had famously uttered the line "Cigarette me, big boy" in her first film—shakes her head no, I couldn't possibly. What's brilliant here is that, over the course of the song, the nature of her reluctance has changed: she declines the ciggie not because she doesn't want her heart broken, but because she's too swooned-out from dancing.

Expressing emotion through dance requires neither speed nor big movements. Sometimes the most interesting 5Rhythms dancers to behold are the ones who stand perfectly still except for, say, their right index finger, which might be making a slow, one-inch rotation as if tracing the anal perimeter of an invisible donkey. Which, as it turns out, puts me in mind of the dank worldliness of Bob Fosse's work. We associate this choreography legend with a lot of flashy, angular moves—my favorites include the one where you put a palm on your forehead and then extend the fingers of this hand outward while tilting your head backward, or the one where you lean back slightly and dangle your arms behind you in order to decisively *snaaaap* your fingers. (I once tried this latter move at a 5Rhythms session and felt like a gay camp counselor who struggles daily with autism.)

Less expectedly, what defines Fosse just as much as his vamping gestures—and what helps make his work still feel subversive and dirty more than forty years after it debuted—is stillness. Look at the Kit Kat Klub dancers' weirdly canted, mangled arabesque legs when the dancers are standing on their chairs in "Mein Herr." Or look at the terrifying stasis of the knock-kneed dancehall girls in *Sweet Charity*'s "Hey, Big Spender." ("He pushed us, like puppets, into these broken doll positions," one of the dancers told Fosse biographer Martin Gottfried.)

By isolating the movement on offer to a single gesture, Fosse could infuse that gesture with a vividness and a terror. Susan Stroman, who danced in the national tour of *Chicago* before going on to much acclaim as a Broadway choreographer, has said that at the point *Chicago*'s dancers drag their palms back and forth over the floor, "Fosse always told us to make believe we had blood on our hands and like we were trying to wipe it off on a wall, kind of how the Manson family did."

Indeed, of all the research I did for this book, the most surprising find to me was dance's relationship to violence. It started when I read that in 1983, the day after the anniversary special *Motown 25* aired on TV, showcasing Michael Jackson performing the Moonwalk for his first-ever time, Fred Astaire telephoned Jackson to congratulate him.

"Man, you really put them on their asses last night," Astaire told him. "You're an angry dancer. I'm the same way."

Fred Astaire, angry? Granted, in *Top Hat*, during "No Strings (I'm Fancy Free)" he taps so hard he unmoors a tile from Ginger's ceiling, and during "Top Hat, White Tie and Tails" he uses his cane to machine-gun a chorus line. In *The Sky's the Limit*, he drunkenly smashes three stacks of glasses and a barroom mirror, and in *The Band Wagon*'s faux noir "Girl Hunt Ballet," he slams a male dancer's cigar down his throat and then elbows him in the face.

But . . . angry? This was odd to me. However, Brian Seibert writes in *What the Eye Hears* that Astaire "liked to think of himself as a gangster, and a violent streak runs through his outlaw style, an urge to startle underneath the formal attire and good manners. In *Top Hat* it's a plot point and a character trait, this impulse to disturb the peace as an American in stuffy London. But across Astaire's career, whenever he's tapping, the violence is there, the suspense of it and the satisfaction."

For Jackson, the violence came earlier on in his life, and was less metaphorical: in the 2003 TV special *Living with Michael Jackson*, the song-and-dance phenom said that his father sat in a chair with a belt in his hands while the Jackson Five rehearsed, and that "if you didn't do it the right way, he would tear you up, really get you." Cue every dance memoir's early-on scene in which a dyspeptic, Eastern European ballet mistress wields her metal-tipped cane to discipline and abuse innocent young ankles.

Or look at Kevin Bacon's unintentionally hilarious "angry dance" in *Footloose*. Bacon, while inhaling a beer and cigarette, irritatedly pulls his car into an abandoned warehouse and, after hurling the beer bottle against a wall and then pounding on the car's hood, launches into a number that lies exactly midpoint on the continuum between a gymnastics routine and a hissy fit. He vaults over a wall like it's a pommel horse, he zooms through the air on a high-placed rope swing, he spins over a high bar and we see his dismount in slow motion seven times. He's *that* angry. This kind of cheese makes Jackson's *Thriller* video or the rumble in *West Side Story* look like documentary.

Read a biography of Gene Kelly, and his fabulous dancing and utter charm and political convictions aside, what comes across is what a hothead he was. The young Kelly is described by one of his biographers as "a tough Irish bantam of a fighter in the Pittsburgh tradition." Kelly told another biographer, "Because I was small, I felt I always had to prove myself and the best way to do this was with my fists."

Kelly's inherent pugnaciousness suited him well for the scorn that his interest in dance would bring him. "My mother sent my brother and me to dancing school in those Buster Brown collars, and we had a minimum of three fights every week walking between our house and the school. The funny thing is that nobody called us sissies when we served Mass in these collars, only when we went to dancing school." In the late 1920s, while a student at Penn State, Kelly and his brother were dancing at a club and got called fags by a heckler, so Kelly pulled the heckler off his bar stool and knocked him down. Around the same time, Kelly's agent one day asked for his 10 percent commission to be paid on the spot, so Kelly punched him in the face. The agent collapsed onto the floor and Kelly wound up with broken fingers.

Kelly turned down his first two Broadway offers (he thought one role was too small and that the other one didn't pay enough). When Louis B. Mayer reneged on his promise that Kelly wouldn't have to do a screen test for *Pal Joey*, a role Kelly had played on Broadway, Kelly wrote Mayer an angry letter that ended, "I'd rather dance in a saloon!" Shortly thereafter, when David O. Selznick said that he wanted to put Kelly under contract without a screen test, Kelly told him about Mayer and said, "I hope I can trust you. You sons of bitches are all alike." Years later, when Kelly was shooting 1948's *The Three Musketeers*, during one scene Kelly pushed costar Lana Turner so forcefully that she fell onto the floor and broke her elbow.

Women get in on the violence, too. One early example is mythological: maenads, the intoxicated and wildly dancing female followers of Dionysus, were said to rip apart the bodies of animals they found in the woods, and then devour them. But ladies in the meatspace have their moments, too. Martha Graham once pushed the legs of one of her dancers as far apart as possible and said, "One day a man will do this to you." In Jerome Robbins's ballet *The Cage*, female "insects" treat male intruders with similar high dudgeon, by putting the male dancers' necks between their kneecaps and crushing them.

Some sensitive souls have seen fit to object. In 1984, while watching a performance of Twyla Tharp's *Nine Sinatra Songs*, which features a thrilling dance set to "That's Life" in which a female dancer is pushed around by a man before ultimately jumping fully onto him, Mark Morris stood up in the audience, yelled "No more rape!" and walked out of the theater.

If all these examples of aggression were confined to acts of physical violence, I'd understand: dance relies on the full spectrum of bodily movement, the more dramatic and vivid of which is sometimes based in aggression.

But it's the emotional violence that I wasn't expecting.

I'm not an angry person and thus have no need to channel fury into a fiery display of scissor-sharp *cabrioles* and pelvic pops. However, sometimes when I'm dancing with a straight dude in his twenties or thirties at an ecstatic dancing or contact improv event, I unleash a rowdy boy from inside me, a rowdy boy who rarely shows up off the dance floor: to emphasize sportiness over sensuality is to put these partners at ease. But it also feels great to have adrenaline course through my body: no salmon can outswim this bear.

That said, I hate the idea, pantywaist liberal that I am, that dance has a strong relationship to aggression, even if the dynamic is primarily one of sublimation. I take succor in the idea that, in my age and in my country—I'm absenting from this discussion voguing and twerking incidents, which seem largely tongue-in-cheek, as well as a 2013 incident in Moscow in which the artistic director of the Bolshoi, having made some unpopular casting decisions, had a jar of sulfuric acid thrown in his face—dance's relationship to fighting would seem mostly to have had a gentler cast to it.

Take, for instance, hip-hop battles. In the Bronx and other urban areas in the 1970s and early 1980s, hip-hop dancers taunted and tried to outdo one another with flashy moves—e.g., popping and locking, or freezing—that sublimated violence. In the summer of 1978, Tee of the High Times Crew told the *Village Voice*, "When you get mad at someone, instead of saying 'Hey man, you want to fight?' you'd say 'Hey man, you want to rock?'"

Chillin' like a villain.

Two years later, members of the High Times Crew were arrested for "fighting" in a subway station in Washington Heights. The dancers explained to the police that they weren't brawling, they were having a dance-off. The police asked for proof, whereupon the Crew came up with a list of dance moves, one of which had the very, very intimidating name "the baby." The cops called what they thought was the dancers' bluff, and asked them each to dance right there and then. The dancers went into their awesome stylin', the legend goes, whereupon the charges were dropped.

* * *

While changing out of my boxer shorts in the Joffrey dressing room one night—my typical 5Rhythms getup is a T-shirt and then a pair of boxer shorts worn over a pair of briefs—I fell into conversation with another dancer. He started evangelizing about contact improv, illustrating same by standing and smooshing the side of his body against mine.

"Ooh, that's personal," I said.

"Deeply personal."

I'd heard of contact improv at that point, but had never seen it performed. I liked the idea that it was, like 5Rhythms and living room dancing, free-form. But its insistence on weight-sharing and partnering made it seem like a step up, or like just enough of an added challenge to keep me on edge. I proceeded to take more than forty contact improv classes, to learn technique.

Contact improv was officially started in 1972, when former gymnast Steve Paxton wed his interest in aikido to the knowledge he'd gained dancing for Merce Cunningham and José Limón. The idiom lists among its early practitioners choreographers Bill T. Jones, Trisha Brown, Lucinda Childs, and Yvonne Rainer. Based in gravity and trust, contact is mostly an improvised duet form in which dancers share their weight with each other, collapsing onto each other, lifting each other up in the air on their backs or shoulders, colliding their bodies.

Because it's not often performed for audiences, contact doesn't have the renown or cred that it probably deserves—but it's been taught at Juilliard and Yale, and a group of Dartmouth students who started messing around with a version of it in the early seventies became the not-so-obscure modern troupe Pilobolus. ("I realized that I couldn't teach them as I would teach dancers, so I started teaching them improvisation and choreography instead," Alison Becker Chase has said of the three men who, in 1971, showed up without any dance experience for her Dance Composition class at Dartmouth. Chase and two of the students, joined by three others, including Martha Clarke, would form Pilobolus, which has been seen contorting and shape-shifting at the Oscars and in Super Bowl commercials, and which won an Emmy in 1997 for its televised performance at the Kennedy Center.)

Outside of traveling to a country whose language I don't speak, or swimming in the ocean at night, I'm not sure I've ever done anything that feels as adventurous as contact improv. My first contact class was the aforementioned attempt to jump into other dancers' arms. In my second class, I removed my partner's feet from my chest—she was doing a handstand and leaning against me—and, holding her ankles, proceeded to rapturously twirl her in the air 540 degrees around me. By my fifth class, another partner somehow put my left hip on top of his left shoulder and then carried me across the floor like an exciting, possibly flambéed, entrée.

One of your first acts as a contact dancer is to buy kneepads. Though the first-ever piece of contact improv, a dance called *Magnesium* that Steve Paxton and others performed on the Oberlin campus in Ohio in 1972, was done on wrestling mats, we contemporary bearers of the flame are not so lucky. When my lumpy, white kneepads come back from being washed at the Laundromat, they look like melted but unbrowned pieces of mozzarella; the first time this happened, I thought, Why is there lasagna in my laundry?

But kneepads weren't enough to quell some of my initial contact-specific anxieties. In one of my early-on classes at Gibney, my teacher Bradley Ellis asked me to do an exercise that foiled me. My partner was on her hands and knees with her back flattened, in the position known as "table." I was meant to gracefully lower my sacrum onto hers, giving her all my weight, and then, while bending my head backwards onto the floor, slowly to lift my legs straight up into the air one at a time in a graceful, slow-motion backwards somersault.

I couldn't do it. Bradley asked what was holding me back. I wasn't sure. He put forth the possibility that I was afraid of falling backward. I readily copped to this diagnosis—I mean, who isn't?

Bradley had an intriguing suggestion: I should go to a swimming pool, put a lot of kickboards and floaties under me, and then practice floating on my back. A few days later I hied myself to the NYU pool, where forty-five minutes of experimentation led to a helpful realization. Namely, if I closed my eyes during a difficult move, as I had been doing in class, I could psyche myself into all sorts of fear: during one eight-minute-long stretch of self-inflicted darkness in the pool, I imagined that my body was spinning, and I thought I heard sirens. But if I kept my eyes open: totally fine.

It was this kind of realization, along with practice, practice, practice, that helped me to build up the confidence needed to start going to contact improv jams—the open-to-the-public dances which are held weekly all over the world. As with jumping into people's arms or backwards-somersaulting over their sacrum, initiating dances with total strangers was daunting for me at first. I remember once trundling down to the studio in SoHo where the Saturday jam is held, full of nervous excitement. New York had just been whomped by a huge snowstorm. As I walked, I thought, This will be amazing—only the true diehards will show up, and together we will honor the dark forces of meteorology, bursting into a joyous ring dance called *Man vs. Nature*!

Indeed, only nine or so of us showed up. But of the five people I felt qualified to dance with, two were sealed off in the cocoon of a duet, and two of the others flitted off seconds after I tried to initiate dances with them (I usually do this by putting my hand on your shoulder). I left the jam after half an hour, and as I trudged home in the snow, I found myself welling up with tears over the failed connection. At this point in my contact improv career, being spurned by other dancers, or being given corrections, felt like a bee sting. I would briefly wallow in the sentiment "I'm a bad dancer" before bottoming out into a mud hole of masochism labeled "I'm not good-looking enough for you." This latter mindset was particularly galling, for all the reasons that we learn in childhood: If someone lets me know that I've made an idiotic comment, or that I am behaving idiotically, then a part of me knows that I can always self-correct if I agree with that person's assessment. But if someone suggests that my *looks* are idiotic, there's a lot less that I can do about it. And thus, this kind of rejection or scorn can, with a masochist's love and nurturing, leave an uglier bruise. (The organizers of Ecstatic Dance NYC events smartly reduce this kind of trauma by announcing that dancers should try to dance with each of the other dancers, but that if for any reason you don't want to dance with someone who's moved near you, you should simply make the steepled-fingers *wai* gesture.)

But I kept going back to the jam because the highs were so high. On the edges of the dance floor, the gymnastics and the weight-sharing sometimes take second place to a looser and more fanciful kind of movement, and it was herein that I started to experience moments that I can only call sublime. One fairly elaborate pageant of swirly sumo-wrestlers-at-the-Ice-Capades staggering and ice-waltzing that a young woman and I laid down caused me to shed a tear of joy upon its completion. I had the impulse to thank her but quashed it, certain that if I opened my mouth the only thing that would come out would be birdsong.

Another time, the sheer romance of a (heterosexual male) partner's and my synchronicity—his anticipation of my every move seemed almost freakish to me—caused me to blush bright red. As anyone who's done a fair bit of social dancing knows: a good dance is better than sex. But if this burst of sensual intensity happens while you're moving with someone you would otherwise have no interest in, it can feel like you've been roofied.

Is a good partnership one where you "talk" 50 percent and "listen" 50 percent, or is it one where the percentages get thrown out the window altogether? I wasn't sure. But I knew one thing: if listening to radio is often more involving than watching television because a radio listener has to work harder, so, too, with contact improv—it's usually done without music, and almost never *to* music. The groove is deeper because it's of your own making. (When, in the late seventies, choreographer Trisha Brown was asked why she'd finally started incorporating music into her pieces, she said, "I got fed up with listening to all the goddamn coughing.") On some occasions I've simply marveled, slack-jawed, at the Pina Bausch–like kookiness of what a partner and I are doing, and felt as if I've just gotten gas at my dentist's: my need to laugh is so all-consuming and enormous that I am incapable of producing sound. Like the time I danced with the young male cellist who told me he was learning contact improv because he hoped one day to dance it while, yes, his cello was strapped to his body. Ten minutes into our dancing, I found myself staring at the ceiling, my feet up on the wall at shoulder level and my upper torso held in the semi-crouched cellist's arms about fifteen inches off the floor. Just as I was forming the thought, "This is an interesting way to spend a Saturday afternoon," a young woman who'd been standing idly by the wall grabbed my feet by the ankles, whereupon the cellist lowered my torso onto the floor and then flitted off to another partner. Then the woman, still holding my ankles, started doing a series of *arabesques*, putting her leg high up in the air behind her like some inexorable insect, all the while murmuring and semi-grunting like she was trying to decide whether to devour me now or to cover me with a preservative mouth spit.

She went a third way. Still in *arabesque*, she started gracefully but forcefully pushing and pulling me across the floor in short bursts.

The insect was vacuuming.

DANCE AS PURE PHYSICALITY

1.

Certain kinds of dancing can seem like pure physicality to me. The tap classes I took at Alvin Ailey in 2016 and 2017, for instance, felt less like dancing than like drumming with the feet.

Throughout the class, we would stand in place mimicking our teacher Marshall Davis, Jr.'s eight-count beats, never moving our tap shoes across the room. The warm and avuncular Davis, who has collaborated a lot with Savion Glover, looks like a scruffy Eddie Murphy. He loved to have us do cramp rolls (go up on right toe and stay, go up on left toe and stay, then come down on right heel, then down on left heel), first on a leisurely 1-2-3-4 beat, then on a peppier 1 and a-2 and a-3 and a-4 beat, then in a crashing waterfall, 1234. Then he'd switch up the order of foot placement: we'd start with our left heel, say. Or he'd drop a bombshell like, "This time, the 3 isn't on the 3, it's *before* the 3"—a statement which caused my universe instantaneously to seem a lot larger. There are beats *between* the beats? Dude.

Davis's point here—a point also stressed by virtuosic tapper Steve Condos, with whom Davis studied—is that all tap routines are made up of a combination of a handful of fundamental steps, so let's get these fundamentals down pat before we add music or start traveling around the room. On the rare occasion that Davis mentioned the upper body, it was to remind us to bend our knees slightly and lean forward lest we topple backwards when we stood on our heels—as Davis himself did during the Broadway production of *Bring in 'da Noise, Bring in 'da Funk* when he encountered a patch of water on the stage. (Davis told us his recovery strategy was to regain his balance and then make a fast and decisive X with his hands like a baseball umpire saying "Safe!")

But there was something else that constricted my worldview to my feet and their ability to make sound. Davis wanted us to take our choreographic cues from him aurally not visually. One night he told us that he was going to stand behind us while he tapped out combinations, so that we could hear him but not see him, and we'd have to guess what he was doing. Looking around the room, I saw a few eyeballs roll heavenward as we students prepared for this big task.

But all six of us found that our ear was better than our eye.

In another class, Davis talked about dancing "on the two," the habit of dancing on the "off" beat rather than the "on" beat, as practiced by many of the more sophisticated Latin and swing dancers. After teaching us four students a routine on a beat of six, he had us stand in a circle. He said the first person was to do the routine on the one, the second person on the two, the third on the three, etc.

We went around the circle a few times. The cascades of rhythm we produced were at once lovely and totally disorienting. It felt like my legs and feet had gone off to wave-making camp without me. I couldn't tell when one wave started and the next began. It can't be pure coincidence that the 1915 publication of Einstein's field equations, which redefined gravity as we knew it and suggested that space-time is malleable, occurred just as swing rhythm was making itself known.

I'd like to be able to tell you that, as the upholder and ambassador of "the three" in this exercise, that my three was *on* the three, or even that each time I took my turn it had the same relationship to the three. But I have to admit that my body does not always do what I want it to, and also that numbers are a tiresome social construct.

Musicians use instruments, writers use keyboards and paper, painters use paint and canvas, but a dancer has only his own body. This is both a blessing and a curse.

The Pure Physicality function is dance at its most inimitable and quintessential; of the arts, only physical theater and certain kinds of vocalizing (e.g., Tuvan throat singing) put such emphasis on the human body. It's here that dance shares more similarities with sports than with the arts. But more tellingly, the Physicality function shines a light on dance's essential pathos, by which I mean that dance is a moment out of time. Dance is hugely dependent on the physical range of the body, which more than any other building block of the arts (e.g., words, paint, clay, music, video, film) is subject to the ravages of time. What is dance if not an attempt to deny that passage?

Viewed in another light, Pure Physicality might also be considered dance's most sophisticatedly human function, too: an animal doesn't make a lot of movements that are purely ornamental (at least, not from the animal's point of view).

"I know my feet, all about them. It's like my feet are the drums and my shoes are the sticks," Savion Glover writes in *Savion: My Life in Tap*, cowritten with Bruce Weber. "My left heel is stronger, for some reason, than my right; it's my bass drum. My right heel is like the floor tom-tom. I can get a snare out of my right toe, a whip sound, not putting it down on the floor hard, but kind of whipping the floor with it. Get the sound of a tom-tom from the balls of my feet. The hi-hat is a sneaky one. I do it with a slight toe lift, either foot, so, like a drummer, I can slip in there anytime. And if I want cymbals, crash, crash, that's landing flat, both feet, full strength on the floor, full weight on both feet."

Every dance idiom, be it jazz or hip-hop or butoh, has its own set of exacting physical demands. Swing dance instructors sometimes refer to dancers who can't bend their elbows as having "Barbie arms." Lil Buck, who performs the style of street dance known as jookin', once spun so hard that he burned a large hole in his low-top Pumas. Whenever I watch *Dancing with the Stars*, I like to imagine a choreographer's assistant writing down "Female: (Scissors kick, lands on Left). Male: (Rips shirt off own body)."

The bodily changes that all my dancing wrought on me were slowish—after doing contact improv for a year and a half, I went from a medium shirt to a large. But other dancers' changes come more rapidly. Alvin Ailey dancer Linda Celeste Sims, for instance, holds the Kirov-trained Madame Darvash, one of the country's most revered ballet teachers, responsible for lengthening her legs after Darvash told Sims one day to straighten her knee all the way. The next morning, Ms. Sims's husband, a fellow dancer, asked, "What did you do? Your legs look long."

Of all the idioms and their demands, it's the rigors of ballet that most amaze me. Once you've stood in your office and tried to go through the motions of a ballerina's Mount Everest—Odile's thirty-two *fouettés* in *Swan Lake*—you get a startlingly real dose of an emotional state that I can only call stomach heave. Similarly, once I learned that the sole of one of Nijinsky's feet could operate in such a prehensile way that it could clasp the back of the other foot's ankle like a hand, I came to appreciate what a tiny amount of podiatric potential most humans have made use of.

Or consider diet. Though the prohibition on unrestrained eating is not specific to ballerinas, they would seem, of all dancers, to bear its brunt most acutely. In 2015, when *Playbill* asked New York City Ballet principal Rebecca Krohn whether she had any guilty pleasures, Krohn referenced Le Bernardin, a high-end New York

City restaurant she'd never been to: "Sometimes I will go online and just read the menu." When Misty Copeland was told by American Ballet Theatre early on in her tenure to "lengthen"—balletspeak for lose weight—she rebelled. She called a local Krispy Kreme franchise, and when an employee told her Krispy Kreme only delivered to corporations and in large numbers, Copeland told them she was a corporation. After rehearsals, she would order two dozen donuts and eat half of them in one sitting.

If you've ever stood in a hallway with a bunch of parents outside their daughters' Beginner's Ballet class for pickup, you may have noticed the parents' bittersweet expression. Typically this expression is composed of equal parts "I am so glad my daughter is acquiring poise while giving me an hour to run errands" and "I hope she loses interest before they get to pointe." When we see or even imagine a ballerina balancing her entire body weight on her ten little toes, we all wail in sympathy, but actually it's even more arduous than what we're thinking: she's really supporting her weight on her two big toes. For comparison, imagine trying to do it on your thumbs.

Moreover, ever since ballet master Jean-Georges Noverre wrote in 1760 that "it is imperative to reverse the order of things and force the limbs, by means of exercise both long and painful, to take a totally different position from that which is natural to them," young ballet dancers have been trying to get their femur bone to adjust within its socket so as to achieve maximum turn-out.

Gelsey Kirkland put it vividly. "By turning a bed into a makeshift rack," she wrote in *Dancing on My Grave*, "I stretched myself out like a victim of medieval abuse. Assuming various positions that forced my extension beyond its natural limit, I told [my best friend] Meg to hold me down no matter how much I might beg for release. She sat on me, disregarding my groans, allowing her body weight to restrain me until the pain became so excruciating that I collapsed into tears."

Not only does Balanchine emerge in this memoir as a relentless taskmaster—"Eat nothing," Kirkland claims he told her repeatedly; or he'd thump on her sternum and ribs and say "Must see bones"— but Kirkland herself is wildly neurotic and self-immolating. Her frantic efforts during her tenure at New York City Ballet to reconceive her physical self led to anorexia, bulimia, plastic surgery, silicone injections, breast implants, major dental realignments, a healthy appetite for cocaine, and an addiction to speed and Valium.

Then she's cast in *The Turning Point* and things get *really* dire: "I enacted my own private mad scene: I starved by day, then binged on junk food and threw up by night; I took injections of pregnant cows' urine, reputed to be a miraculous diet aid; I stuffed myself with laxatives, thyroid pills, and celery juice; I emptied myself with enemas and steam baths. During the wee hours, I often made desperate trips to the drugstore to pick up ipecac, the emetic that I used to induce vomiting. I became an expert with the technique of shoving two fingers down my throat. The blood vessels around my eyes erupted with the constant strain."

Kirkland's weight fell to eighty pounds. And in the end, she was replaced in the cast of the movie.

Kirkland's book is scarifying. I couldn't put it down. I have no problem understanding how a professional dancer's life would revolve around maintaining the physical phenom that she has spent years turning her body into. I cooed in sympathy when Toni Bentley's memoir, *Winter Season*, quoted the nightly regimen of one of Bentley's fellow New York City Ballet dancers: "First I rub this aspirin ointment on my foot. . . . Then I put Saran Wrap around it, then an Ace bandage, then a sock and a heating pad—all night. Otherwise I can't *plié* when I wake up." I found it lovely when modern choreographer Paul Taylor writes about being on tour and stuffing the grids of air conditioners with tissue paper so as to block the cool drafts that would tighten his dancer's muscles. I developed weird admiration for actor and dancer George Raft—he plays the main gangster who's chasing Jack Lemmon and Tony Curtis in *Some Like It Hot*—when I learned how, in the 1920s, he was able to pull off what Astaire called "the fastest Charleston I ever saw": he'd numb his feet by lacing his shoes with piano wire.

But Kirkland's particular brand of mortification of the flesh struck me as overkill—unnecessary and pathological. That is, until I read *New Yorker* critic Arlene Croce's review of a 1975 Suzanne Farrell performance, when Farrell had just returned to New York City Ballet after her long absence. This review gave me a better sense of what dancers—particularly ballerinas—are up against.

> Although this tall, incomparably regal creature could be nobody but Farrell, it was not the same Farrell. She has lost a great deal of weight all over, and with it a certain plump quality in the texture of her movement. The plush is gone, and it was one of her glories. The impact of the long, full legs was different, too. If anything, they're more beautiful than ever, but no longer so impressively solid in extension, so exaggerated in their sweep, or so effortlessly controlled in their slow push outward from the lower back. The largesse of the thighs is still there, but in legato their pulse seemed to emerge and diminish sooner than it used to, and diminish still further below the knee in the newly slim, tapering calf. Yet the slenderness in the lower leg gives the ankle and the long arch of the foot a delicacy they didn't have before. And it shaves to a virtual pinpoint the already minute base from which the swelling grandeur of her form takes its impetus. Farrell is still broad across the hips (though not so broad as before); in pirouettes she is a spiraling cone.

Were the subject a model or actress or athlete, we'd cry foul, right? How dare a critic wax so body-specific. But something about ballet's quest for perfection keeps an assessment like Croce's from being wantonly cruel.

Granted, dancers know what they're getting into. For ballerinas, the bodily rigors of their craft are well advertised from the outset: a bloodied toe inside a toe shoe is a sign of good luck, especially if the dancer is wearing her first pair of toe shoes. Moreover, all professional dancers know that their efforts to harness the full potential of their bodies is a race against time. As Jamie Bishton, the Tharp dancer, put it to me, "The sad part of dancing is that when you're seasoned enough as a dancer to fully carry out a choreographer's vision is also when you can't really continue to do what you want your body to do."

I asked him, "You mean, you have to have enough experience to fully realize the work, but that's the same time when . . ."

". . . You're done."

Toni Bentley was done at age twenty-six. She'd danced for New York City Ballet for ten years, but had been diagnosed with osteoarthritis in her right hip three years prior. Decades later, when her doctor replaced her hip, Bentley, who'd gone on to become an author, made an unusual request of him: she wanted to keep the hip bone. She liked the idea, as she wrote on the *New York Review of Books* website in 2010, of having "a parched white Georgia O'Keeffe bone" that would be a tangible, viewable hedge against the thousand of hours she'd devoted and lost to the ephemeral art.

But when her doctor's office manager presented Bentley with the hip bone, it was no parched white O'Keeffe beauty. The femur head had been cut in half and it, along with lots of unidentifiable bits, was floating in formaldehyde in a Tupperware container. The office manager told Bentley that she needed to have a taxidermist extract the fatty tissues from the bone so it wouldn't go rancid.

Bentley boiled the bones and soaked them in bleach. ("But, what if, as they came to a boil, there was a smell?" she writes. "What if my cats started yowling like they do when they smell chicken broth?")

The bones did not emerge white. Bentley dried them in the sun. Still, not white. Moreover, Bentley couldn't pinpoint the arthritis. "Like a child, I thought my bad hip was my fault," she writes. "I wanted to face it now, to confirm somehow that I could not, with all the will in the world, have overcome it and danced again."

So she took the bones back to her doctor. On seeing them, he, ironically, wrinkled his nose and recoiled slightly. He told Bentley that the smooth, marble-colored side of the femur head—the only part of the bones that Bentley found beautiful—was the "arthritis," meaning the place where the cartilage was gone entirely. Bentley writes, "Arthritis is an absence—pure, smoothed-down bone surface."

In trying to create a monument to absence, she ended up with absence. She reached into the sea of nothingness and dredged up a different kind of nothing.

2.

Because I caught the dance bug late in life (age forty-nine), it's easy to view my doing so as an effort in part to stave off the ravages of time. This view is not inaccurate. Like a lot of people, I tend to think of myself as being perpetually thirty-one years old: seasoned enough not to commit the atrocities of adolescence and my early twenties, but not so old as to have cut off any of my options in life. I'd like to think that, if I really wanted to, and if I really committed myself to it, I could still become a novelist or playwright or pastry chef—because to believe in these possibilities is to live at the misty intersection between hope and faith, far from resignation. A lot of my other ships in life have sailed, but in the harbor, safe behind the breakwater of my delusion, I keep a small fleet, the sails of which are perpetually luffing.

Part of this magical-thinking mindset is the concurrent belief that a thirty-one-year-old's optimism about life need not be supported by a thirty-one-year-old's body.

I never said I was a realist.

I came to Zumba in 2011, as I mentioned earlier, via a writing assignment: my *Times* editor Laura was interested in hearing about the combination of Latin dance and cardio workout that, in 125 countries, has whipped some 12 million people into a lather. I was intrigued by the fact that you can fry to a crisp five hundred to a thousand calories per sweat-soaked hour.

I started on the zumba.com website. I learned there how, one day in the mid 1990s, the Colombian fitness instructor Alberto Perez, called Beto, forgot to take his aerobics music to a class he was teaching. Using instead some salsa and merengue tapes he had in his backpack, Perez started improvising what would attain immortality as Zumba. He moved to Miami in 2001 and was soon cranking out DVDs and an infomercial. In 2005 Perez and his business partners opened an academy to train instructors, of which there are now more than twenty thousand.

Typing my zip code into the website, I learned that there were 648 classes within five miles of me. As the Hollywood adage runs, you could die from the encouragement.

I consorted with the Z, as I came to think of it, for two months before writing about it, and then another six months after that. Most of my frantic gyrating and quick quick-stepping took place at New York University and at three Manhattan YMCAs. Though there are specialty classes like Aqua Zumba and Zumba Gold (a slower-paced variety for seniors), the great majority of Zumba classes are open to practitioners of all levels, and follow this format: an instructor arrives wearing stretchy black clothing and a facial expression of militant excitement; he or she turns on some music (lots of Ricky

Martin and salsa, with a smattering of the Latin-Caribbean hybrid known as reggaeton) and wordlessly starts dancing. We fifteen or twenty (primarily female) students, all in workout clothes, erupt in a Broadway kickline-ish cavalcade of flailing mimeo-choreography: squats, lunges, grapevines, cha-cha-cha.

Zumba's slogan is "Ditch the workout, join the party." At the Z-fest, no one is going to count out the song's beat for you, or demonstrate the choreography before the song starts. There's no and-a-five-six-seven-eight that transports you back to your childhood school trip to see *A Chorus Line.* You're here to party, my friend, not to audit a graduate seminar at the Dance Notation Bureau. Indeed, one of my Chinatown Y instructors told a group of us, three of whom looked to be closing in on seventy: "You need to relax your face. You don't go to a nightclub and look all tense. Imagine there's a great-looking guy or girl at the club."

The effort at face relaxation alone made this the most physically exhausting party I had ever attended. Exhorted again and again to kick my feet as high as my shoulder and, on one occasion, to propel myself across the floor purely through the magic of buttocks-clenching, I made my body ache. I bent parts of my body previously unbent. I got caught up in the excitement and overdid, overextended. Meanwhile, during the slow songs, I configured my face in the classic, tragic-pensive mode of the tango dancer, trying to convey equal parts tragedy and urgency: I'd been shot in the stomach but was late for an appointment.

I operated at about 50 to 60 percent mastery of the choreography, which is average. Certain stuttering Latin beats, and the fancy footwork they foster, eluded me. But my Achilles' heel was my overly literal approach: anytime an instructor telegraphed a coming move by, for instance, pointing to the right or holding up three fingers to denote repetition, I was sure to make these prescriptive actions the very centerpiece of my dancing. I was like the language student who greets passers-by with "Lesson 1: Good morning!"

My favorite instructor was named Yvonne Puckett. When I read on the Zumba website that this seventy-three-year-old showbiz veteran had danced with Astaire and with Marge and Gower Champion and had been in two Elvis Presley movies, I hied myself to Chelsea Piers to take her class.

In the soaring, bustling hangar that is the Chelsea Piers Sports Center, I pegged Miss Puckett at first sight: a warm, pixieish Carol Burnett type in boysenberry cargo pants and black-sequined sneakers. I gushily introduced myself, and asked, "Do you think Fred Astaire would have embraced Zumba?"

"Oh, definitely," she said. "As all dancers would."

I told her, "I'm trying to get some of the Astaire buoyancy and lightness into my Zumba work." She smiled at me indulgently, as if I had told her that there were tiny people living inside my mailbox.

Unlike some of my other instructors, who use war and combat metaphors ("Punch it!," "Kick it out here!") to fire up a class, Puckett proved to be all unicorns and rainbows; she trilled "Bee-you-tea-full" to us no less than five times during the hour. I wafted home on a cloud of lavender Tofutti.

I hurt myself only once. Hoping to up my game, I took a class one Sunday morning at Ailey, where I had heard the crowd was younger, and the workout fiercer. My instructor, Ben Byrd, a puckish redhead in his twenties wearing a navy do-rag, complimented my speed walking in place during one song, which led me to think, I'm in. But some five minutes later, my cloddishness about touching the floor with my hands while crouched in a frog stance caused him to yell at me, "Get lower!" I complied, whereupon he smiled, grabbed one of his own buttocks diagnostically and gave me a sign of encouragement. I didn't know how this translated to dance professionals, but to this amateur it meant: Ben was as concerned about my keister as I am.

The dancing ramped up in fiery intensity, which was thrilling. I hurled my will into the air and hoped my body would follow. At hour's end, Ben led us through fifteen additional minutes: seventy-five jumping jacks, seventy-five push-ups, and seventy-five sit-ups, of which I completed one-fifth. The next day my body was a lake of fire. I looked like the Baryshnikov chapter in a public library's copy of Gelsey Kirkland's memoir. I got three massages in five days; I swore off the Z for almost a week.

When, post-Ailey, I returned to the relative oasis of the China-town Y, it was with some of the hauteur of the Broadway veteran who has been asked to perform Chekhov monologues at a Cracker Barrel. Suddenly I was Mr. Juilliard. When I started to slide in a puddle in the locker room, I thought, Where is this facility's toe chalk?

Soon enough, my inflamed ego cooled, and I returned to an effort to improve my 50 to 60 percent mastery.

After three months, I noticed that I could touch my toes, an improvement of an inch or so. I'd lost seven pounds. Stretch and drop.

DANCE AS RELIGION AND SPIRITUALITY

1.

I WAS HAVING LUNCH WITH A RADIANTLY WARM DANCER IN her forties named Wendy Heagy. Wendy is a Christian praise dancer—yes, she dances for the Lord in churches, but more often she does it in shelters, halfway houses, and prisons.

We were both tucking into our bowls of curry at a Thai restaurant in Jackson Heights, Queens, near where Wendy and her husband and son live, when a question occurred to me.

"Do you think God accounts for technique?" I asked her. "Like, if you do a *grand jeté*, is that more of a commitment to Him than if you just do a tiny little *pas de bourrée?*"

"No," Wendy said smilingly. "But I'm very honest with my students. Some of them may have seen a video, or seen some dance performed, but they can't pull off what they've seen. So I say, "If you want to do those long, beautiful movements, you need to take a ballet class, you need to take a jazz class. If you want to articulate His word, you need to have the technique. I mean, I want to give God the *grand jeté*."

"That makes sense," I said. "He's the ultimate authority. He's the ultimate stern old Russian lady who uses her metal-tipped cane to whack at ankles."

"Hello. Madame Darvash."

You can't describe the relationship between dance and religion as "larky."

If you go to a wedding, you might dance. But if that wedding takes place anywhere in the Western world, the odds are that you'll be dancing at the wedding's reception, and not during the service. This is because the Judeo-Christian tradition, unlike most non-Western traditions, makes a distinction between the sacred and the secular. This distinction has, over the course of time, made life a whole lot more complicated for us dancers at the proverbial party. There ain't no Shiva at the shiva.

In many respects, the Religion function of dance overlaps with the other functions. This kind of dancing might, especially if it takes the form of ecstatic dancing, be an effort to elicit Emotion and Release; it might be a kind of Healing; it might, in its appeals to God, be the ultimate form of Social Entrée.

But it is also the function of the art form that has most caused dance to be beaten about the head.

"Judging from the volume of condemnations from on high," Barbara Ehrenreich has written, "the custom of dancing in churches was thoroughly entrenched in the Middle Ages and apparently tolerated—if not actually enjoyed—even by many parish priests." That said, the Church had begun prohibiting dancing in churches in the middle of the fourth century; this censure would reach its apogee from 1200 to 1500. From the Renaissance onward, dance in Western societies has tended to be a purely secular pursuit.

Praise dancing took off in the 1980s, perhaps aided by the increased number of women in leadership roles in the church, and by the increased use of video and contemporary music during services to raise attendance. It's particularly popular with Pentecostal congregations, who have a tradition of being literally moved by the Spirit.

Throughout its long history of ambivalence on the topic, the Church would sometimes differentiate between appropriate and inappropriate kinds of dancing. Dance history is full of examples of similarly unaccommodating people drawing lines in the sand—Plato, for instance, approved of educated men dancing in order to keep their bodies ready for battle, but he hated the jumping and leaping thing; one eighteenth-century choreographer thought that arms raised above shoulder height suggested loss of control or an SOS signal. Some naysayers even take action: in the 1830s, Christian missionaries in Hawaii insisted that hula dancing be performed in high-necked robes with sleeves.

That dance is sacred in some cultures but profane in others is perhaps only to be expected, but it's fascinating when it's both things in a single culture. In the nineteenth century, whenever the Zezuru tribe in southern Africa was about to be attacked by marauders, the Zezuru would send out a chorus line of topless tribeswomen, who would distract the hostiles with a lascivious shaking of their breasts. Yet the Zezuru, like most Africans, decried Western-style touch dancing as vulgar.

Or look at modern-day Christian evangelicals in the U.S. Fifty or sixty years ago, evangelicals linked dances like the Lindy Hop and the Jitterbug to miscegenation and truancy and other forms of wildness. But today, in a world that's host to much wilder forms of movement like twerking and krumping, some of these Christian parents who were forbidden in their own youth to dance now urge their kids to take up the old-timey steps.

We should not overlook the fact that, outside the confines of mainstream religion, we in the United States have a long tradition of ecstatic dancing. The Shakers used dance as a way to worship God;

after marching around a room in a procession and then swaying and turning in unison, the men on one side of the room and the women on the other, the Shakers would then form an oblong circle and wait to see if any dancer had received a "gift" or inspiration to move. This gift typically expressed itself with closed-eyed twirling, as if you were at a Grateful Dead or Phish show.

Or it might get a little more wiggy. One observer of an 1850 Shaker service wrote, "They fall a groaning trembling, and every one acts alone for himself; one will fall prostrate on the floor, another on his knees and his head in his hands; another will be muttering over articulate sounds, which neither they nor anybody else understand. Some will be singing, some will be dancing; others will be agonizing, as though they were in great pain; others jumping up and down; others fluttering over somebody, and talking to them; others will be shooing and hissing evil spirits out of the house, til the different tunes, groaning, jumping, dancing, drumming, laughing, talking and fluttering, shooing and hissing, makes a perfect bedlam."

Native American culture, too, has long included collective exaltation via movement as one of its ways to contact the forces that rule the world. In the Ghost Dance, which arose in the 1860s, dancers paint their bodies and then stand in a circle with their arms around one another, an effort to reunite the living with the spirits of the dead, and to get these spirits to protect the mortals and to promote unity. The Hopi's rain-bringing ritual called the Snake Dance honors the creatures seen as brothers to the weather spirits. Dancers carry live snakes—including rattlers—in their hands and mouths, while chanting about the need for precipitation. At ceremony's end, the snakes are returned to the earth (and not, as white men would probably favor, stuffed with a savory ricotta and eaten).

Before I went out for Thai food with praise dancer Wendy Heagy, I saw her perform—or, as she puts it, minister—at the Bowery Mission, which, since 1879, has offered food, shelter, and medical care for New York City's homeless. Wendy ministers in the mission's chapel every second Sunday of the month.

When I entered the chapel one blustery Sunday afternoon in January, I saw about eighty people sitting in the pews, almost all of them men. Because most of them had come in off the street, all but two of them were wearing their winter coats and hats. Some of these men were canted at a thirty-degree angle, asleep. Many had brought their worldly possessions in rollaway luggage. When a Mission employee caught me staring at a six-by-six-foot luggage storage area at the back of the chapel, he told me, "We call that LGA, or LaGuardia."

Noon. Time for Wendy to dance. I expected to see her up on the stage, but instead she was down in the aisle. Dressed in a red T-shirt, black dancewear, and sneakers, Wendy waited for her music—a Christian ballad called "This Place," sung by LaShun Pace—to come over the PA system. Then she launched into one of the more emotionally fraught and interactive dances I've ever seen. Her self-devised choreography incorporates a lot of American Sign Language and mime—when the lyrics mentioned "a terrible place," Wendy looked pained and fashioned her fingers into cat claws; when the lyrics ran "I ask these questions many a time," Wendy counted on her fingers from one to eight.

Then, after some lovely arm extensions and a nice blast of *pir-ouettes*, Wendy started moving down the aisle and interacting with the men, touching them, staring and smiling at them. The first man she moved on was a bedraggled gentleman in his seventies who, when Wendy clasped his face in her hands (lyric: "You're my peace"), rolled his eyeballs ever so slightly. But when, ninety seconds later, at the song's conclusion, Wendy came back and touched this gentleman's shoulder, he pointed at his heart, smiled, and then pointed at Wendy.

After her dance, Wendy sat in a pew and listened to the pastor's sermon. Then she joined the pastor in the aisle for the altar call, the opportunity for the men to talk to the officiants and to receive God. A few walked up to her, but mostly she wandered amid the pews.

Some fifteen minutes later, once the altar call had dissipated and a singing group had assembled on the stage, I introduced myself to Wendy, who was still standing in the aisle. "We had a healing today!" she said. One of the men she'd walked over to during the altar call had said he was having trouble breathing. "I lay one hand on his back and one on his chest. He started to stand and I felt this release, and he started breathing much better."

"Amen!" two bystanders chimed in. One of them added, "Good for you, Wendy."

Wendy shook her head.

"That's all Daddy," she said. "All Daddy."

Wendy drove me out to Queens for lunch. Once at the Thai restaurant, she unspooled her life story for me. She'd grown up Catholic in Montreal. She wasn't devout, but she loved church, even though she knew that some of the priests looked down at her for being black. An alcoholic by the age of sixteen (who would lose her sister to drug addiction some years later), she tried to pour her energies into her dance classes at Montreal's Dance Factory, one of whose teachers recognized Wendy's chops and encouraged her to go to New York. Once in New York, Wendy got a scholarship from the Broadway Dance Center. She graduated from BDC and then launched a successful career that included dancing on Broadway and touring with both the O'Jays and Kurtis Blow.

She was saved in 1996 during the run of an Off-Off-Broadway gospel musical called *Promises of Gold.*

"At my callback," she told me, "the first thing they did was stand in a circle and pray. I was like, Seriously? I had this whole thing in my head about Christians, how they can be really hardcore and Bible-thumping. But these people were phenomenal, both as performers and people. Over the course of the show, my heart was endeared."

Cut to the final week of the show, being done at the Lamb's Theatre in the Theater District. Wendy was backstage when she felt a tingling sensation all over her body. "I fell to my knees. It was like a surrender." The cast gathered around her, and prayed with her. Shortly thereafter, while standing in her living room one day, she heard the voice of God.

Putting my spoon down next to my bowl of curry, I said, "I read somewhere that when God spoke to you, he told you, 'I'm going to take you out of the dance world for a while, but then I'm going to put you back in it.'"

"Right," she said, nodding.

"So my first question is, Does God sound like Morgan Freeman?"

"No. Noooo. It's my own voice. It's more like he's informing my mind."

My second question was, What did he say?

He said he wanted her to teach others to dance in his name.

Wendy chuckled and looked down at the floor next to the café table we were sitting at. She said, "In my mind? My finite mind? I thought God was going to send me all these Broadway dancers. But when I saw the people he was sending me, I was like, Are you *kidding me*? Never danced in their lives. Older. They could move, but no technique."

Wendy founded her Raise Him Up Praise Dance School and Ministry in 2003. She started by holing up in a dance studio in Jackson Heights, coming up with choreography. Many praise dance ministries incorporate ASL, the dancers signing out scripture during songs; not knowing ASL, Wendy cooked up some of her own signing, but later also looked online at an ASL website. She knew that the ASL and miming would make dancing easier for her dancers, by providing them specific moves and technique. She also teaches her team members—unlike her solo piece at the Bowery Mission, she prefers to perform with three or four other dancers—to interact with the audience, because all her dances include a section where the dancers wander among the onlookers and touch them.

"I've met a lot of really shy dancers," I told her. "Do you ever get a student or team member who can do all the dance moves but who's shy about the physical contact stuff?"

"I make it very clear to people when they come to my classes. We start in prayer. I ask them to share testimony—'I helped my mother when she was ill,' etc. No testimony is too small. And I tell them, mine is not a praise and worship team. Praise and worship teams are the ones with all the costumes and the flags; the dancers are mostly looking upward. That's not the kind of team I have. We're evangelists. There's outreach. I'm a minister, not a performer. And it works because dance is a universal language."

"Yes, dance is a universal language," I said. "But many people, particularly men, are made hugely uncomfortable by it. That's why your ministering this afternoon struck me as so brave—you touched those men's faces! So many men—even if deep down they crave that kind of physical contact—are scared of it."

"But I'm not Wendy when I do that. It's the Lord summoning me. It's a spirit touching a spirit. It's not just Wendy coming up to them, and them thinking, She's cute! It's literally the touch of God coming through that person."

I also wondered if she'd met with resistance from the church itself. I said, "Joe Dell Hutcherson, who founded the dance ministry at Bethel Gospel in Harlem, has said that the first time she ministered through dance, all twelve people in the room walked out. Has anything like that happened to you?"

"No. She was a pioneer. When she started, the church was like, Really? Seriously? She told me that they made a dance studio for her, but when she started teaching they said, 'We can't get with this.'"

I said, "Other world religions don't separate the religious from the secular as Christianity does. So that's part of the problem. But then there's also this idea that Christianity doesn't see the body as holy in and of itself."

"Once the pastors see our work and see who we are, they invite us. I could see the apprehension on their faces because they're thinking VH-1 or the person down at the club. I asked the Lord, you tell me what's appropriate for your altar. In the Bible, it talks about how to dance appropriately. But it also talks about Jezebel. I mean, I'm not going to pick a Beyoncé song. I have nothing against Miss Beyoncé but that's not for church."

We talked for a while about some of the practicalities of having a team. Wendy told me that prior to ministering in a new location, she'll call the location and find out what "the issues" are there, so she can pick or tailor a song to those specific needs.

I asked Wendy about her favorite success story, and she told me about traveling to a small foreign country seven years earlier, and ministering to a young prostitute who saw Wendy and a team dance in a town square. Wendy told me, "I saw a lot of pain in her. So I prayed for her. Remember when Sylvester ran into Tweetie, who was acting like Frankenstein? It was like that. The scales were falling off her as I prayed for her. About three years later I get an e-mail from her: she's an interpreter at the United Nations now. She said, 'After you prayed for me, God took me, sent me to school, and brought me to the United Nations, where I met my new husband. Here is a video of my wedding.'"

Our conversation drifted to Wendy's career. I applauded her for having essentially lengthened her career as a dancer by taking up a less physically demanding idiom than doing the Running Man for Kurtis Blow. "You'll be able to praise dance until you're ninety."

"What we say in the ministry is, I'm gonna dance till Jesus comes."

"And then when he comes there'll be no more dancing?" I asked.

"There'll be a lot of dancing, but we'll all have recovered our glorified bodies. We'll be like"—she looked down at her torso here—"'Thank the Lord!'"

I laughed. It was then that I asked Wendy if God accounts for technique and Wendy told me, "I want to give God the *grand jeté*."

Which led me to another question: "Do you give corrections? Some teachers, like the great jazz teacher Luigi, don't, because they know certain students won't come back."

"I correct," Wendy told me. "If you're in my class, you're standing before God. Also, if you don't execute something properly, you can injure yourself. I'm known as the Lady with the Shoe."

"Because you're tap-tap-tapping with the shoe . . . or because you're throwing the shoe?"

Wendy smiled sheepishly.

"Look at *you!*," I gushed. "A thrower! A little Old Testament in the studio, yo!"

"Honey, you don't *know*. I've got the grace of the New Testament and the remedy of the Old."

2.

For its more ardent practitioners, it's also possible for dance, or one's life in the world of dance, to become a kind of religion. I don't mean to disrespect thousands of years of church-inspired piety here; but any individual whose livelihood and survival are dependent on strangers paying for things that they don't need is an individual who lives at the behest of forces unknown. In certain hands, this act of faith can become an entire system of belief.

"Why do you want to dance?" the ruthless impresario Boris Lermontov (Anton Walbrook) asks the aspiring ballerina Vicki Page

(Moira Shearer) in what is, alongside *Cabaret* and *Singin' in the Rain*, probably the most beloved dance film of all time, 1948's *The Red Shoes*. Ms. Page replies, "Why do you want to live?" to which Lermontov responds, "Well, I don't know exactly why, er, but I must." Page tells him, "That's my answer, too."

Though this compulsive approach to one's art would seem to be more prevalent in the worlds of ballet and tap, let's look at a celebrated name in jazz. Who, as it turns out, had some grounding in traditional religion, too.

Bob Fosse grew up Methodist on the North Side of Chicago. His father, a Hershey's chocolates salesman, taught young Fosse and his siblings social dancing at home. But the more formative event came from a local dance teacher and agent named Fred Weaver. When Fosse was twelve, Weaver paired him up with another boy in a tap act called the Riff Brothers. The Riff Brothers played Chicago "presentation houses" (movie theaters with live acts) as well as strip clubs.

This latter type of venue would shape Fosse's life for years afterward, as evidenced by the Fosse canon's allegiance to swivel hips, popped shoulders, and a louche, worldly knowingness. The seedy venues would also provide Fosse with incidents for his psyche to gnaw on: the strippers liked to lick Fosse's ears, or to prankishly grope him so he'd have a hard-on when he went onstage.

"I was a very religious kid," Fosse once said. "I mean, I did know all the Bible verses. I really believed that there was a god who was watching me all the time, who knew whether I was thinking the bad thoughts, the impure thoughts. I would concentrate on Bible verses if I ever thought about, uh, anything I thought was dirty . . . and being attracted to pretty women at the same time, it was a struggle, this terrible, terrible struggle, and thrown into these stripper joints when I was young, the battle that was going on inside me was just tremendous."

As an adult, however, the creator of the most distinctive choreographic style of the twentieth century was not particularly pious. "I think he would say he was an agnostic," dancer Ann Reinking, one of his longtime colleagues and lovers, told Fosse biographer Sam Wasson.

Yet the adult Fosse's relationship to his art had many of the attributes of religious devotion, particularly when viewed in terms of three qualities: his humility, his devotion to his craft, and his interest in confession. It seems all too fitting that *All That Jazz*, his heavily autobiographical and self-excoriating film about the psychic toll of show business, was called by author and Catholic priest Andrew M. Greeley "perhaps the most religious film ever made."

His humility could border on the abject. For the mordant Fosse, the world was a fraud, but he was an even bigger one. Even the hat trick he pulled off in 1973 (an Oscar for *Cabaret*, an Emmy for *Liza with a Z*, a Tony for *Pippin*) couldn't convince him of his talent; he earnestly told friends at the time, "I fooled everybody."

Indeed, the man who wasn't sold on his own talent sometimes needed a helping hand from on high—which in a few instances meant his partners. After his first major break, the 1953 film *Kiss Me Kate* (in which choreographer Hermes Pan had allowed cast member Fosse to choreograph his own duet), it was Fosse's wife Joan McCracken who persuaded theater director George Abbott to hire Fosse as the choreographer for Broadway's *The Pajama Game*. Fosse's work here, which would win the Tony, would be so vivid— the automatism that would increasingly be a part of his style is on display in the great "Steam Heat" number, wherein the dancers' bowler hats appear to be lifted heavenward by invisible steam—that Abbott would hire him the following year for *Damn Yankees*. Five years later, Gwen Verdon, Fosse's muse and longtime wife, would get him his first job as director-choreographer, by insisting he be hired for the 1959 musical *Redhead*, which she was starring in. From thereon, Fosse would serve as director-choreographer on almost all her projects. (Partners: they can get you jobs.)

You could see his humility in his everyday behavior, too. "I threw up twice a day when I was a performer. Now I throw up three times a day," Fosse said once he started directing. He almost always introduced himself to others with his full name lest people ask "Bob who?" Sometimes his rejections of dancers at auditions were so thoughtful that the dancers would write Fosse a thank-you note. He was slightly defensive about never having gone to college, and about not working in ballet: "Everything I know I learned from *Hollywood Squares.*"

His focus and devotion to his craft could come off as a kind of zealotry or penitence. Like pious people who reject colored clothing in order to keep their priorities straight, he wore all black. "Naturally hunched, he had an almost collaborative complicity with the sidewalk, a rehearsal space he could engage at any time," writes Sam Wasson in his terrific, if occasionally purple, biography *Fosse*. A perfectionist, Fosse sometimes got to rehearsal spaces before dawn; occasionally his concentration during rehearsals or filming was so intense that a colleague would have to flick the cigarette from his lip lest Fosse be burned. Verdon said of his rehearsal demeanor, "His face changes. He gets ropey looking. His eyes sink into his head. . . . I've worked in insane asylums and the inmates didn't look as weird as Bob."

After Verdon asked for a separation in 1971, Fosse's hard partying escalated—he upped with Dexedrine and downed with Seconal, padding them out with double margaritas and four packs of Camels a day. By 1977, when the director of the film *Thieves*, starring Marlo Thomas and Charles Grodin, needed someone to play a street junkie, Fosse volunteered himself and pulled off the role convincingly.

His overinvestment in his work had started earlier. To tell the cast of Broadway's 1961 *The Conquering Hero* that he'd been fired as director-choreographer, he dressed up as the character Pal Joey, whom he'd played to acclaim in summer stock a decade earlier. He sported a trench coat, its collar up; a fedora pulled over one eye; and the ever-present ciggie, like a kick from his mouth. After Fosse unspooled his sad news to the assembled cast onstage, he strolled stage left, said goodbye, dropped his cigarette to the floor, stubbed it out with his toe, pulled his fedora's brim down even further, and disappeared into the wings. Jesus wept.

As he got older and a grimness seemed to settle over both his life and work, the zealotry got even wiggier. During the filming of the autobiographical and painful-to-watch *All That Jazz*, he sometimes wore lead actor Roy Scheider's costumes. During the *Star 80* shoot, Eric Roberts was having trouble portraying Paul Snider, the sleaze-ball who, after discovering *Playboy* bunny Dorothy Stratten, killed and then raped her. So Fosse screamed at Roberts that he should just play Snider as if he were playing Fosse, because Snider *was* Fosse, but without the success. "Now show me *me*," he told Roberts.

Yes, Fosse's working methods struck some as a kind of fanaticism. But this fanaticism was preferable to the one that came when he *wasn't* working. Fosse's assistant Pat Kiley told Fosse biographer Martin Gottfried that Fosse would get depressed at the end of projects: "He had to start on something new before the old one ended"— otherwise, according to Fosse, "my pain would be so great that I wouldn't be able to deal with it."

Indeed, for Fosse, show business was an all-powerful juggernaut with long, dangly puppet strings. When telling friends and colleagues, after the failure of his first film, 1969's *Sweet Charity* with Shirley MacLaine, "I got so cold. No one called me," he would hunch his shoulders and punctuate his statement with a drawn-out, hollow whistle. (The film's failure nearly killed off the much-ailing MCA-Universal; as biographer Gottfried put it, "That was his stigma.")

Or look at the *The Little Prince* episode. In 1974, while lying in a hospital bed after his heart bypass surgery, Fosse was visited by filmmaker Stanley Donen, who'd directed the film of *The Little Prince* in which Fosse danced "Snake in the Grass" (a number that Michael Jackson adored—and, some say, stole from). In the hospital, Fosse cajoled a reluctant Donen into watching a critic on television deliver his review of the just-released film. When the review turned out to be abysmal, Fosse became exercised and had another heart attack.

No, his lamentations were not whispered. "He hid none of his troubles," the critic Joan Acocella has written. "He was one of those people, often veterans of psychoanalysis"—Fosse was in psychoanalysis during the 1950s—"who feel that if they admit their sins they are somehow absolved of them." Fosse sometimes used the mediums of dance and film as a confessional booth. We see this most clearly, of course, in *All That Jazz*, with its chain-smoking, sex-obsessed, pill-popping workaholic choreographer whose stress about his work puts him in the hospital for coronary artery bypass surgery, directly after which he has another heart attack.

But we see signs of the confession booth elsewhere, too. The great womanizer Fosse, who cheated on Verdon throughout their marriage—one theory runs that Fosse's having worked with strippers as a child made him try to prove that all women were whorish—loved threesomes. So he saw fit to have the character Pippin watch two women make love at one point during *Pippin*. Though there's no evidence that comedian Lenny Bruce partook of amorous triads, Fosse slapped one into his 1974 biopic, *Lenny*.

Sometimes the impulse to confess had a more moralistic edge. He punished girlfriend Reinking for an affair he thought she was having by choreographing a pornographic ballet number for her in 1978's *Dancin'*, and then casting as her partner the male dancer that Fosse thought she was having an affair with.

It's possible to view Fosse's injection of self into narratives as an extension of his larger influence on Broadway. Prior to Fosse's rise,

in the 1950s and '60s, the dancing in Broadway shows was meant
to emerge naturally from the characters: Anna is at first slightly
cowed by the King of Siam, but, with time, the two of them will swirl
together in dizzying circles. Agnes de Mille's dream ballet in 1943's
Oklahoma! had severed musical theater from its European operetta
roots by using dance to portray the heroine's emotional troubles,
rather than as mere distraction or scenery. (This orientation, and
its subsequent reign on Broadway, was not without a price for de
Mille; some call her "the woman who killed tap.")

Fosse followed the dance-as-mirror-of-emotions approach up
through the sixties, "but then it started to look corny to him," Acocella writes. So he returned to his vaudeville roots, making lots of
self-aware dances that are "justified" (meaning, overtly theatrical,
and often occurring on a stage that is on the stage). Look at his
two most beloved works—the spectacular film version of *Cabaret*,
and the stage version of *Chicago*, which he cowrote in addition to
choreographing and which, decades after his death, would be his
first blockbuster hit. Neither has much in the way of mortal beings
breaking out into dance; we see a lot of musical staging as opposed
to full-out dance numbers.

Or look beyond: "In much of his later work," Acocella writes,
"there is little or no story to humanize the dancers, or to objectify
them. We can't separate them from ourselves, can't say, 'That's Lau-
rey and Curly.' They come from nowhere, or—as Fosse, with his *hypo-
crite lecteur* philosophy, appears to be saying—from within ourselves."

The end game of confession, of course, is absolution. Which
brings us back to *All That Jazz*, with its angel of death played by
Jessica Lange. At the end of the film, Fosse's stand-in, Joe Gideon
(the role Roy Scheider played), is lying in his bed during his bypass
operation. While thusly "dead," he jumps off the bed, runs into
the theater that the hospital set is located in, and starts to hug the
audience, which is composed of all the people in his life—his wives
and daughter, the movie executives, the strippers from the clubs he

played in when young. There's lots of cheering, and then Gideon rematerializes on the hospital bed, but this time zipped into a body bag, whereupon we hear Ethel Merman sing "There's No Business Like Show Business." Fosse seems to be suggesting here that, though working in show business can be a kind of penance, death affords man a gentle exoneration.

As they were rehearsing the scene, Fosse said to Scheider, "You know, that must be exhilarating, running into the house like that." So Scheider suggested that Fosse try it himself. Fosse got up on the bed, paused, and then ran out into the audience and hugged everyone.

Afterward, he sidled up to Scheider and said, "Jesus Christ, that was terrific, and you know, Roy? The best part of it is, they forgave *me*, too."

3.

Many of us have had the experience of watching dance that is so transporting that we can only call the experience sublime. To see a corps of women wafting flawlessly across a stage as if they were all swans can make me think that there's a force that is larger than man or any literal or temporal entity. There's a section of Paul Taylor's *Esplanade*—in the fifth movement, a little less than three minutes in—that similarly moves me. To a score of ever-beetling Bach, the dancers do a lot of big, loose, outstretched-arms full spins while *relevé*-ing on one foot, and then they crash to the floor. But then when one of the dancers (Carolyn Adams in the YouTube video) starts doing the spin, just as she's about thirty degrees into her backwards fall, her partner catches her, and then gently helps her onto the floor. She does another spin and he catches and helps her again. Then again. Again. Again.

But as someone who himself likes to dance, I don't know where I fit in on the dance-as-religion-or-spirituality front. I believe in a higher power, but I don't call it God. Organized religion often gives me the willies. And, given that I'm a social dancer, and that I've been dancing in earnest for only seven years, I'm not like one of those ballet or tap people whose commitment to his or her craft or whose quest for excellence naturally gives way to discussions about cherubim or grace. I'm excited by a quote from *Brave New World* author Aldous Huxley that runs, "It is with their muscles that humans most easily obtain knowledge of the divine," but my connection to the quote is almost entirely notional.

It's when I'm watching dance, as opposed to dancing myself, that I seem to empathize most with this part of Paul Taylor's memoir: "Some folks, especially those who find organized religion unappealing, may, like me, find in dance an ordered discipline that signals the existence of Order. Yet dance is only a symbol, not the real thing. But it can relieve instinctive cravings for ritual, ordered magic. Something tells me that when churches started making their rituals more understandable, that was when churchgoers started to look elsewhere."

DANCE AS NOSTALGIA

1.

I CAN MEASURE MY LIFE IN PRODUCTIONS OF *HAIR*.

1969: I'm seven, and I'm starting to fall in love with the original cast album, which one of my older siblings has left near the family turntable. There are words in here that are dark and exciting to my impressionable young mind: sovody, fellatio, cunnilimbus, peberasty.

One day, while we're driving around Worcester, Massachusetts, in our VW bug, my two sisters enthusiastically sing along to "Aquarius/ Let the Sunshine In" when it comes on the radio, waving their arms like air traffic controllers who've ingested a lot of muscle relaxants. So I join in, too, desperately hoping to be mistaken for cool.

1977: In Cambridge, Massachusetts, I see a group of gushy young actors in fruit-colored leotards perform a highly aerobic showcase of some of the show's better-known songs. I leave the theater feeling like I've eaten more than one piece of cheesecake on a humid day: the hallmark of overexposure to the Danskin crotch panel.

1979: I'm seventeen, and trying not to be gay, but when I watch the new Miloš Forman film of *Hair*, I'm strangely attracted to John

Savage, who plays Claude. But I'm also drawn to the horses in the film, who, like Twyla Tharp's dancers, can be seen prancing sideways.

The horses are side-stepping, and so am I.

2008: I'm forty-six. I'm gay and happily coupled, which is to say, I go to the theater like some people go to Costco. It's a sport. If I run into you in the lobby before the show, I might leave you with "See you out on the ice."

Greg and I get tickets for Diane Paulus's terrific production of *Hair* staged outdoors in Central Park. When it starts raining fifteen minutes into the show, the cast, mid–dance number, flees backstage. I notice one chorus member glare at the surrounding woodland as if one of the older and crankier maple trees had called the cops and shut down the party. An air of doom pervades the audience as we're told to wait out the meteorology.

Greg and I trudge to the front of the theater, where we linger under the eaves and try to sublimate our disappointment by making up synonyms for "rainstorm." When, fifteen or so minutes later, just as we've abandoned "torrentula" and moved on to "spittledammerung," the squall slowly shifts to a palpable and granular mist, all us audience members cautiously trickle back to our seats. Back in the theater, we see stagehands mopping down the lawn that the cast has been dancing on; they're using rolled-up towels that look like the world's largest tampons.

When the show resumes, it's as if both the audience and the cast and crew have surmounted some personal tragedy: we're in this thing together now. This camaraderie is only deepened by the fact that Karole Armitage's thrashy choreography will now be done on a lawn that may or may not have been tamponed to total dryness. Here is suspense. Here is possible injury. I imagine felled hippie dancers receiving shots of cortisone and then suddenly reanimating: Unbathed and Undead!

I watch the remainder of the show in a state of dazed exhilaration. My breathing is altered. When, after the curtain call, audience members are encouraged to get up onstage and dance with the cast, I long desperately to go, but am too shy to act on the impulse: the ice, she seems icy.

2010: For my forty-eighth birthday, I take Greg and two friends to the Paulus/Armitage production, which has now transferred to a Broadway theater. At the show's conclusion, I bustle onto the stage and dance with the cast. I start center stage, but on realizing that the audience can see me, I move upstage center so that I can see everyone but no one can see me, the hallmark of the closet exhibitionist.

2014: Greg and I are in Chicago, visiting the two friends I took to the Broadway production four years earlier. Scanning the *Chicago Reader* one Saturday afternoon, I see a listing for a storefront production of *Hair*, and impulsively buy four tickets. As I rattle off my credit card number to a phone representative, I think, This is becoming a thing—if it is not already a thing.

When we think of nostalgia with respect to dance, we tend to think of the obvious—the glassy-eyed and beatific *Nutcracker* veteran who has never convincingly returned from the Land of Sweets; the nattily dressed dance enthusiast who applies to the human race the not unreasonable binary (1) People who are Fred Astaire, and (2) People who are not Fred Astaire. It's easy to catch the bug: if you and a love interest have a great dance together, the memory of it can live on in your consciousness like a phantom limb.

Books and photographs have long provided inspiration for the sentimentalist, but the huge crop of dance film clips unearthed over the past thirty years or so have whipped these smoldering embers into a bonfire: the ability to spend one's lunch hour excavating YouTube clips of Margot Fonteyn dramatically increases one's desire to be Margot Fonteyn. Though the majority of them are admittedly not dance-related, four hundred hours of video are uploaded to YouTube every single minute.

Depending on where you live, live performances of historical dance are often readily available, too. If you live in a major metropolitan area that does not annually offer a variation on a Jazz Age lawn party, then you need to write a strongly worded letter to your chamber of commerce, and sign it Daisy Buchanan.

The dance function that I'm calling Nostalgia is one of the hardest of the functions to define. With respect to other functions, it's probably most similar to Emotion and Release, Intimacy and Socializing, and to Healing; it may be all of these things or some combination thereof. When we refer to people watching dance (as opposed to dancing themselves), the Nostalgia function usually works much as it does in the other arts—audience members, particularly at either end of the age spectrum, love the reassurance of the familiar, but an overabundance of this same reassurance can feel like kitsch. When it comes to dancing ourselves, the Nostalgia function may derive some of its power from an unexpected inquiry: if muscles have memory, are some of these memories more fondly remembered by our muscles than others?

What's clearer is that, in a world in which "LOL" and emoji pass for communication if not banter, a blast of ye olde charm is decidedly a tonic. While the contemporary world's allegiance to practicality and speed makes certain dance idioms seem ever more charming by the hour—hello tap, ballet, swing, and ballroom—this is not to say that other dance forms are without a nostalgic component. Hip-hop dancers love to get "old skool with it" from time to time; modern dance companies are forever resurrecting decades-old material from their repertory; ask a jazz dancer about Michael Bennett's work on *A Chorus Line*, and prepare to have more of "The Music and the Mirror" performed than you were hoping for.

As the success of *La La Land* and the 2017 remake of *Beauty and the Beast* attests, it's hard for many to resist nostalgia's appeal.

Whether, like me with my *Hair* obsession, you're after beads, flowers, freedom, and happiness, or whether you gravitate to the swoopy elegance of the Viennese waltz and the many complicated, buttery baked goods such an allegiance conjures up for you, it's pretty clear that pursuing these ends is as close to time travel as we're likely to get in this lifetime.

Fortunately, nostalgia, as the saying goes, isn't what it used to be. The Swiss doctor who coined the term "nostalgia" in the late seventeenth century defined it as a "neurological disease of essentially demonic cause." The high incidence of this "disease" among Swiss mercenaries abroad was, bizarrely, thought by doctors to be the result of damage caused to eardrums by overexposure to clanging cowbells.

Today we know better, thanks largely to research done by a psychologist at the University of Southampton in England named Constantine Sedikides. In the same way that people in concentration camps during the Holocaust figured out that remembering meals they'd eaten could imbue them with a sense of optimism, so, too, Dr. Sedikides realized, do fond memories lift spirits for people who are not in crisis.

Studies have shown nostalgia both to foster inspiration and creativity and to make subjects more tolerant of outsiders. Subjects who've been made to feel nostalgic have shown decreased levels of anxiety, boredom, and loneliness.

In one experiment, subjects who'd been induced to a state of nostalgia were asked to set up a room for a meeting; they placed chairs much closer to one another than their non-nostalgic counterparts did. In another experiment, nostalgic subjects were asked to write essays; an impartial panel judged these essays to be more creative and imaginative than their counterparts' were.

To be sure, there's a dark side to nostalgia, too—this bittersweet emotion can cause some people to dwell on absence or regret in a way that becomes counterproductive, and that can even hurt them. I asked swing dancer Ryan Martin, the cofounder of the Hot Rhythm Foundation, a nonprofit organization that promotes jazz music and dance forms that originated in the early part of the twentieth century, what he thought about dancers who use slang from another era, and he said, "That's usually a warning sign. No one really does that."

Audiences can get trapped in a kind of nostalgia, too: Jennifer Grey has said that, after the success of *Dirty Dancing*, she didn't dance for twenty-five years, even at weddings, because the pressure to meet onlookers' expectations was too staggering.

But Dr. Sedikides's research suggests that looking back on the past typically makes people less fearful of death and more optimistic about the future. Which may be related to my hunch that the more dire the era you live in, the more rose-colored the nostalgia you engage in. During the oil-poor, crime-infested 1970s, we all gravitated to a candy-colored gloss on the 1950s called *Happy Days*; in the throes of the 2000s' global banking crisis, we binged on the stylized cool of *Mad Men*; in the rocky early days of the Trump administration, many clung to the throwback-y charms of *La La Land*, a giddy, gee-whiz musical about a young actress rescued from obscurity by her jazz-snob guy pal.

2.

Early on in my tap dancing career—which is to say, before I had taken a single class—I got to dance on the stage of the Apollo. Admittedly, this is like putting a seven-month-old infant in charge of an oil rig. But let me explain. The American Tap Dance Foundation, a school located in Greenwich Village, was offering a tour of the illustrious Harlem theater, at the conclusion of which all tour-takers would get a chance to strut their stuff together. So I signed up.

Some seventy of us—mostly students in their twenties from the foundation—trickled into the theater at the appointed hour and took seats, marveling at the theater's neoclassical splendor. "You're all sitting so far back," a friendly young tour guide named Sally said on beholding us, "like you're afraid of the Apollo."

Maybe we were. I mean: Bill "Bojangles" Robinson. James Brown. Aretha. Diana Ross and the Supremes. Michael Jackson. We were staring at eighty-two years of genius-making.

Sally encouraged us to move closer. We did so cautiously, as if walking in sand.

Sally launched into a brief history of the theater, and we started to relax. After her speech, she led us first to the Apollo's smallish, dimly lit greenroom, where she asked us if we knew the origin of the name "greenroom." Nervous chuckles, but no answers forthcoming. So I tried, "Is this where you got paid?"—using the past tense to acknowledge the demise of window envelopes and little deerskin bags filled with wampum. Sally smiled at me and said, "Boom!"

Then we climbed a bunch of stairs backstage to look at "the stacks," four small, cinderblock dressing rooms the cramped charm of which landed midpoint on the college dormitory/prison continuum. Only about a third of the group could fit in at one time; trying to squeeze past one another without committing frottage felt like our first piece of choreography. Sally told us, "People like Paul McCartney and Rod Stewart and Maurice Hines ask for these dressing rooms instead of the newer ones because they're so full of history."

Then, downstairs in the stage right wings, we checked out the autograph wall, a black expanse twinkling with Sharpied flickerings of Alicia Keys and Janelle Monáe and Beyoncé. It would have held our attention for longer if the stage hadn't been six feet behind us, dully throbbing with golden light.

The stage. Some of us edged onto it, others zagged like bugs from a jar. There was a big bolus of slightly yellow light center stage;

to enter it was to lower yourself into a swimming pool filled with butterscotch pudding. It felt *good* in there. You're up about three feet from the first row, which is comforting in the manner of piloting an elephant or an SUV—if anyone wanted to throw a punch at you, you'd have ample warning. But then looking out at a sea of 1,506 red seats—the house lights were on—was disorienting and kaleido-fabulous, like holding a zinnia a centimeter away from your face.

Sally told us that, before we danced, we would follow Apollo tra-dition by each touching the Tree of Hope for good luck. Hollowed-out and the size of a large watermelon, the Tree of Hope is the trunk of an elm tree that once stood near the theater. Black performers liked to stand under the tree for good luck. As I swiped my right hand against the tree's smooth surface and thought of the thousands of people who'd done the same thing over the years, I thought, I bet this trunk used to be twice as big.

Then it was time for us all to perform the Coles Stroll. This is a simple circle dance devised for nonprofessional dancers by legendary tapper Charles "Honi" Coles who, prior to performing in the duo Coles & Atkins and playing Tito Suarez in *Dirty Dancing* and winning a Tony for *My One and Only*, was a stage manager and performance coach at the Apollo from 1960 to 1976.

Tony Waag, the head of the Tap Foundation, told us to form a large circle on the stage. Forty-eight of us moved into place. "You all know this, right?" he asked.

Uh, no. Later, of course, I would read all about the Stroll, and learn that it was an encapsulation of Coles's famous saying, "If you can walk, you can tap," because you simply walk or bop in a big group circle while adding a beat every eight bars. But I didn't know that yet. Moreover, given that at least four people were filming us, and that another tour group of about seventy were sitting in the balcony watching us, I felt a little pressure not to look like an idiot. So I said to the well-dressed, forty-ish woman in front of me, "They're going to teach us how to do this, yes?"

"They will."

"I mean, I know Honi Coles devised it for non-dancers, but . . ."

"It's easy. Just look like you know what you're doing. Sell it."

I nodded my head and gave her a tentative thumbs-up sign. At which point the irritatingly noisy twenty-something dude standing behind me asked, "What did she just tell you?"

I whispered, "She told me, 'When you get to the other side of the stage, take off your pants.'"

He laughed nervously.

Tony Waag started us all off humming "Take the A Train," and then we went into the Stroll, moving in a circle in big, slow steps. You put your heel down first, then lightly slap your toe down. Then on the other side. One after another.

Easy. Afraid no more.

3.

His friends call him Save.

Before he was born, his mother didn't know what to call him. Then, while in the hospital to deliver him in 1973, Yvette Glover had a vision: she saw a blackboard with the word "Savior" written on it. But she knew that she couldn't saddle a child with the weight of a name like that, so she switched the r to n.

Savion Glover, who some consider the finest tap dancer who ever lived, has done a lot to help keep the perpetually dying art of tap alive. This is no small thing. Tap's heyday was in the 1920s and '30s; when the greatest luminary of that period, Bill "Bojangles" Robinson, died in 1949, a one-hundred-car funeral cortege drew more than a million onlookers along its route. But during the 1960s, tap all but vanished from the cultural landscape, probably because no one wanted to tap to rock and roll or soul or Motown. During the seventies, the historically black idiom saw a slight resurgence thanks largely to white women like Brenda Bufalino and Jane Goldberg, but by the late 1980s, the fervor was starting to diminish again.

Enter a certain cherubic, hip-hop-loving child prodigy and his surprisingly appropriate nickname.

Savion was one of three sons, each born to a different father. He grew up in a housing project in Newark, New Jersey. He was shy and skinny. He mumbled a lot.

Many tap dancers have played the drums (Bill "Bojangles" Robinson, Harold Nicholas of the Nicholas brothers, Fred Astaire, Gregory Hines), and so, too, did Savion: in fact, he drummed before he could walk. He'd pull out all his mother's pots and pans and start whacking on them. Or he'd whack on the walls, or on people. When single parent Yvette would come home from work as an administrative secretary, Savion would say, "Mommy, sit down and collapse yourself," and then put on a show for her.

Yvette Glover put the four-year-old Savion into a Suzuki drumming class at the Newark School for Performing Arts. Soon, he was given a scholarship at the school, the youngest person ever so honored. Then in 1982, while he was playing drums in a benefit at the Broadway Dance Center one day, two auspicious things happened: Savion became enraptured by a performance given by the hoofers Chuck Green and Lon Chaney (not the actor Lon Chaney), and his mother enrolled him in the dance school. At the school, Savion wore cowboy boots for the first seven months because he couldn't afford tap shoes.

In 1983, Savion successfully auditioned for a workshop that the producers of Broadway's *The Tap Dance Kid* had started at Broadway Dance Center to foster a pool of talent. By the fall of 1984 Savion had taken over *The Tap Dance Kid*'s title role, doing eight shows a week for three hundred performances at the age of eleven. A limo would pick him up in Newark to take him to the theater; his mother has said, "Even the neighborhood drug addicts were so proud of him."

But it was his subsequent turn on Broadway, in the blues revue *Black and Blue*, that really laid the groundwork for Savion as a preservationist and respecter of elders. Not only was the show choreographed by a murderers' row of hoofers and swingers (Henry LeTang, Frankie Manning, Charles "Honi" Coles's former partner Cholly Atkins, and Fayard Nicholas of the Nicholas Brothers), but the cast itself was studded with luminaries. During the show's run, Savion pestered some of the old-time hoofers in the cast like Jimmy Slyde and Bunny Briggs with so many questions about tap and life that they started calling him "the Sponge." He became so close to tapper Dianne Walker that he started to call her Aunt Dianne.

Savion also bonded with the *Black and Blue* cast member who would become his mentor, Gregory Hines. "Remember, I had no father image in my life," Savion writes. "And these cats were accepting me, and I was just this little kid. . . . We went out. We went to clubs. You ask what they taught me? Everything. About life. About being a man. About how to be."

Inspired and dazzled by Hines and the old-timers and what they were teaching him, Savion increasingly made a distinction between tap dancing and hoofing. The former was about entertainment, and came with graceful arms and a big smile. But Savion, like most of his *Black and Blue* colleagues, was more drawn to hoofing, in which personal expression is primary, and what a dancer looks like is much less important than the sounds he makes. Hoofing's mandate is summed up in the expression "hitting"—for Savion, it's high praise to be told "Yo, you hit last night!" because hitting means to express yourself fully, or to capture the rhythm of life. (Conversely, a tapper like Tommy Tune, according to Savion, doesn't hit—Tune does "classroom stuff.")

This orientation would seem to have affected Savion's work both for good and bad. On the positive side, you'd be hard-pressed to find a dancer, let alone a tap dancer, whose footwork and sense of rhythm is more virtuosic: "whirlwind" does not begin to describe the sweet hell that Savion can rain down upon a stage. (He's known in the trade for having a "heavy foot." As Hines once put it, "He can tap dance faster and harder and cleaner than anyone I've ever seen or heard of. He hits the floor harder than anybody, and to do it, he lifts his foot up the least. It doesn't make any sense.")

On the negative side, Savion has been accused, particularly when he was younger, of neglecting his audiences. In wanting his work to be viewed as music more than dance, and in putting all his attention on the beat rather than on how that beat is produced, he has sometimes alienated audiences by refusing to look at them or by performing with his back to them. When Greg and I went to see Savion at the New York City jazz club the Blue Note in January 2017, he did something odd. The announcer said, "Ladies and gentleman, Savion Glover!" On walked three band members, who picked up their instruments, but did not start playing. No Savion. Forty-five seconds in: a fourth band member sauntered onto the stage. Still no Savion. Still no music. Audience members started looking at one another, coughing. One minute in: the bass player looked offstage awkwardly and said, "All right." The audience grew increasingly restless, their sympathy skyrocketing for the band members, at whom we were all staring but who still weren't playing. Two minutes in: still no Savion. The audience writhed in discomfort, sure that we'd been trapped in some weird example of Antonin Artaud's Theatre of Cruelty.

When, some two and a half minutes in, Savion finally appeared, he did not talk to, look at, or apologize to the audience for the next forty-five minutes. But so fiery and innovative was his dancing—he can dance on the side of his feet! He walked *en pointe* across the stage! He can make at least three different sounds by scraping his toe!—and so contagious was the rhapsody he felt while doing it (he tends to beam his joy at the floor or at the musicians), that all the awkwardness of the show's opening was dissipated. Thrillingly, Savion was simultaneously dancer, drummer, and bandleader—he was driving the beat, and changing it so the musicians all had to follow. What dancers do this?

By 1991, young Savion was appearing regularly on *Sesame Street*, as himself or someone just like him named Savion; he'd wear a baseball hat sideways, and teach tap to the likes of Big Bird and Shelly the Turtle. A year later, he was on Broadway with Hines again, in *Jelly's Last Jam*.

In 1995, Savion and *Jelly*'s director George C. Wolfe opened their spectacular theatrical collaboration, *Bring in 'da Noise, Bring in 'da Funk*. The show—an informal history of the black struggle as chronicled through the progression of "da beat" from African drumming to Stepin Fetchit–style tap dancing in Hollywood to street drummers—made Savion a star and won him a Tony.

As *Hamilton* would continue to do years later, *Bring in 'da Noise* made Broadway safe for hip-hop. For us audience members, this paradigm shift first revealed itself with the slight smell of ganja that seeped into the Ambassador Theatre from backstage, but then solidified at the sight of Savion himself: by now he'd acquired his trademark Rasta-man dreadlocks, thus heightening the surprise to be found at the intersection of a dying profession and slangy, ghetto cool.

"When I was a kid," Savion told the *New Yorker* just before *Bring in 'da Noise* transferred from the Public Theater to Broadway, "I looked up to Honi Coles, Sammy Davis, and Sandman Sims. A 15 year-old kid today is now trying to do Savion." Or maybe the inspired kid was only nine: when one of today's most esteemed young choreographers of ballet, Justin Peck, saw *Bring in 'da Noise* at that age, he was so gob-smacked that he started training.

To a certain degree, the trope of honoring one's elders is built into the DNA of tap. A longtime element of tap dancing is something called the hoofer's line. "That's where everybody's doing a paddle and roll and one dancer at a time takes a solo turn," Savion explains in his book. "There are rules, but the rules are unspoken, almost secret. The main thing is you got to finish the phrase of the man before you, finish it and then add something of your own. And if you don't, you'll be cut by the next man, embarrassed, you'll have your own step flipped back on you. You can spit on someone through the dance. You can murder someone through the dance."

But Savion takes the practice of honoring your antecedents to a new level; as he told *60 Minutes* in 2000, "I'm on a mission to brainwash an entire generation." When he performs in his own shows, he often bedecks the stage with large photographs of the dead masters of tap. After Hines died in 2003, Savion would sometimes perform with a photograph of Hines hanging around his neck. Sometimes his desire to honor or resurrect is baked into the project's DNA: in 2016, Savion collaborated with George C. Wolfe again to adapt for Broadway 1921's *Shuffle Along*, the first Broadway musical to feature a romantic duet between a black man and a black woman.

He also pays it forward via teaching. During the national tour of *Jelly's*, he taught in all sixty-five cities that the show visited. In 2009, he opened a school of tap in Newark called the HooFeRzCLuB (named after a small room in the back of a comedy club that was the informal headquarters of tap in Harlem during the 1920s and '30s).

You can't read an interview with Savion, it sometimes seems, without encountering him banging on about Jimmy Slyde or Honi Coles or some other overlooked legend of yesteryear. Take his experience with the 2006 animated hit *Happy Feet*, for instance. Savion was the inspiration for Mumble, the penguin protagonist who was voiced by Elijah Wood. Traveling to Australia several times to work with director George Miller of *Mad Max* fame, Savion devised the choreography for, and did the motion capture dancing for, Mumble.

He wore a black body suit with forty reflective sensors attached, and was filmed on a small soundstage with some sixty light-sensitive cameras. When the film came out—it would take in more than $384 million at the box office, and win the Oscar for Best Animated Feature—*USA Today* interviewed Savion, who told the paper, "I see a lot of my mentors and tap pioneers like Jimmy Slyde in the steps and patterns. I do a special move that was given to me by Gregory Hines. Now this penguin is doing it."

4.

There's at least one dance community—that of swing dancing—wherein the attraction to nostalgia is so prevalent that it's the dancers who *don't* buy into the reminiscence machine altogether who make the strongest impression.

In January of 2017 I went to Austin, Texas, to attend Hot Rhythm Holiday, a weekend devoted to swing dancing and jazz. (I went alone, Greg having declared himself too antisocial for social dancing.) The festival is held in the gorgeous 1931 Georgian Revival mansion that is the headquarters for the Texas Federation of Women's Clubs. USO dances were regularly held at "the Fed" during World War II; Duke Ellington, Cab Calloway, and Benny Goodman all played its ballroom. With its period furniture and oil paintings of large-jawed bluestockings, the Fed feels like visiting the home of an impoverished noble and her slightly dusty dishes of Jordan almonds.

The day before the festival started, the organizers sent us all an e-mail stating "To help preserve that vintage vibe, we request that attendees not wear screen-printed t-shirts (a.k.a. "graphic t-shirts") and/or jeans to the Friday and Saturday night dances. If you want to stay casual try a plain color or striped t-shirts with slacks for a vintage look." So I was not surprised, on entering the mansion on a Thursday night, to find myself amid a lot of people in their twenties and thirties, many of them turned out in high-waisted pants, dresses with shoulder pads, spectator shoes, suspenders, snoods. Very fetching.

Over the course of the weekend, I took classes, attended panels, went to dances, listened to great music, and holed up in my hotel room watching clips of swing dancing in old movies. At a class in creating vintage hairstyles, I talked to a young woman who told me that at the first swing weekend she ever went to, "I realized I was much more into vintage hair than I am vintage dancing." I talked to a former punk rocker and skateboarder who told me that his adoption of the swing lifestyle was only natural, given that in both skateboarding and swing, "there's tricks."

One night, about 250 of us dancers, having declared ourselves either leaders or followers, lined the two long sides of the four-thousand-square-foot ballroom. Then, starting at one end, the two lines started snaking inward toward the middle of the hall, creating lots of pairs. I grabbed the hand of the jolly, twenty-something woman who was to be my partner. We couples moved rapidly down the length of the room together like fertilized eggs down a gigantic fallopian tube.

I wondered if there was a correlation between the dancers' level of nattiness and the particular form of swing they were doing. Indeed there was, I was told by various people. Lindy Hop, the first kind of swing to be revitalized—this happened in the 1980s, with later boosts from the 1988 "Khakis Swing" GAP commercial and the movies *Swing Kids* (1993) and *Swingers* (1996)—is the most popular form, the gateway drug of swing if you will, and thus has the lowest percentage of people who wear vintage. The more smooth and elegant Balboa, the second of the weekend's featured dances to be revitalized, has a lot of vintage going on, perhaps because its smooth, intricate moves are less sweat-producing than its two cousins', and thus less likely to dissolve the armpits of your mint-green voile jumper. Finally, the weekend's most recent revival, the collegiate shag, though bouncy and calisthenic, also draws a lot of dandies because it's an outlier that appeals to the bold or eccentric of spirit.

Indeed, the most fun I had during Hot Rhythm Holiday was a class in collegiate shag. Fifteen of us assembled in the mansion's library, which is lined on two sides with glassed-in bookshelves, some of them bearing one-foot-tall doll figurines of former presidents of the Texas Federation of Women's Clubs. These eerie porcelain ladies stared down on us dancers as we hopped and shuffled around the library; you could almost hear them murmuring, "We never should have let these young people into our home." Because shag, which is danced on a six-count, unlike the other two forms, which are usually on eight, is a bit of a nutshow. In one of its variations, the leader holds his left arm against the follower's right arm up at eye level, resting the section from his wrist to his elbow against his partner's; then he hops on his left foot (and the follower on her right), then hops on the other foot, and then runs in place. You look like a pair of spastic Statues of Liberty.

Moreover, the dance's bounciness is, particularly for beginners, exhausting. "Shag is my happy dance!" Irina, one of my group's instructors, yelled. Her partner Jeremy said, "It's my workout dance!" My partner looked at me and said, "It's my sweaty rabbit dance."

But the two moments from the weekend that left the longest-lasting impression were both anti-nostalgia, or, rather, to the side of nostalgia. In the first instance, I interviewed one of the weekend's Balboa instructors, a super-cheery young woman named Jenn Lee. "I don't have a vintage lifestyle," Jenn confessed to me. Then when I asked her what video clips of Balboa dancing she recommended to her students, she said, "I show them modern dancing rather than vintage clips because that's more like what they'll be able to do."

Interesting. So, I wondered, if you're not 100 percent invested in the Bygone Era of it all, then what's the draw?

As it turns out, the Seattle-based Jenn—who is forty-two but looks fifteen years younger—is an ophthalmologist who owns her own practice. "When you're a small business owner and a surgeon," she told me, "a lot of your personality is not allowed to shine. You're not allowed to be jokey. You're not allowed to have blue hair. You're not allowed to be silly and make faces. It makes you a bit one-dimensional. But when I'm swing dancing, it's almost like I have a different personality."

Indeed, when Jenn dances, she can often be seen beaming rhapsodically, if not actually laughing. Which I'm sure many licensed professionals would say is related to her success as a competitor: Jenn holds first place titles from Lindy Focus, the Snowball, California Balboa Classic, All Balboa Weekend, the Eastern Balboa Championships, Montreal Dance Festival, and Lindy Fest.

My second strong memory is of Norma Miller, aka the Queen of Swing, who, along with Frankie Manning, is one of swing's probably most revered dancers (e.g., she and Manning are the only two dancers Ken Burns highlighted in his ten-part 2001 documentary, *Jazz*). The rubber-limbed Miller lights up two of the best video clips of swing dancing on YouTube—one from the Marx Brothers' 1937 *A Day at the Races*, and an even more spectacular one from 1941's *Hellzapoppin'*. In this latter clip, she's part of a group called Whitey's Lindy Hoppers, and at one point she dives into a handstand between her partner's feet; he grabs her thighs and hoists her over his head; she flips in the air, landing faceup, inches from the ground between his legs, her arms around his thighs; he hoists her up into the air again, causing her to frog-leg in the air before landing and then bouncing backward offscreen. Every time I watch it I lose five pounds.

But it's a video clip from a 2016 interview that Miller gave at age ninety-six that I keep returning to. Miller was teaching at the time in Sweden, at the Herräng Dance Camp, an annual swing event. Seemingly anchored into her chair by her huge wig and her buggy,

Jackie O–style sunglasses, the rail-thin Miller dutifully answers question after question from her interviewer, an earnest young dancer named LaTasha Barnes. An hour or so into the session, Miller starts to wax increasingly ambivalent and irritable, possibly hangry. Asked what she thinks about the modern resurgence of swing, Miller says, "It don't matter. If you like it, wonderful. I don't care. . . . That dance was thrown to the curb—we had to rezitate it! Nobody was talking about no jazz dancing! Frankie Manning spent thirty-two years working in the post office because he couldn't get a job!"

Then, when Barnes asks Miller where she'd like the idiom to go in the future, the Queen of Swing huffs. "I don't care what they do with it. If they can walk, that's all right with me. . . . If I can participate and give you something, leave you with something, I'm very happy to do so. But if you don't take it, I don't care!"

When you care enough to not care.

5.

About a month after I'd missed the *pas de deux* performance at Peridance, I threw my back out for the third time in four months, on this occasion when I tried to lift someone at a contact improv jam. The injury was much more severe this time. I limped for a month. To sneeze or to cough was to set off a seismic occurrence around my spine, like a donut-shaped cloud of dust quickly rising in a mine shaft; twice when this happened I grabbed a wall for balance. I couldn't tie my shoes for a week, or bend at the waist at more than a thirty-degree angle; one morning when Greg had gone off to the gym early, I couldn't pull my boxer shorts up around my waist, so I used salad tongs.

When the pain subsided, it was replaced by a kind of blankness: on some days it felt like I had a two-inch-wide band around my waist that was nothing but air. I called this strange new anatomical feature my "band of uncertainty."

I didn't want to go see my doctor: two injuries prior, he had said, "I'll give you one more injury," intimating that contact improv was not a good fit for me. So instead of exposing myself to further dire warning, I visited two massage therapists, an acupuncturist, and a chiropractor. All provided temporary relief.

And then I remembered having read about Luigi.

When his steelworker father was killed in a car crash in 1930, five-year-old Eugene Faccuito (fuh-CHEW-toe), the eighth of eleven children, started singing on the street corners of Steubenville, Ohio, to bring in money for the family. In his teenage years he'd go on to sing and dance on the vaudeville circuit.

But in 1946, a few months after moving to Hollywood, he was thrown from a car that slammed into a telephone pole. He hit the curb headfirst. Doctors did not expect him to live; he emerged from a two month–long coma with the left side of his face and the right side of his body paralyzed. But when his doctors told him he wouldn't walk again, Luigi thought, I don't want to walk, I want to dance. (In my mind, there's always an exclamation point at the end of that sentence.)

It took him three years to achieve that dream. He did it by developing a regimen of stretching, standing at the barre, and careful bending. "I didn't want people to see my face," he would explain, "so I did things to make my body look good."

Once rehabilitated, he started getting work in the chorus of musical films (his face would remain paralyzed for the rest of his life, so larger roles were tough for him to get), including 1949's *On the Town*, where he befriended the movie's codirector and costar, Gene Kelly, who became Luigi's mentor. Kelly thought that having two Genes on the set was confusing, so he gave Faccuito the name Luigi. When Kelly noticed that Luigi tended to hide his face while dancing, Kelly told him, "Keep doing what you're doing but lift your face. It's beautiful."

While Luigi continued to work on films—*Annie Get Your Gun* (1950), *An American in Paris* (1951), *The Band Wagon* (1953)—he would do his stretches on the set, and dancers started joining in. He opened his first school in Los Angeles, in 1950.

Then he moved to New York, where in 1957 he opened a school where his dedication and amazing roster of students—Alvin Ailey, Twyla Tharp, Susan Stroman, Michael Bennett, Ben Vereen, Ann Reinking, Donna McKechnie, Robert Morse, Barbra Streisand, John Travolta, Tony Roberts, Jane Fonda—would earn him another nickname, "the father of American jazz dancing."

I started googling. One of the first things to come up was Luigi's 2015 *New York Times* obituary, a fairly staid affair much enlivened by the sudden injection of Liza Minnelli. The fifth paragraph opens with a quote from her: " 'A lot of the people who came to his class had been injured—and damn it, he got all of us well,' Ms. Minnelli, who worked with Mr. Faccuito for decades, said in a telephone interview on Friday. 'I broke my back a few months ago. I've been doing "Luigi" every day, and I can walk and I can run because of that technique.' " The obit lists all of Luigi's accomplishments, and then ends, " 'He was truly one of the great influences in my life,' [Ms. Minnelli] said. 'I made all my dancers that I worked with go to his class. Darling, if you watch *Liza's at the Palace*'—her 2009 concert film—'all those dancers are Luigi dancers.' "

Oh, to have one's obituary graced with a presence as fabulous as Miss Minnelli's—and then to have this presence refer to the reporter as "Darling"! This is definitely the way to, uh, go.

I hied myself to the current location of Luigi's school, the Luigi Jazz Centre. It's located on the Upper West Side and shares a basement space with several other dance schools, including a children's tap school called Shuffles. Seated behind the registration desk was a deadpan, compact gentleman of a certain age named Francis Roach, a Luigi protégé who has long run the studio and taught most of its classes.

"Are you the teacher?" I asked, handing over my $20.

"I am today," he said expressionlessly.

"Just to say, I'm injured. So if it looks like I'm holding back, it's because I'm holding back."

"Do you know the origin story of the studio?"

"I do."

"It's the only dance form to emerge from a tragedy."

Though I'd found Luigi's triumph over physical disability to be both affecting and inspiring, it was too extreme for me to use as a template for dealing with my own comparatively modest setback. So I explained to Francis, "I also know the Liza Minnelli story. I'm trying to follow in her footsteps, actually."

"I'll get your Tony ready."

In a typical Luigi class, you spend an hour stretching, and then half an hour on a routine. The technique is heavy on *épaulement* (turning the body from the waist upward and bringing one shoulder forward and the other back); while you're oozing thusly, you're slowly extending your arms in front of you as if plucking ripened figs to store in your prodigious cleavage. When you put *épaulement* on its feet, stepping forward with your right foot while leading with your left shoulder, and vice versa, you're doing a "jazz walk."

There are two iconic Luigi stances, both of them aids to balance and spine lengthening. One has you put your arms out in front of you, and then press down as if on an invisible barre. This is likely attributable to the fact that, during the three months Luigi spent in the hospital, he practiced a series of angular *port de bras* that were devised by a eurythmic dancer named Michio Ito to help musical conductors develop arm strength.

The second move gives you fierce balance. You put your legs in a closed or locked fourth position by bracing one knee and lower quad behind the other leg's knee and lower quad. This stance helped Luigi when, a year after he got out of the hospital, he kept falling on the floor, particularly during the barre-less "center" section of ballet classes.

Francis proceeded to put five of us students through our paces, invoking the deceased Luigi frequently, at one point pointing to the sky and saying, "Luigi wants me to tell you this." I loved the signature Luigi moves, though they both seemed like things you'd only ever do in a dance studio.

Jazz is the type of dance that I'm worst at. I blame nostalgia. The many hours of my life that I've spent watching theater and TV and film have erected a blocky, multistoried research facility between me and any jazz move I try to do. I'm not moving my body through space, I'm accessing archival clips. I'm not dancing, I'm "dancing."

Francis really wanted our *épaulement* to be chesty. At one point he had us pretend we were each wearing a $30,000 necklace while we danced. This felt very showgirl to me; my imaginary $30,000 necklace was nothing compared to my imaginary two-hundred-pound headdress. It's hard to achieve "Nipples firing!" when they're aimed at the floor.

Next, when demonstrating how to bend at the waist while keeping a flat back, Francis said with each successive bow, "Thank you for this Tony," ". . . this Emmy," ". . . this Grammy." Then, looking at me, added, "Or all three, like Miss M."

Then we tackled a combination that Francis had choreographed to Peggy Lee singing "Fever." If the essence of ballet is, in the words of one of its most esteemed former coaches, Maggie Black, "Up! Up!

Up!" then the essence of jazz is more like "Up but down! Up but down! Up but down!": the essential slink and cool of jazz dancing is rooted in a dancer's ability to be simultaneously pulled into the ground and pulled into the sky. This is difficult for those of us whose posture brings to mind the phrase "heavy backpack." Much more manageable for me was one of jazz's other signature tendencies, isolation: Daddy likes to roll only his rotator cuff forward on three because it means everything else can rest until four.

At class's end, Francis, who'd become much more animated through the course of dancing, motioned me to come talk to him. He was standing on the side of the studio, next to the stereo speakers. Eyes twinkling, he unearthed a black-and-white photo of an exhausted-looking Liza wearing dance clothes and leaning against a barre. Then, to show me where the photo had been taken, Francis pointed at the barre that was less than two feet behind me. I whooped with delight.

He asked how I was feeling and I said, "Energized, not whipped."

"That's how it should be," he said. "So you can do your class and then get to your show for a seven o'clock call time."

As it was only 12:30 p.m., my supposed Broadway-performing self had about six hours to dust off my trophy cabinet and then start self-medicating.

A week later, I found myself handing Francis my $20 at the registration desk again. "I haven't been practicing," I confessed. "But I did watch *Liza's at the Palace.*"

Francis, who, off the dance floor, often looked stilled or becalmed, simply stared.

This totally fun 2009 Broadway offering, which I watched on YouTube, was itself an act of nostalgia—in the first act, a slightly wobbly sixty-three-year-old Liza reworks the vaudeville tribute that her mother Judy Garland performed at the same Broadway theater, the Palace; the second act is a redo of the nightclub act performed by Liza's godmother Kay Thompson, the *Eloise* author who during the 1940s was MGM's vocal coach and choral director. Yes, we get some crowd-pleasers ("Maybe This Time," "Cabaret," "New York, New York"), but we also get some less heavily trod stuff ("If You Hadn't, But You Did," "I Love a Violin"). More important to me, though, was the fact that Liza can be seen pressing her arms down on an imaginary barre twice, and doing the knee-lock once.

Liza at sixty-three is not Liza at twenty-six, the age at which she made *Cabaret* and *Liza with a Z* and at which she could, as dance critic and *Vanity Fair* contributor Laura Jacobs has written, "send a shiver from head to toe with a fleshy little seal-like frisson—the hot mama on an Arctic ice floe." Rather, what gives this newer offering its immediacy and crackle is not Liza's singing and dancing (her voice is hoarse, and she can't really kick anymore) but the volcanic effort she makes to try to get us to like her: surely this film, and not Ms. Riefenstahl's, would be the one most accurately titled *The Triumph of the Will*.

Seated at the Jazz Centre's registration desk, Francis pointed to the studio behind him and said, "It was choreographed right in here. We were all there opening night."

I'd like to tell you that I am immune to such intimations of glitter. But I would be lying. I loved hearing this—just as, half an hour later, I loved it when Francis corrected my diagonally slanted body with "Straight ahead, Henry. You're at the Palace, let them see you!" or, a few months later, "Henry! Chest! We're on Broadway!"

This kind of individualized attention reminded me of the Liza/Luigi relationship. Luigi was Liza's godfather. She called him Papa. They'd met on the set of *An American in Paris*, which Liza's father, Vincente Minnelli, directed. Liza was four. "She was a little girl," Luigi recalled for a *Wall Street Journal* reporter who visited the studio in 2013. "She was hoping to feel it and that's what she learned. A lot of these kids I taught them how to feel."

A self-described "studio brat," Liza would ride her bike to MGM every day after school and sit in rehearsal halls and watch the likes of Cyd Charisse and Gene Kelly and Fred Astaire rehearse. Kelly said of her at a young age, "She's gonna be a dancer!" Indeed, dancing would come first for her—she saw a production of *Bye Bye Birdie* that galvanized her—but she would come to consider herself an actress first, a dancer second, and a singer third.

When Liza moved to New York in her mid-teens to pursue a career, she enrolled in Luigi's school, where she would continue taking classes throughout her career. Liza would often bring her *Cabaret* colleague Marisa Berenson to class; *Modern Family* actress Sarah Hyland, who studied with Luigi in the late nineties and early aughts, was sometimes in class with them.

In 2002, Luigi walked Liza down the aisle at her fourth wedding, to David Gest, joining best man Michael Jackson and maid of honor Elizabeth Taylor.

Liza has always been hard on her body, and I don't mean just the partying and self-caregiving. Susan Stroman, who choreographed her in 1992's *Liza Minnelli Live from Radio City Music Hall*, has praised Liza for never "marking" or walking through a rehearsal but for always rehearsing full out.

The bodily ravages that Liza would have had to contend with when she did *Liza's at the Palace*—scoliosis, two false hips, three fused discs, a wired-up kneecap, and arthritis in her feet—must have seemed like mere static compared to the brain encephalitis she contracted from a mosquito bite in 2000. "I was told I'd never move again, let alone walk and talk," she told author Rose Eichenbaum. "I blew up to 180 pounds. I went to Luigi and asked, 'You think I'll dance again?' . . . 'Sure. You'll dance better than ever.' I went to class the next day and never stopped. In six months I was rehabilitated. I'm able to speak today because of dance. I'm living because of dance. There's nothing more important in the world to me."

The loveliness of Liza and Luigi having latched onto each other had a way of continually reasserting itself. Sometimes Luigi's ministrations to his young charge were less about feeling than *not* feeling. Liza's character on the cracked sitcom *Arrested Development*, Lucille Austero, had chronic vertigo, and would fall to the floor when nervous. In 2009, Liza told NPR listeners about her first day of shooting: "It came time for the line right before I fell down and they said, 'OK, cut.' And they brought in a lot of pads for the floor and a stunt double, and said, 'She'll fall down for you.' I said, 'Are you kidding?' I went to my dance teacher, Luigi, and he taught me seventeen different ways to fall down."

I was heartened by the fact that the students drawn to the Jazz Centre skewed older than most in my other dance classes—lots of folks forty plus amid the younger professionals. As with doing Zumba at the Chinatown Y, this made me appreciate my comparative youth. My dancing was, yes, emotionless and awkward—but it didn't lack in the oomph department.

The fact that Luigi had died less than two years earlier seemed, on some days, to cast a slight pall over the proceedings. Did the woman on my left who kept looking up at the skylight expect Luigi to come barreling through, Santa-style? And what of the older woman who sometimes danced not alongside us other students, but off on the side, diagonally facing the corner of the studio: showgirl gone rogue?

There is an occasional tendency among the Luigi followers to speak of the past in a way that would bedevil fact-checkers. If you call the studio, for instance, the outgoing phone message tells you that Luigi coined the expression "a-five-six-seven-eight," which very well may be true, but how would you substantiate it? Or, in the documentary *Broadway: Beyond the Golden Age*, Liza tells us that Luigi's car crash shook his eyeballs "out of his head, and they put them back in." One sixty-plus Luigi student told me that she sometimes performs hip-hop. One day in class Francis told us that blind ballerina Alicia Alonso's detached retinas were the product of too many pirouettes.

But more typically, Francis's nods to the past were conversational goads. They'd take the form ". . . and once Luigi started giving classes on the movie sets, some interesting people started to show up. Like you may have heard of George Chakiris."

ME: *West Side Story!*
FRANCIS: Yes. Or Vera-Ellen.
OTHER STUDENT: *On the Town! White Christmas!*

Combining as it did a dance class with a round of *Jeopardy!*, this was highly diverting. It was also a nice distraction from the part of the warm-up that always made me quail. Namely, the part where you bend forward at the waist and reach your outstretched arms as far between your legs as possible—and then do it seven more times in succession, two of them while lightly bouncing. Yes, this kind of reaching is something that I wanted my body *ultimately* to be able to do, but right now, with my still slightly sore back, it felt like waving a T-bone in front of the lion's cage.

So, after my third class with Francis, I added to my Luigi training a weekly session of Pilates, the highly effective but highly expensive ($100–$200/hr.) body conditioning popular with dancers. Pilates has you pulling pulleys, mostly while you're lying down. If the Luigi method's twin dragons (the knee-lock and the invisible barre) had struck me as moves that I would only ever do in a class, Pilates gave me a move I could employ anywhere, anytime—while walking down the street or doing the dishes or lying in bed. Namely, collapsing my bellybutton, which is what you're meant to do while carrying out all of Pilates's stretching and pulley-yanking.

One day I excitedly asked Stephen, my Pilates instructor, "Are you saying to me that sucking in my gut—the same method I use to try to look thin—is helping my back? Because, if so, that is a win-win situation."

Well, yes—more or less, Stephen answered, though Pilates wants more of a gentle tuck than a belly-wide suck.

And so I embraced what I thought of as the Gentle Tuck.

Once armed with the rudiments of both Luigi and Pilates, I could feel dramatic improvement. My spine was getting stronger. Ever since this most recent injury, whenever I needed to pick up something that I'd dropped on the floor, I'd been doing something like a *grand plié* to retrieve it, but now I downshifted to a *demi*. Flushing a low-slung toilet no longer necessitated a delicate crab walk. I could get into bed without lowering myself like a knight in armor onto a horse. I was Edward Saladtongs no more.

Around this time I'd also started taking some jazz classes at Joffrey, with a short, funny, faux-furious teacher named Bill Waldinger. Bill teaches the Luigi technique, which, like Francis, he studied for many years with the master himself. I relayed to Bill that I was combining Luigi and Pilates—"I call it Lew-oddies," I said—and he enthused that the two methodologies were very compatible.

Indeed, pinging back and forth between the Jazz Centre and Joffrey and Noho Pilates added a geographical heft to my rehabilitation: the fact that my renewed strength wasn't specific to one location somehow made it seem stronger. Seen from the air, the three outposts of my recovery would form a triangle—a giant athletic supporter on the Manhattan skyline. That I was still unexceptional at the dancing itself now seemed less pressing to me: I was getting something else from my studio hours.

Handing over my $20 to Francis at the registration desk one day, I told him, "I wanted to thank you. My back feels much better."

"That's very nice of you to say, thank you," he said, looking up from a real estate brochure.

I continued, "I'm feeling very bendy and pretzel-like. There's a new pertness to my buttocks, too." Then, trying to sound as much like Joel Grey in *Cabaret* as possible, I added, "Even the orrrrchestra is beautiful."

"I wonder where you got that line," Francis said drily.

"But I will say, the hard part of this technique has been all the bending over. I've sort of been anxious that I might get stuck in that particular position and that, in addition to talking and writing like someone whose head is stuck up his ass, I'd start looking like one, too."

Francis gave me a withering smile, and drew my attention to a real estate ad for a $32 million town house that had once belonged to Gypsy Rose Lee.

Francis can do a lot with a look, but Bill can do a lot with a finger flick. "Tiny. Nothing," Bill would sometimes say enthusiastically of a single extended finger or an isolated hip-check that he'd put into one of our routines. One time he paired a jutting shoulder move with "Tiny. Don't do it for the audience—make the audience come to you." I wasn't hearing this kind of talk much in ballet or ballroom or tap.

It occurred to me that, since Bill and Francis both studied with Luigi for many years, they were probably either best friends or mortal enemies. So, one night at Joffrey with Bill, I allowed as how I was also taking classes with Francis. Bill smiled and suggested that he and Francis were not thick as thieves. When I confessed that I loved my classes at the Jazz Centre but that there was a slight air of tristesse to the proceedings, Bill said, "Well, you know, Francis wasn't just Luigi's protégé, he was also his life partner."

I hadn't known.

Bill continued, "I don't advertise this as a Luigi class because that's Francis's thing. Luigi left Francis the school, and that's what Francis has. The school."

I nodded my head.

Bill finished, "And the school should live on."

That did it. Previously, all the strands of nostalgia swirling around my Jazz Centre tenure—the story of Luigi's accident, my love of Liza, Francis's allusions to yesteryear—had charmed and delighted me. They'd gotten me to show up. But they were part of my nostalgia problem, chunks of bacon in a thick soup of reference. But now, on concluding that Francis's downbeat demeanor off the dance floor was the result of his having lost his partner, I had something palpable and human to work with.

That my next available Tuesday—the day I usually went to Luigi's—was Valentine's Day seemed like a cosmic nudge. Francis was in a whimsical mood—ebullient, even. Two not-yet-unwrapped bouquets of roses sat on the registration desk. When I pointed out that one student had signed the sign-in sheet merely with his initials, Francis shrugged his shoulders and said, "Everyone adds his own je ne sais quoi." I said, "Well, then I guess I'm Henry with a y."

In the studio itself before class had started, I chatted up a woman in my age bracket who was wearing a gorgeous calf-length fur. "It's seal," she told me. "I got it when Fosse put me in the national tour of *Chicago* as Roxie."

I swooned slightly. Fosse, seal coat, money—I wasn't sure which was the source of my enthusiasm, it all seemed juicy.

She continued, "But it's not my *good* coat. The good coat I got with my *Grand Hotel* money."

This the Broadway veteran Penny Worth, who understudied Dorothy Loudon as Miss Hannigan in the original production of *Annie.* I introduced myself and said I was honored to meet her.

Francis put nine of us students through our paces. When he saw me delicately negotiating the arms-between-the-legs move, he said, "Just one more, Henry, then we'll call the paramedics."

The routine was set to the Bee Gees' "How Deep Is Your Love," and included in its line-up were two bouts of jazz walk, two *pas de bourrées*, a *passé* on either side, and two full spins. Francis did the routine with us three times without music, and then broke us up into two groups so that one group would watch the other.

As is always the case when I'm delivered of a bunch of choreography on the spot, I found myself able to remember, and to perform to lower mid-level competency, a little more than half of the moves. I simply cannot do the routine in its entirety, so what I've learned to do is to try to "master" the three critical moments: the opening, the close, and the climax or flashiest move. Everything else, I let go of, absolving myself from any bloodshed or unbeauty; all is dissolved in an inch of Vaseline on the camera lens.

When Francis said that Penny's and my group would be up first, I was thrilled to hear Penny say, "Shall we do this, Henry A.?"

"Absolutely!"

She continued, "Henry A. and Penny W.: it sounds like we're in AA."

Yes, I thought, and I should probably be on the step where you call everyone in your life and apologize.

There were four of us in our group, but to me it was just me and Penny. At first blush I'd thought that having a seasoned pro standing next to me would make me self-conscious, or amp up my tendency toward gestural schtick, but it did the opposite: none of the five students standing against the barre would bother to look at me, I realized—they'd all be looking at Miss Hannigan. (Partners: let them deflect attention from you.)

We positioned ourselves and commenced. Before coming to class, I'd cooked up a little visualization exercise. I now went into it. I tried to imagine how I'd feel if Greg passed. I pushed my shoulders forward like I was pushing a tackling sled of heartbreak; I spun like I was winding up to kick loss in the face.

On one of the six run-throughs of the routine that Francis gave each of the groups, I watched myself doing it in the mirror. My work had so much more resolve than my usual harried, Sorcerer's Apprentice flailing did. During another run-through, one of the other dancers raised her eyebrows while nodding her head at me: the first time I'd ever been "complimented" by another student at Luigi's.

Half an hour later, as I was leaving the Jazz Centre, I ran into Francis in the hallway.

"That Henry, he sure likes to dance," he said to me.

"It's true! And today was the first time I ever got any emotion into it."

"That's good," he said, smiling. "No, that's not good—that's huge."

DANCE AS INTIMACY AND SOCIALIZING

1.

ONE OF THE BEST WEDDINGS I'VE EVER GONE TO TOOK PLACE in an old, crumbling farmhouse in the Catskills. A groovy young filmmaker of my acquaintance was marrying her groovy young film-maker boyfriend. What put this wedding up on its feet, both liter-ally and metaphorically, was the dancing. After a brief ceremony, lots of funny toasts, and a heap o' barbecue served under a tent, there was no awkward or conscience-driven need for us guests to hit the dance floor so as to show support for the couple or to fan the party's flames, as sometimes occurs at the beginning of wedding dancing—people were simply joyous and tipsy and ready to shaaaake it. Someone started blasting B-52's and Talking Heads from inside the house; a bunch of us rushed in and commenced gyrating in the living room, spilling over onto the stairs and the screened porch.

Around midnight, having danced for two hours, I was sweat-soaked and still happily boogying on the porch when a crazed and torrential rain started. The wide sheets of water pouring off the porch's roof looked like a dried Fruit Roll-Up if it were made of jellyfish. The dancing got even wilder; it was as if the sheets of rain on three sides of us were pressing in on us at foot level and lifting us slightly off the floor. That moment when you've been bodily thrashing for a couple of hours and realize that you've burned off the alcohol in your bloodstream but have seamlessly replaced it with something equally enlarging? I was there. I felt lighter than air, a gaseous vapor.

Around 1 a.m., the rain slowed to a speckled scrim, and some fifteen of us stumbled onto the lawn like newborn gerbils struggling to form eyelids. I saw a big flare-up of flame startlingly close to my face: the person standing next to me had ignited a gnarled wooden club, turning it into a torch. He started walking toward the woods. We all followed behind, as did, at the far end of our mob, another torch-wielding guest. Walking for about six minutes through the eerie, drippy woods, I was impressed by how little effort I had to make—it felt like we were motored by vestigial pull. I shared a look of expectant glee with the person behind me; I had no idea where we were going, but I sensed that animal sacrifice might be in my immediate future.

We stopped at a clearing, and two of the guests started to take off their clothes. I thought, No one wants to get the animal sacrifice all over his clothing.

But, then, our mission became clear to me when one of the torches lit up the area directly to our left: a swimming hole.

And behind that: a waterfall.

The part of this evening that I can't seem to let go of is the one-two-three of dancing, then huddling in the dark, then scuttling through the woods in group formation carrying torches. It was all so caveman. So *what* if our loincloths were wash-and-wear separates bought 30-percent-off at a Donna Karan sample sale? Each rain-speckled tree and bush was a potential woolly mammoth—but, as with the Fosse amoeba that my high school pals had formed outside Studio 54, we were impervious due to our number.

Which intrigues me because most anthropologists think that the original evolutionary function of dance was to allow humans—and maybe even encourage them—to live in groups larger than tiny clusters of close relatives, thus making themselves less vulnerable to predators. After all, if you encounter a lion or bear on the trail, what are you supposed to do? Wave your arms, jump up and down, appear large.

I am Hugh Jackman, hear me roar.

Ask enough dancers why they dance, and the word that keeps cropping up is community. Whether we're fleeing our family or our stifling job or the dead-eyed but occasionally vituperative fish that is the internet, many of us find in dance a primal, fully immersive experience that allows us to meld with other people, be it for three minutes or for three decades.

On its face, the Intimacy and Socializing function would seem to have a lot in common with Social Entrée, but I hasten to point out that the intimacy and socializing I'm referring to is unmarked by social ambition. Indeed, the Intimacy and Socializing function can often be distinguished by what it's *not*. In many instances, Intimacy and Socializing is the function (with the possible exceptions of Politics and Healing) that is the least interested in or dependent on artistry. (To be sure, intimacy wants a gentleness and a sensitivity, but these qualities are more aids than necessities.) Intimacy and Socializing is less about a well-executed *pirouette* than about the coffee afterward.

Dance's power to draw its practitioners together reminds me of two things. The first is my godson Ruslan Sprague, the son of my high school friend Carl and his wife, Susan. Ruslan has danced a lot with the Albany Berkshire Ballet, and has studied with Boston Ballet and Ballet West. He loves the work of Czech choreographer Jiři Kylián, and would one day like to have his own company.

Ruslan came into my life in 1995 when Carl and Susan decided to adopt. Carl and Susan went through the requisite year or two of bureaucratic rigamarole—lots of filling out of applications and notarized forms, lots of waiting. Finally, they flew to Russia to pick up three-year-old Ruslan. On their first visit to the orphanage they were accompanied by a group of other parents also meeting their adoptees for the first time. Carl and Susan immediately fell in love with the affectionate and charming Ruslan. However, lest the children get worn out, the adoption agency had stipulated that the parents' first visit with their kids should be short, about half an hour.

Thus it was hugely gratifying to Carl, on his and Susan's return to the orphanage the next day, to have Ruslan immediately recognize him among the scrum of parents. Ruslan ran to Carl and threw his arms around his legs. Carl was moved to tears.

I had a coffee with twenty-six-year-old Ruslan two years ago at a café in Chicago, where he was doing a residency at the nearby Hinsdale Dance Academy. I asked him what keeps him dancing, given the rigors of his field—the low pay, the lack of job security, the physical exhaustion, the absence of medical insurance, the built-in obsolescence of one's talent.

"I love the family aspect of it," he told me. "Everywhere I work, even if it's only for a week, I form a little family with the other dancers."

My second thought is of *Paris Is Burning*, the 1990 documentary about drag ball culture and voguing. If you've ever used the expressions "throwing shade," "yasss queen," "werk," or "fierce," you can probably trace it back to this film, which paved the way for, if not outright inspired, both Madonna's "Vogue" video and *RuPaul's Drag Race*. Drag balls had been held in Harlem since the 1920s, of course, but until Jennie Livingston made *Paris Is Burning*, few people outside the scene were aware of them.

Seven years in the making, the project started in the summer of 1985 when Livingston was walking through New York City's Washington Square Park and stumbled onto a group of drag queens. Despite the fact that it was raining, the queens were voguing while calling out moves like "Witch queen in drag" and "Saks Fifth Avenue mannequins."

Soon Livingston found herself and her camera immersed in the world of drag ball competitions, where the mostly black and Hispanic queens flamboyantly strut the runway and then dance, all the while emulating movie stars or the stratum of society most likely to reject them—society types in jodhpurs, military personnel, Wall Street bankers (complete with briefcases loaded with credit cards and airline tickets). "This is white America," the emcee of the ball featured in the movie explains. "And when it comes to the minorities, especially black, we as a people, is the greatest example of behavior modification in the history of civilization. . . . That's why in the ballroom circuit it is so obvious that if you have captured the Great White Way of living or looking or dressing or speaking, you is a marvel!" A queen's ability to embody a given type—e.g., "Executive," "Alexis vs. Krystle," "Town and Country"—is, of course, called "realness."

That the participants in these balls usually have their tongues firmly planted in their cheeks is what makes the pageants hilarious. The queens—many of whom, we're told, are working as hustlers— have such sad backstories that the balls could easily come off as a pity parade. But what keeps the individual performers' quixotic pursuit from seeming abject or pathetic is the fact that each of them belongs to a "house"—a group of friends or "children," who are presided over by a mentoring "mother" and sometimes a "father." As one interviewee points out, houses are gay street gangs.

"When someone has rejection from their mother and father, their family, when they get out in the world, they search. They search for someone to fill that void," one mother says, shortly after telling us how her own homophobic biological mother had angrily burned her child's mink coat when she found it, angry at her son's sexuality and the fact that his breasts were bigger than hers. "They can talk to me because they're gay and I'm gay. That's where a lot of the ball and the mother business comes in. They look to me to fill that void."

But, as we all know from our own biological families, living in small groups of people is a lot of work. The queens vent their complicated feelings toward one another through dance in the same way that b-boys and breakdancers do. In the film, choreographer Willi Ninja, the mother of the House of Ninja who would go on to dance for Janet Jackson and Karole Armitage and to help Naomi Campbell and Paris Hilton with their runway walks before dying of AIDS in 2006, explains, "Voguing came from shade because it was a dance that two people did because they didn't like each other. Instead of fighting, you would dance it out on the dance floor and whoever did the best moves was throwing the best shade basically. . . . I make my hand into a form like a compact or makeup kit, and I'm like beating my face with blush, shadow, or whatever, to the music. Then usually I'll turn the compact around to face that person, meaning almost my hand is a mirror for them to get a look. Then I start doing their face because what they have on their face needs a dramatic makeup job."

Three years after the film's debut, when journalist Jesse Green attended a memorial for one of the cast members—Angie Xtravaganza, the former mother of the House of Xtravaganza—the mood among the surviving queens was bleak. Not only had the mainstreaming of drag that the film had inspired limited, ironically, the queens' performance opportunities, but most of the film's survivors felt betrayed by the film's success. Though they'd signed release forms and were aware that the subjects of documentaries are not typically paid, all but two of the surviving principals from the film had hired lawyers, given that the film had taken in $4 million after only costing $500,000 to make. One of the queens, Paris DuPree, whose 1986 ball was featured in the film and provided its title, sought $40 million for unauthorized and fraudulent use of her services. Though Pepper Labeija had called her ball Paris Is Burning to suggest that the fashion capital of the world would be jealous of her ball's competitors, journalist Green invokes the earlier, darker reference—Hitler asking "*Paris brennt?*" in 1944 to find out whether Paris had fallen—and lands on the withering observation "Paris has burned." (Though the passion for voguing has mostly subsided in the States, it flourishes in Europe.)

In the article, the tiny tendril of hope that pokes through the rubble comes from one of the mothers, Dorian Corey, who emerges sanguine about her brush with fame, and full of wise counsel for the brood she looks over. "I love all that madness," Corey says to Green about the drag ball scene. "But I tell the children to think very serious, and if it's at all possible avoid the drag life. It's a heartache life. If you do pursue it, make sure you get your education, some kind of skill."

2.

Tommy Tune tells a story about the time that Martha Graham visited his college in Texas in the early 1960s. "She was so dramatic, we were all in awe," he told the authors of *Conversations with Choreographers*. "She said in her lecture, 'All great dance comes from the lonely place.' This little girl in the back of the room in a real Texas voice said, 'Miss Graham, you said that all great dancing stems from the lonely place. Where is the lonely place?' Martha Graham raised herself up and said, 'Between your thighs. Next question?'"

Martha may have been onto something. For its participants, dance's purchase on intimacy—sexual or not—is one of its most powerful attributes. It takes only one seismically wonderful dance with a partner to confirm the aforementioned "a good dance is better than sex." Lindy Hop pioneer Frankie Manning used to describe the dance as "a series of three-minute romances." In 1994, for his eightieth birthday, he started a tradition of dancing with one partner for each year of his life, thus conducting, in a single night, eighty three-minute romances.

Some people seem to get their dose of intimacy from *watching* dance. In 2016 alone, roughly 2 million people, most of them women, saw a Chippendales show, and the touring revue *Magic Men Live!* sold some $5 million of tickets at 148 shows all over North America. Viva the pectoral implant industry.

For social dancers, who may have shown up at a dance event with the express purpose of finding a mate, the question of intimacy has a special piquancy. Indeed, psychologists have even gone so far as to use motion-capture technology to determine what kinds of dance moves win admiration from others. In research published in the journal *Scientific Reports* in 2017, these researchers determined that women were most admired for swinging their hips (but not too much), keeping in time with the music, and asymmetrically moving their arms and thighs. Meanwhile, men were most admired for tilting and twisting their necks and torsos in a variety of positions (the majority of men, the researchers pointed out, only move their arms and legs, and do so in a repetitive fashion).

However, we should also note that two kinds of peril lurk at the dance/intimacy crossroads. The first is the presence of creepy men (and the very, very occasional creepy woman). This tends to be a gentleman forty-plus years old who is on the chase, and who sees in any dance-based gathering an opportunity to vent unwanted ardor. On two occasions I've momentarily felt like I was one of these fellows, and both occasions were searingly awkward.

In the first instance, I bought a ticket for a Beginner's Ballet class which was to be taught by a New York City Ballet dancer. On hying myself to the appropriate part of Lincoln Center for the class—a floor above the School of American Ballet—I found lots of little girls tottering around the hallways in tulle, but no dressing rooms. So I went into a stall in the men's bathroom and slipped into my tights and ballet slippers, which felt a little like I was an aspiring superhero with a terrible, dark secret.

Out in the hallway, I presented myself to the young woman at the registration desk, who was poring over a list of names. She gave me a faint look of horror. I said, "Hi. Alford. A-L-F—" She stopped me: "Um, this is a children's class. The adult class is in a few months." I gasped, and apologized. Then I walk-sprinted back to the bathroom, where the stall now seemed like an echo chamber of shame.

The second instance: Though I don't normally wear jewelry, when I went to the swing dancing weekend in Austin, I decided to wear a ring on my wedding finger to reduce some of my potentially perceived creepiness. While standing in the lobby of the Fed on Day 2, I grew hot, and removed first my jacket and then my turtleneck sweater. This second item, when peeled from my body, clung slightly, so I yanked it—which dislodged the ring from my finger, causing it to shoot across the lobby and hit a twenty-something female dancer in her stomach. She popped her eyes in surprise, then looked down at the ring on the floor, then looked at me. Fluttering over toward her to retrieve the ring, I gushed, "Oh my God, I'm so sorry!"—flapping my arms and trying to sound as homosexual and flummoxed as possible.

The other kind of peril that intimate dancing sometimes traffics in, of course, is infidelity. One day on the street last fall, I ran into a friend I'll call Samantha, whom I hadn't seen in a long time. I asked Samantha how her husband of three years, whom I'll call Tim, was. Samantha's eyes grew saucer-like and pained; she told me that Tim had started taking dance classes on his own. "Tango lessons," she said, "and they have these things called *milongas*?"

Milongas are tango parties, usually held weekly, and often preceded by a lesson. Typically at *milongas*, several songs are played in a row (this is called a *tanda*), followed by a musical break (a *cortina*) so that people can change partners.

Well, at the *milonga* Tim had been frequenting, he'd met someone.

I told Samantha that I was sorry, and said that I hoped she and Tim figured it out.

Samantha and I made a plan to get together for a drink the following Friday. But when I asked if Tim might like to join us, she said, "Nah, he'll be off fucking Suzy Milonga that night."

The intimacy struggle can be particularly acute for dance partners who compete or dance at exhibitions or get paying gigs together. Swing dancer Ryan Martin told me, "In this community, there are a lot of married couples who are also partners, but there aren't a lot of married-couple partners who've been doing it for a long time." Ryan's colleague Jenn Lee, the Balboa dancer, explained, "A dance partnership is almost more complex than a spousal relationship or a boyfriend. You travel together, you're often housed together in the same room. You're giving each other feedback, sometimes during competitions, which are already high-pressure. There are a lot of different, crazy situations that on a day-to-day basis you probably wouldn't have with your best friend or partner. Sometimes you spend more time with your dance partner than you do your regular partner. It's intense."

I got off lucky, I guess. In 1995, when I competed twice as a ballroom dancer, I was partnered with my dancing instructor, a warm, wonderful woman named Reba Perez. Not only did Reba and I genuinely like each other, but the specific nature of our relationship flooded it with deference—I was a shaky beginner, eager to let my follower be the covert leader; she was not getting paid for competing with me, but was hoping that I had enough of a good time that I would come buy more lessons.

This outing was a writing assignment. Ballroom dancing had just been granted provisional status as an Olympic sport, and a men's magazine had asked me to write about taking ballroom lessons and then competing.

Up at DanceSport, a studio on the Upper West Side where Al Pacino had learned to dance the tango for *Scent of a Woman*, an administrator told me that competitors needed to have a working knowledge of five "smooth" dances (waltz, fox-trot, quickstep, tango, and Viennese waltz) and five Latin dances (cha-cha, rhumba, samba, *paso doble*, and jive). This administrator paired me with Reba, who, over several months, painstakingly tried to morph my stolid mass of flesh into something more fleet and jaunty. I had a fairly good frame—the chest-up, shoulders-back, arms-outstretched carriage that ballroom wants—but my feet were dogs looking for a fight. The Latin dances required the right shoulder/left hip and left shoulder/right hip opposition that goes by the name "Cuban motion," and my efforts on this front bring to mind the statement a Native American made to Agnes de Mille when de Mille visited his reservation in Zuni, Colorado, one summer: "You're white. Bad for the dance."

After fifteen lessons with Reba, six group lessons, and two social dances at DanceSport, Reba and I proceeded to two competitions. The first was held at the Kismet Shriners Temple in New Hyde Park on Long Island, where we spent a lot of time schmoozing with students and teachers from the other twelve competing studios—a group united by their shared passion for the immovable hairdo. In our Newcomers category, we took second place in waltz and third place (out of three couples) in tango. Two months later, after lots more classes, we hit the Sheraton in Stamford, Connecticut, for the Constitution State Challenge, where we took a first (out of two couples) in rumba.

When, twenty years after the fact, I sat down and tried to read the account of our competing that I'd written, I could barely make it through the piece, so full was it of snoot and cheap shots at ballroom. I'd spent a lot of time during lessons trying to access my "inner Eduardo." I'd shown Reba a flimsy, red sequin cummerbund that I was intending to wear, and she'd more or less slapped it out of my hand. I'd asked Reba if, when competing, she ever wore "face jewelry."

So I now decided to track down Reba, who, wholly due to passivity and attrition, I hadn't spoken to in fifteen years. After running her own studio for many years, she has retired as a dancer and instructor, gotten married and moved to the suburbs and had two kids, and become a life coach. Dance-wise, our trajectories, I realized, were opposite, and I had happened to luck into the moment at which they'd crossed.

We met up at a bakery in Queens. Reba's lovely brown hair is now threaded with salt and pepper. She still has the heartwarming grin and the infectious energy that I remembered. Reba has always had a Ginger Rogers duality to me—when you talk to her, she's vivacious and slightly goofy, and as film critic Pauline Kael wrote of Rogers, "Maybe it's her greatest asset that she always seems to have a wad of gum in her mouth." But as soon as Reba starts dancing: total elegance.

"I wanted to apologize to you," I told her. "When I reread the article, all I could think was, What a wiseass. The tone was so snotty."

She smiled and said, "No need at all. But thank you. I had assumed the story would be humorous and that you'd be using your ironical, outside eye."

"Well, twenty years later, I now realize that I should never write these sorts of first-person stories unless it's about something that I would do in my real life, something that I actually want to do. Which, at the time, ballroom wasn't."

She nodded sympathetically. We talked for about an hour. When she told me that she had married an Orthodox Jew, I asked what ramifications this would have if she wanted to dance again.

"I'm allowed to dance," she told me. "But I'm not supposed to touch a man."

I choked on my tea.

"I hugged you hello," I said, embarrassed. "I'm so sorry!"

"It's okay. I do it. As many people as there are, there are versions of Orthodox Jews. It'd be hard to teach social dancing and be Orthodox: not a good fit. I mean, I could maybe do it, but . . ."

We kept talking. I decided to revisit with her the main plots of the article as I remembered them, to see if she had any memories to add.

"So, we tried ten dances," I started, "but you choreographed routines for us in three—rumba, waltz, tango."

"I probably did that because I would base some choreography on a box step and optimize what you were learning. You didn't have endless lessons."

True dat. I recounted how we practiced a lot over four months' time, at which point I bought more lessons. "And then, shortly before the first competition, you simplified the choreography significantly."

Reba laughed. She said, "I just thought that that would highlight your talent."

"I know, dear. And I love you for that," I said. "Then, at the class before our first outing, you said to me, 'There are only two things I want to see at the competition. Good posture. And don't get in my way.'"

"I remember that. I'm stuck with it."

"Then, at the competition, we gazed for a while at something called the Connelly Charm Trophy. We were in one heat where we were the only couple, so I told you, 'I'm gunning strictly for the Connelly this time,' and then you made your bombshell response."

"Which was?"

"You told me, 'Start exuding.'"

"I was so funny."

" 'Start exuding'—It's a direction *and* a threat."

"I was so funny."

If you ever do some googling on the topic of *Dirty Dancing*, you can see Jennifer Grey trying to learn the iconic "angel lift" that is the film's climax. Though she'd taken some classes, Grey wasn't a professional dancer when she was cast in the film as Baby. Baby's anxieties and struggles about learning the lift were also Grey's. Thus, the film's moment of triumph is doubly sweet.

I felt a little bit of this doubled sweetness from talking to Reba. We'd had a really good time dancing together, but, nevertheless, over two decades, I'd harbored doubts. So it was hugely relieving to have her tell me that my trespasses had been taken in the right spirit.

After we'd paid our check, we headed out to the sidewalk to say goodbye. We did not hug in parting, but the hug was wholly implied.

3.

Dancing is almost always a narrative about physical intimacy—the politics and consolations thereof—and on this front, contact improv is an industry leader. I have rested my cheek on other contact improvisers' cheeks, butt, armpits, feet. I have laid my entire body, from ankles to forehead, on top of the body of a heterosexual economics professor whose name I think is Arnold. I have held my body against someone else's long enough for the patch of sweat on her T-shirt to transfer to my T-shirt.

As with gynecology and football tackles, contact improv is, on its surface, so seemingly sexual that you can't acknowledge it as such, or the whole enterprise would implode. In a class one day, I reached out to my tallish female partner's upper arm to twirl her, but instead got a healthy handful of side-boob and a smaller portion of boob-boob. So we both snort-laughed and proceeded as if nothing had happened. Another time, at a jam, a muscular twenty-something professional dancer on whose back I was frontally spread-eagled decided to back up to a wall and pin me against it with his shoulders such that my feet were five inches off the floor. Once he let go of me, we, too, snort-laughed, whereupon I offered the wildly articulate "Wow!" and he responded, "Yeah, I just thought I should put you up against the wall"—a statement which, strangely, did not make me feel like we were minor players in the hot tub scene of *Hannah Does Her Sisters*.

In the face of all this intimacy, I devote, before jams and classes, what nevertheless seems an eccentric amount of time to finding the right underarm deodorant. I started out wearing the Tom's no-aluminum, Mountain Spring–scented deodorant that Greg stocks our medicine cabinet with, but found that it petered out mid-dance, like a foreigner who has run out of possible combinations of the fifty-six words and phrases at his command. Then I had a brief and disastrous turn with Gillette High Performance gel, a viscous, transparent goo whose ammoniated vapors caused my eyes to smart each time I put it on. Then I had dalliances with Malin+Goetz's eucalyptus deodorant (lovely, but as fleeting as a sunset), Old Spice Classic Antiperspirant and Deodorant stick (pungent on arrival, but exhibiting a vinegary afterglow reminiscent of longshoremen scurrying to complete tasks before a holiday weekend), and finally Mitchum Advanced Gel (no).

I've settled on the wonderful Dove Secret. Although it is, like the Gillette, an extruded crème, one which looks like it wants to adorn cinnamon buns more than human bodies, Dove Secret surrounds my person with a nimbus of powder-smelling inoffense and fantasy. Gone is the rank, slightly salty tang of my underarms and their desperate need to hand out business cards to all within their environs; welcoming is the soft, talcum cloud of my muffled under-boudoir.

But no amount of propylene glycol would have prepared me for the experience that dancer Barry Hynum had in 1988. Hynum went to the annual jam held in Harbin Hot Springs, California, where he and a group of dancers spontaneously started doing contact improv in the buff. As Hynum described it in the contact improv newsletter *Contact Quarterly*, "It was like Velcro and silk. Initially I felt glued to my partner like Velcro. This permits some unusual perches and unexpected locks. Then the perspiration set in and I slide around like sliding the length of the high school shower on my butt. It wasn't that bad but I never knew when I would stick or slip. I perspire heavily so I became concerned over others slipping on my slicks so I stopped, but not before rocking back on my back for a long slide across the floor. My dances with men were shorter than usual and I had some inner reservations like those I went through when I first started dancing with my community brothers long ago."

I've yet to see anyone in his starkers. But I did have a wonderfully fraught moment with my friend Lucy. Forthright and intense, the pigtailed, sixty-something Lucy first danced with me in a class wherein one partner danced a solo while the other partner tried to follow the first dancer's feet as closely as possible with his or her own. This was fairly mirth-making. After the exercise, all seven of us in the class huddled, and our instructor asked us what we thought. Lucy, the first to speak, gushed, "Delicious!" The dancer sitting next to her—a ruggedly handsome, fifty-something male choreographer—concurred, saying how fun it was to let your feet "run all over the room, looking for meals."

A week later, I ran into Lucy at the same class. For one exercise, the teacher idly suggested that we find a partner whose feet were somehow different from our own; Lucy walked over to me and said, "Feet are how we met."

"Uh-huh," I said self-consciously, looking across the room as if in search of a dog to pet.

Fifteen minutes later, Lucy and I were rolling over each other log-like when our teacher mentioned that some contact improvisers like to think of the floor as a duet's third partner. The teacher added that he'd just read something interesting in *Contact Quarterly*: dancer Martin Keogh had written that he sometimes finds it helpful to give this third partner a name.

The teacher suggested that all six of us dancers name the floor. So, while Lucy started to bodysurf over me, stretching her arms out over her head so as to reduce her impact on those of my body parts less blanketed with adipose tissue, she glanced at the slats of wood beneath us and said "Mud," drawing it out slightly so it sounded more like "Muuuud."

My turn. I gazed at the dull, weathered floorboards and went with "Denise."

At which point Lucy put her lips up against my right ear and whispered earnestly, "*Is that your mother?*"

It's probably unwise to put anything that you love under a microscope. I've considered contact improv my home in the dance world for the past three years and thus am not in a hurry to pathologize my attraction to it. That said, it occurs to me that marriages or couples usually owe their longevity less to shared interests or physical compatibility than to the two people's having a mutual task or question that they're addressing together: you think you've been married to John for twelve years because he has chocolaty, understanding eyes and takes care of the bills, but more likely it's because you both lost your fathers the summer before you met, or that now you have two children.

Hindsight suggests to me that two "problems," both of them related to the theme of public vs. private, kept me coming back to the jam week after week. The first of these led to a counterintuitive conclusion. In my initial contact dances, I used mostly my hands and lower back to support my partners' body weight, as this felt practical, safe. I also like merely touching fingertips while moving around the room—a move that contact luminary Nancy Stark Smith dubbed "finger ouija" but that I think of as E.T.-ing. Then I started using my feet. Now I use my head and chest a lot—I'll put my forehead in between your shoulder blades, prompting you to lean back slightly onto me, and then I'll slide my forehead down to your sacrum; or I'll press my breastbone into your sacrum or chest (unless you have enormous breastesses) so that you can collapse or lean thereon. Alternatively I like to hold your forehead in the palm of my hand.

What emerges from all this is the realization that when it comes to making searingly intimate body configurations with others, the more you commit, the less weird it feels. If my placing my forehead on your back causes you to lean away from me or respond tentatively, then you've turned down my invitation and welcomed your difficult teenager, the floor-staring and anxious Scrutinella, into the room. Whereas, if you give me your weight, we're a-sail. Similarly, if you try to initiate a dance by gently brushing your fingertips against my triceps, then I'm not sure what you're after, and a small amount of uncertainty or weirdness will bloom. Whereas if you jam your butt into my crotch with vigor, I know exactly what to do: flop over onto your spine like an octopus being dried on an overturned boat on Santorini.

I still have miles to go here. It took me two years of doing contact regularly to be able to engage in any kind of eye contact whatsoever with my partners; even now my headlights remain intermittent, blinky. I'm also trying to initiate more cheek-to-cheek dancing. Contrary to expectations, cheek-to-cheek dancing in the contact scene is, despite the close attention that the idiom pays to bodily collision, rare, and retains the vivid quality of its intimacy, particularly for the less unbuttoned of spirit. (Intriguingly, the only two people who, among the group of sixty or so regulars to the jam, initiate cheek-to-cheek with any regularity are both straight men in their twenties. Which says something good about that generation.)

The second task I've worked on is related to newcomers. New York's Saturday jam has a reputation for being less friendly to newcomers than other jams because it draws so many professional dancers. Among the regulars—all folks I've danced with now—are dancers who've been in *The Lion King* on Broadway and in Off Broadway's *Sleep No More*, who've danced for Merce Cunningham, Lucinda Childs, Risa Jaroslow, and Bill T. Jones. Some professionals are reluctant to dance with the less seasoned because they fear injury, or because they want to challenge themselves or enjoy the coziness of dancing with a friend. This insiderism and its resultant chill can, to some newcomers, be amplified by the laissez-faire nature of the jam itself: although, yes, the jam ends at four fifteen with the moderator having everyone sit in a circle and say his or her name and make any dance-related announcements, the preceding three hours are—as they are at almost all jams—unguided. No one takes your $5 from you when you arrive (you just leave it on the desk), and if you're a newcomer you'll probably need to initiate most of your dances. This can be a mountain. I felt, as alluded to earlier, staggeringly self-conscious at the first four jams I went to, until I saw one dude arrive, lie down on the floor and sleep for fifteen minutes, then get up and leave—at which point I concluded, So it's *that* kind of party.

Thus my mission here, particularly before I threw my back out the third time and became more cautious, has been to try to dance with newcomers as often as possible, particularly if they look shy. Typically this goes well, and, in an ideal world, a third person ultimately joins us, and then I can winkle off into the crowd, knowing that the newcomer now has two familiar faces in the room. I told one newcomer, "If you want someone to dance with, hit me up. I'm advanced-beginner, but with delusions of grandeur." I told one regular who has a nice sense of noblesse oblige, "I'm a self-designated slut. I'll dance with anyone." She responded, "Don't take my job away from me."

One day early on in my jam-going I was down on the floor with a partner, emerging from a slo-mo backwards somersault, only to find myself staring into the face of a guy I'd hooked up with fifteen years prior, when I was single. Hello. This was the sly shavehead Paul Fischer, a fellow writer who has been doing contact for more than twenty-five years, ever since going to college at the dance form's cradle, Oberlin. We started dancing together and have continued to do so. Because I am happily coupled, and because Paul had recently started a new relationship when I ran into him at the jam, I sensed that "private dancing" was unlikely to lie in our future; nevertheless, early on in our new friendship, I found myself saying in his presence, primarily for my own ears, "I dance the dance of sublimation." Cards, table.

Looking over our e-mails from the past two years (Paul lives in Tel Aviv during part of the winter and summer, so e-mail is a good way to keep in touch), I see this theme borne out again and again.

What distinguishes Paul as a dancer, besides killer partnering skills that make him much sought after at the jam, is that he is the chattiest person on the dance floor. To dance with Paul is to catch up with each other's news from the past week—and, if possible, to cover some new facet of our mutual preoccupation, baked goods. This is big fun. Indeed, our new friendship really kicked off the Saturday I told him that I needed to travel a birthday cake that I'd made out to Brooklyn, probably on the subway, but that I didn't have a cake caddy. So Paul invited me over to his apartment to borrow his cake caddy, joking that, when I returned same, it would not be inappropriate to include within its domed sanctuary "a thank-you cake."

Two days later, I left the borrowed item with Paul's doorman. Less than an hour after the drop-off, Paul sent me a message on Facebook: "Thanks for the container. But where's my cake?!"

ME: I know. The pathos of the empty cake caddy. It's like we lost our firstborn.
PAUL: Sure, rub it in. Though, technically, our firstborn should be a teenager by now.

ME: [Coughs. Stares at floor.]
PAUL: Is that where the kid ended up?

We started getting in the habit of occasionally checking in with each other the day before, or the morning of, the jam. One Friday I wrote him, "No jam for me tomorrow, alas—we have ballet tickets." Paul wrote back, "Listen, Twinkle Toes, you better remember where your loyalties lie. With me on the floor!"

A few months later, Paul had gone back to Tel Aviv. I went to go see *Anomalisa* one day, and remembering that Charlie Kaufman is one of Paul's favorite filmmakers, sent Paul an e-mail saying, "Saw the Charlie Kaufman puppet movie without you. I am trying to hurt you."

PAUL: Now you owe me two cakes.

A couple of weeks later, on an unseasonably warm March day, I wrote him, "75 today. You can come home now." I'd recently seen a picture of his still-newish boyfriend on Facebook, and so found myself adding, "Your dude is cute. Is that going well (I hope)?" Paul wrote back, "Yep, everything's going well. He'll be coming with me to NYC for two weeks so maybe I'll lure him to the jam."

ME: That's so cool—congrats, sir! I will try to dial down my passive-aggressive campaign of ambiguous affection, except in instances of a certain postmodern dance idiom so excellent at sublimating undefined longing into choreo-somatic splendor.
PAUL: You don't have to dial anything down.

We kept dancing together. Because we live near each other, we often walk home together after the jam; during these walks we've stopped for coffee with other dancers, run errands together, bought shoes. Sometimes when you're walking with Paul and he wants to cross the street, he will simply lean into you, gently pushing you in the right direction: contact improvisers, takin' it to the streets.

I got a laugh out of Paul the day I told him that, during my ballet training, I'd thrown my back out while sexing. An hour later, walking home from the jam, I found myself referencing something we'd both just overheard: "That contact workshop that they were just talking about in the closing circle? Its title is 'The Nuance of the Pelvic Bowl.'"

"Nice."

"But is the pelvic bowl actually nuanced? I feel like most of them work in big, broad strokes."

"Well, *yours*."

Another time, after a dance floor conversation about the calm and Zen that I get from doing needlepoint and that Paul gets from baking, I said, "Maybe your tahini cookies want to meet my needlepoint sometime," which is about as Mae West as I ever get. The next week Paul came over to Greg's and my apartment for a tea party à deux that I'd billed in an e-mail as "Cookies and Wool: An Interfaith Symposium."

Two nights after "Cookies and Wool," Greg, who had not mentioned Paul's visit—they'd overlapped in the apartment for less than a minute, and were meeting for more or less the first time—now brought him up.

"Your friend Paul. Is that his name?"

"Yes," I said, caution seeping into my voice.

"He's really charismatic and sexy."

Boom. I raced to Facebook and stared at pictures of Paul. Yes, foxy. I felt a lightness in my chest, like a bodily smile. Then my heart started pounding. I thought, Why haven't I tried to have an affair with him?

A few days later, after the jam, I found myself at Paul's apartment. I asked him, "Is there a cuddling option here?"

"Kosher cuddling?"

Kosher cuddling. We sat on the couch. I leaned my back against him. It felt consoling, reassuring. It did not feel sexual. It was just like when you're doing contact with someone, and, bodies entwined, you both pause for ninety seconds as if having pulled into a scenic rest stop on the highway. It's sensual, but not leading-to-sex sensual. Sensual like you're nuzzling a beloved pet.

Ten minutes later, a friend of Paul's having showed up to pick up a houseplant, I was walking home, my mind a welter of thought. First thought: Why wasn't our time on the couch more erotically charged? Had we reflexively gone into dance mode? Additional thought: Friends should probably cuddle more. This would dramatically reduce the rates of alcoholism and karaoke. Final thought: If it's your boyfriend's enthusiasm for your dance partner that makes you see your dance partner in a different light, then maybe it's your boyfriend's enthusiasm that you're really turned on by?

Came the day I sustained my serious back injury, the one I got at the jam trying to lift someone. That evening I e-mailed Paul, "Thanks for the dance, hon, that was lovely. Sorry I boogied abruptly, but I was feeling my back."

PAUL: Indeed that was a lovely one. You feeling better today?
ME: Yep. I bought a hot water bottle at the drugstore. The only one they had also doubles as an enema and douche—so I guess I know where MY evening is headed . . .
PAUL: You can heal your back and then throw it out again.

Over the next six weeks—my Salad Tongs Days—I wondered if I'd ever do contact again. It felt like a bridge too far. I wondered if I had replaced the traditional medium of the male midlife crisis, a red Corvette, with a series of sweat-soaked, blue American Apparel

V-necks. This hugely depressed me. I'd never before dwelled on the fact that most of the people at the jam were ten or twenty or even thirty years younger than me, but now, in my decrepitude, it was all I could think of. Granted, there are some (but very few) people who go to jams and never engage in contact's mandate, weight-sharing, preferring instead to freestyle it, which would be much less stress on my back; and granted, the three or four episodes of sublimity I've experienced at jams have fallen into this looser kind of dancing. So I hadn't totally injured my future away. Yet nevertheless, there was something deeply humiliating about having rendered myself unable to perform the idiom in question. My mind fixated on two messages: I am old. And I do not know my limits. Was I the office drunk?

Slightly hunched over for weeks, I starting walking to the office I rent by a different route, hoping not to run into Paul. Or, if I was within a couple blocks of his apartment, I'd direct my line of vision at the sidewalk.

Five weeks in, I contemplated showing up at the jam and just standing on the sidelines, but I knew I'd feel weird, or that I'd get sucked into the fun.

So I think you'll understand me when I tell you that one line in the next e-mail from Paul made me cry. Not "Missed you at the jam today. Hope your back is okay and just that you were busy." But this: "I ended up sleeping on the floor for most of the jam. I was zonked."

In the year and a half that I'd been dancing with him, I'd never once seen Paul sit on the floor during the dancing, let alone lie on it. He's a dance-through-er. I thought, He's made this up to make me feel less like a loser.

All I could see was: Come back, you don't have to be Atlas, we miss you.

What does feeling like a member of a group bring you? In my case, confidence. If, during a duet at the jam now, I'm saddled with a desire to do something off-road like make a tiny starburst with my fingers and say "Shrponk," I feel comfortable enough to make a tiny starburst with my fingers and say "Shrponk." I'm not going to be mistaken for a Kardashian anytime soon, but increasingly I can be private in public. Sometimes the more acrobatic moves in contact prompt or require you to whisper to your partner something along the lines of "Is this okay?" or "I can't sustain this [hold] very long." I've started to import this form of voice-over narration into my personal life. The other night over dinner in a restaurant, an acquaintance-but-not-quite-a-friend told me a heartbreaking story, and I had a strong desire to respond by laying the palm of my hand on her head, but I wasn't sure if it would be weird. So I said, "I'm going to put my hand on your head now," and then did so, and it felt right.

Hobbies are hope. Knowing that, on any given Saturday, five or six of the people I really love to dance with will be at the jam makes even a grueling workweek bearable. On Wednesday, I start to feel a tingle of interest; by Friday, I'm anxiously checking Facebook and thinking about who I hope will show up the next day; by Saturday morning, I'm fairly vibrating with anticipation, and anxiously deciding which three of my twelve blue American Apparel V-necks are the *right* blue American Apparel V-necks.

I'm loath to use the word "crush" here because I know that all crushes are narcissistic, but the attachment I have toward some of the other dancers is nothing if not crush-like. Two days after I've danced with G, I'm trying to remember how I ended up standing eight inches off the floor with my right foot on the wall and my left foot on his upper thigh; the minute H flounces off to dance with another partner, I'm wondering if I should change back into my street clothes because there's no way I'm going to top the jagged swirl of tipsy-boulevardiers-in-the-Bois-de-Boulogne that she and I just concocted.

Maybe what I'm getting at here is the power of metaphor: when two dancers really give themselves over to the metaphorical approach to romance that a duet provides, the duet, like any successful piece of art, seems realer than real. While the other 166 hours of my week more or less happen to me, and are the product of millions of unseen workers and wires, the two hours I spend in a silent, all-white dance studio on a Saturday feel purely willed—which, ironically, has the effect of subjugating me all the more. This nothing can feel like everything—which might account for my bursts of emotion (the blushing, the rapture) on this particular dance floor.

My favorite-ever moment from a dance class occurred at a contact class at Gibney. Our teacher, Tim O'Donnell, divided us into groups of threes. My two partners stood on either side of me. They were each to use both hands to press down firmly on my adjacent hip bone. You'd think this would render me immobile or veal me into confinement, but the overriding sensation was just the opposite—my upper torso was buoyant like a kickboard or a pool noodle that's been pressed down in the water; it seemed to pop up from the resistance. I felt wonderfully floaty. Then Tim told all us hipbone-conjoined trios to start moving across the room. The floatiness could travel! The dirigible had been untethered from the loading dock. My arms went all *Swan Lake*. Then Tim told those of us in the middle of the triads to lean back slightly and look up at the ceiling: whoa, the tethers were flapping in the wind below me now, I was somewhere between the roof of the building and the asteroid belt.

Then Tim offered his last prompt: "Do what you can't do alone!"

Now and again I wonder if I've stuck with contact improv because it causes me to interact with other movers in a way that I've never interacted with other people before. Most kinds of dance make me feel like I'm happily swimming across a pool or lake, but contact makes me feel like my partner and I are conjoined and swimming underwater in unison. About a year ago, I nerdishly asked myself which of the other seven functions of dance that I've written about in this book—besides Emotional Release and Intimacy, as I've just discussed—apply to contact. Certainly, Pure Physicality and, post-injury, Healing (which I'll write about in the next chapter). I suppose all the touching, not to mention the same-sex dancing, could fall under either Politics or Rebellion, as could the fact that I'm engaging in an activity that my medical doctor would prefer I didn't. Social Entrée, I guess, is covered by my having danced with some of the pros in the room. And maybe the jam's 1960s-ish hippie be-in vibe—shades of my beloved *Hair*—falls under Nostalgia.

But I couldn't quite place contact in the context of Religion and Spirituality. That is, until I started appreciating the beauty of the group conglomerations that tend to happen in the last ten or fifteen minutes of the jam. These are traffic jams of ten or fifteen bodies in an area suitable for six, human pileups that look like luggage retrieval gone awry, a Brueghel painting in stretch fabric. When I lift my right arm, it will cause Hector's left arm to lift, too, which will cause the right side of his torso to shift downward, where it will brush against Martha, who's balancing on Luisa, who's a Verrazano-Narrows Bridge between Kwame and Colette. Why does this make me so profoundly happy? You spend your waking life figuring out how to interact successfully with others, and here is compelling evidence that you might not be terrible at it. You spend almost all of your working life trying to pinpoint how you feel or what you think about stuff—the phoneme shared by the three words "Why I write," Joan Didion once pointed out, is *I, I, I*—but here in a tangle of bodies, none of that matters. If my fifty-five years on the planet have led me to believe anything, it's that we're usually drawn to specific people or activities because they have a lesson to teach us, but it's never the lesson we thought it was going to be. You'd think a group conglomeration would flood you with a sense of interconnectedness, or make you realize how you can support other people, or how you differ slightly from all the other participants, or how you can ward off the people you don't trust by blanketing yourself with the people that you do, or why anthropologists are always saying that the human brain is hardwired for living in small groups and knowing every group member's name. But wedged in close in a crowd of bodies, the feeling of astonishing calm I have doesn't result from having defined myself in relation to others, but rather from the fact that, for one of the first times in my life, I'm not even part of the equation. I don't have to think about whether I'm supporting others' weight or whether some newcomer is standing by bashfully waiting to be removed from his or her isolation or whether someone is going to reject me: these things are givens. Because these things exist, and because I know they exist, I don't have to pay them heed.

Never have I felt so gloriously empty.

DANCE AS HEALING

1.

LOS ANGELES, FIVE YEARS AGO. AFTER THIRTY OR SO FOLKS had left a literary salon that my friends Sandra and Frier had held in their living room, my two hosts and I moved all that room's chairs and other furniture aside, put on some Motown, and danced for an hour or so à trois. We stomped from room to room, transforming a Craftsman bungalow into an impromptu Bouncy Castle; we swung and punched our arms like a group of ebullient monkeys. At a certain point in the proceedings, Sandra unearthed a hip-length white mink coat from a closet, and then the three of us took turns wearing it while dancing. The kitteny lushness of fur against your skin could render you either a Saudi potentate embarked on an extravagant, cocaine-fueled shopping spree, or a Detroit pimp strutting through a trash-strewn barrio. The choice was yours.

Three years later I visited Sandra and Frier again. This time their union was fraught. They argued so much during dinner that on taking the last bite of food from my plate, I uncharacteristically stood, walked into the kitchen, and started doing the dishes while they continued eating and arguing. I had to escape the wall of bickering.

Fifteen minutes later, Sandra emerged from her office bearing a dance mixtape, and minutes later the three of us were grooving and shaking again in the living room and den, this time to the Commodores' funk classic "Brick House." Frier started doing a move so catchy that Sandra and I copied him: with your palm up, you extend your arm out in front of you invitingly, and then, while slowly pulling your opened palm back to your mid-side, you take five small quick steps backward, as if drawing a curtain to unveil the future.

We all started laughing.

And Sandra and Frier's bickering: gone.

Healing is one of dance's more promising and vibrant functions. Given that dance is so commonly a locus of social trauma in one's childhood and adolescence, it makes sense in a hair-of-the-dog way that boogying would be an effective form of therapy in adulthood. Moreover, of the nine functions that we've discussed, Healing is the one that most stands to give dance its proper due among the arts: humans being humans, we admire results, and I'm going to hazard that the medical and psychological advances that dance can bring are much more tangible to the world at large than, say, the latest choreographer-of-the-moment's danceography.

If we take the long view, dance's use as a form of healing probably goes back to archaic Greece. The classicist Walter Burkert has written about *orpheotelestae*, itinerant charismatics, who, as early as the fifth century BCE, traveled around Greece offering to cure both physical and mental illnesses by dancing a circle around the unwell person.

Such acts of magicking no doubt still occur in the modern world, albeit on a very limited scale. In a world wised up to the glories of penicillin and sanitation and surgery, the use of dance as a form of therapy is much more likely to be found in cases of stress or trauma or Parkinson's. In the 1990s in Christian Uganda, for instance, some of the children who were experiencing trauma as a result of having been involuntarily conscripted into the brutal guerrilla movement the Lord's Resistance Army were rehabilitated through dancing.

In the United States, dancing has been used to treat a host of conditions. Indeed, many luminaries of the dance world originally came to the art in order to overcome shyness, or to recover strength after having an illness. The shyness group includes Arthur Murray and 1930s and '40's film star and hoofer Eleanor Powell, who some consider to be rivaled in dancing talent only by Fred Astaire (unlike many tap dancers in film, including Debbie Reynolds in *Singin' in the Rain* and Ginger Rogers in all hers, Powell dubbed all her own taps). The folks who've gravitated to dance as a form of convalescence include *Singin' in the Rain* and *The Band Wagon* star Cyd Charisse (polio), Jacob's Pillow founder Ted Shawn (diphtheria), tap dancer Ann Miller (rickets), and Joffrey Ballet founder Robert Joffrey (asthma). Israeli choreographer Ohad Naharin, the artistic director of the Batsheva Dance Company, developed the idiom known as Gaga as a way to treat a back injury.

When the wounds that a dancer carries are psychological as opposed to medical, the rigors of choreographed movement are an especially powerful haven. In her history of ballet, *Apollo's Angels*, Jennifer Homans says of Lucia Chase, "After her husband's sudden death and in a state of intense grief and mourning, she took refuge in the discipline of ballet." Chase formed the company that would become American Ballet Theatre.

When Mikhail Baryshnikov was twelve, his mother hung herself, after which Baryshnikov, who'd enrolled himself in ballet school three years earlier, threw himself ever more assiduously into his work. Baryshnikov's teacher Juris Kapralis told writer Joan Acocella that, during breaks in classes, the other dancers would go into the corners of the studio and play, but "Not Misha. He is still working, practicing steps till he gets them right. Very serious boy." As Acocella put it, "He was filling, with something beautiful, the void this beautiful woman left in his life."

But the most vivid example of ballet-as-recovery is probably that of Michaela DePrince, a soloist for the Dutch National Ballet who danced in the "Hope" sequence of Beyoncé's *Lemonade*. Born in war-torn Sierra Leone in 1995, DePrince lost both her parents at age three: rebels killed her father at the diamond mine where he worked, and her mother died shortly thereafter of starvation and disease. Thought by her uncle to be a "devil child" because she had the skin depigmentation disease known as vitiligo, DePrince was sold to an orphanage, where she was abused and starved and referred to as "Number 27." When the orphanage was bombed, DePrince and some of the other orphans escaped to a refugee camp in nearby Guinea, but not before trekking past "hundreds of dead bodies . . . sprawled on the ground with their eyes and mouths open in terror." At age four, DePrince and her best friend were adopted by an American couple from New Jersey. Just before leaving for the States, DePrince found a picture of a ballerina on the cover of *Dance Magazine*; this picture became her lodestar, one of the only things "that reminded me I was alive."

She trained at the Rock School in Philadelphia and at American Ballet Theatre's Jacqueline Kennedy Onassis School. Before getting hired by the Dance Theatre of Harlem, she was the subject of a lot of discrimination: At age eight, she was told she couldn't be Marie in *The Nutcracker* because "America's not ready for a black girl ballerina." A year later, a teacher told her mother that black ballet dancers weren't worth investing in.

As DePrince puts it in *First Position*, the 2011 documentary about aspiring ballerinas, "It's a miracle I'm even here."

If the aforementioned prompt to all my own recent dancing—reducing work-related stress—feels, in comparison with these other examples, to be weak tea, I'd use stronger words to describe all this motion's combined benefit. When Greg started joining me in my living room dancing, I knew that I was a truly lucky individual in having a partner who not only indulged me in my strange new pastime, but wanted to join along. (Two summers ago we took two salsa classes together, given outdoors on a local pier, but we've found that our own living room is a better fit for us.)

Greg and I, unlike most couples, don't fight, or even bicker. We prefer to internalize and then to passively aggress; it makes for a very rich silence.

You can imagine how, as I fell under the spell of contact improv, and kept coming home with bulletins from the land of spaceship travel and the Nuance of the Pelvic Bowl, many spouses would have felt threatened. But Greg took it in stride, sometimes even incorporating into our living room shakings some of the moves I described to him. It says everything to me that, after having taken scores of classes and been to hundreds of jams and other dances, my all-time favorite move is something Greg devised: standing behind me, he puts his two palms on the small of my back, which allows me to lean backwards at a fifteen-degree angle while I dance. Just as I'm about to topple, he catches me.

You need to make frequent efforts to keep a fourteen-year-long relationship from becoming routinized or predictable, yet dancing never feels like effort. While the large majority of Greg's and my boogying is done in partial darkness and without responding to, or looking too much at, each other, it's the moments when we take each other in our arms, or lean slightly on each other, that I'll realize, This is my first sensual act of the day.

2.

I don't have the performing bug. I don't mind being watched dancing, and occasionally I even enjoy it a little, but it's not what gets my fanny into the proverbial leotard. It's no surprise that I'm a writer: I want to be the center of attention, but I'd rather not be in the room while it's happening.

That said, sometimes performing can be a helpful measuring stick, a barometer of ground gained. So when two young filmmakers in their twenties named Luke Smithers and Derek Johnson walked up to me at the Saturday contact improv jam one day and told me—without knowing that I write for several big-deal publications—they liked the way I moved and were interested in having me do contact improv in the four-minute art film they were making, a bell went off. Here was an opportunity to avenge my flameout on the morning of the *pas de deux* presentation at Peridance.

I could have stopped at the mere invitation. That two discerning, style-obsessed creative types would watch some forty-five or so people dancing and then pick me (and two others) from the crowd was wildly flattering and consoling; it was the psychological equivalent of being handed a check covering every dance class and Pilates session and massage I'd ever paid for. I don't know how to say this without sounding like an asshole, so I'll just say it: the month directly following being asked to be in the movie was Endorphin City for me. It was like having three glasses of wine at lunch and realizing THAT IT WAS GOING TO BE AN ALL-CAPS KIND OF AFTERNOON.

Once home from the jam, I went on Luke's and Derek's websites and checked out their work, which included sleek and accomplished videos made for up-and-coming fashion designers, models.com, *Fiasco* magazine, and the Zaha Hadid Foundation. More than one of their short films featured gorgeous, biracial anorectics writhing on expensive furniture. Most memorable and beautiful to behold was *The Body's Witness,* a seven-minute short in which a naked young man in his twenties emerges from darkness and encounters a naked man in his early seventies.

Did I tell Luke and Derek that I have an occasionally iffy back? I did not: I was trying to get (or keep) the (unpaid) gig. But, in the month between meeting these guys and our filming, I took every precaution: I swam a lot and went to Pilates weekly, but went to no dance classes and only one jam.

The film was to be titled *Fragile Machines,* and would be shot in suburban Sheepshead Bay, Brooklyn, in a small, darkish Airbnb house that Luke and Derek rented for the weekend. Pre-shoot, Luke kept us cast members (me and three other contact dancers, four or five young fashion models, the naked actor in his early seventies) updated by e-mail. "This piece is collaborative and will mirror a contact improvisation dance jam," he wrote early on. "We will transform the house into a world unto itself. Displaced objects (e.g., a mirror submerged in sand, an ode to earthwork artist Robert Smithson's *Leaning Mirror*) will occupy corners of the various rooms of the house that we will ask you to engage with. Over the past few weeks, Derek & I have collected prompts from the field of physical theater that will guide us on our exploration of our bodies and this alien space. From these surreal tableaus we hope to generate ruptures in the quotidian. Attached below is our moodboard, informed by the aesthetic of Matthew Barney's works and the concepts underlying Roy Andersson's films. Tony Hoagland's poem 'America,' which you can read here, is a rattling distillation of our thinking."

I admired the seriousness on display. Ruptures in the quotidian, I heard myself thinking: *hell* yeah!

The moodboard—a collage of images that fashion designers create for inspiration—was composed of five menacing photographs, including someone walking into a dark wood and a woman drowned in her living room. Between Luke's e-mail and the photos, you could tell exactly the kind of David Lynch-y noir that he and Derek were aiming for—which may help explain my utter lack of nervousness about the filming. In the weeks before the shoot, I kept scanning my body and consciousness for pools of anxiety or even the slightest tremor of uncertainty or regret, but found only excitement. Indeed, even once I'd showed up at the house for Day One of the shoot and learned that, though all the young models were being gussied up by Hair and Makeup, me and the other fifty-plus male contact dancer would receive merely a little rouge on our cheeks (I think because we were meant to look mysterious or slightly ghoulish-looking?), I didn't care. In their e-mails and conversation, Luke and Derek had been so respectful of contact improv that I wanted to help them and to meet them more than halfway. As I'd explained to a friend the day before the shoot, "I'm open to anything except a genital cuff."

Luke and Derek sometimes identify themselves as fashion film-makers, so the wardrobe for the shoot, some of it bearing the name Yves Saint Laurent, was fairly fabulous. For one dance the costumer put me in a backless, quilted fencer's shirt (it's called a lamé) over low-slung, cream-colored, wool palazzo pants. For another dance I wore mid-calf black wrestling boots, a heavy wool military-green trench coat, and underpants but no shirt or trousers: after-hours SS officer.

Sometimes Luke or Derek would give us prompts ("Slightly ro-botic, like your arms are moving of their own will"), but mostly they would put me and another dancer in front of the camera with a prop or set-piece, like an antique surgery chair or a mid-century, bungee-like chest expander, and tell us to respond to each other or to the prop.

Outside of boogying-in-the-rain-and-then-swimming-under-a-waterfall at my friend's wedding, or waxing rhapsodic during my early days as a contact dancer, I can't remember enjoying myself more while dancing. Indeed, even when it became clear, on Day Two, that my pale pale body and its waist-level bumpers would, in one scene, be shown to disadvantage in nothing but white wres-tling boots, a vintage wrestling helmet, and my underpants, I didn't blanch. I thought, Move so well that no one focuses on my flaws.

But I wasn't pure pedal to the metal. A week later, Luke would write me and ask me—in a sweet and non-pushy way—if, for the second day of shooting, I'd feel comfortable doing nudity. I thought about it and thought about it, and finally demurred. If I were in my seventies or eighties, I would have done it in a heartbeat: everyone would have thought me *so brave*. But nudity at fifty-five is more likely to elicit the reaction "Get a hobby."

Was I being intransigent? Was I putting too much emphasis on receiving credit for my actions? I couldn't tell. All I knew was, everything else that Luke and Derek had thrown at me had struck me as nutty and delightful and slightly subversive, but the nudity proposition had set off a lot of introspection. Everything I'd learned from dancing seemed to be anti-introspection. I thought back on my Twyla misstep, when I'd filmed Savannah Lowery doing my eleven seconds of *The One Hundreds*. I concluded, No. Cease and desist.

But I've buried the lead. I haven't told you about the part of the filming where I surprised myself, the part that helped re-colonize the part of my brain which, ever since the *pas* presentation at Peridance, had fixated on the thought, "I am a flight risk."

On the first day of shooting, after I'd filmed two dances with two other movers, Derek turned to me and gave a direction that we had not discussed: he told me to stand in the middle of the living room where we'd been shooting and do a solo.

If, five years ago, you'd asked me to stand in front of a group of new acquaintances and their movie camera, and then to improvise a dance of three or four minutes' duration, I would have become giggly or schticky, and maybe then, after self-effacing or self-abnegating for a bit, coughed up something tame and minimalist.

But instead, I walked to the center of the living room—I was in the after-hours SS officer wardrobe at this point, which helped—where I took a deep breath and then launched into what I would later describe to a friend as "a modern dance shitstorm." I outstretched my arms as far as possible to my sides, *relevéed* on my left foot, lifted my crooked right leg just above my navel, and held it like a dancey Jesus. I collapsed onto the floor and dragged myself forward using the palms of my hands, like I'd been abandoned in a desert and was in desperate search of nourishment. I landed two credible *arabesques*. I did three floor-based backwards somersaults. I leaned the crown of my head against the wall and then spun 360 degrees while helicoptering my arms and keeping my head wall-bound. I lay on my side on the floor and, using my right deltoid as an anchor, frantically ran 360 degrees. I *releveed* on both feet and Christ-the-Redeemered my arms again. I sunk to my knees and then heartlessly cascaded my face to the floor, breaking my fall with the palm of my hands at the last possible moment, and then did it two more times.

The room got very quiet. Even the Hair and Makeup folks, sitting on a couch some thirty feet away, were staring. I kept thrashing about, but soon, sensing that I should draw to a close, I remembered reading that in her dotage Martha Graham could still lock her knees together and then manically skitter backwards, so I did that, and followed it up with some collapsing and more somersaulting.

Soon Derek was whispering, "That's great," signaling the segment's end.

I stopped. I was drenched in sweat.

The cameraman, big-eyed, said, "That was *felt*."

3.

Here in the carpeted and brightly lit classroom of the senior center, time is playing tricks on us all. Our teacher, Karen Ritscher, dressed today in a flowing, floral smock over black leggings, is sixty-one but looks twenty years younger. The flashiest moves on the floor are being done not by one of the dancers in her sixties or seventies, but by a ruddy gentleman in his eighties who is doing knee lunges with his arms akimbo like some heavily decorated officer from the land of Gilbert and Sullivan. Meanwhile, I'm the youngest dancer but, because I danced too hard the day before, am moving as if in illustration of the term "load-bearing."

Just as I'm starting to appreciate the time warp of it all—a state enhanced by the fact that we're dancing to Elvis Presley singing "Viva Las Vegas," a song recorded when I was one year old—reality rears its head.

Karen, gently rotating her shoulders and hips in elliptical undulations, proposes to the twelve of us, "Imagine that instead of blood you have sparkling water in your veins."

The eyes of one of the male dancers—a bespectacled, hale man in a flannel shirt and jeans—widen, and he asks Karen, "Would I be permitted to use the bathroom?"

Muriel, a tiny, birdlike woman in her seventies who's dancing right next me, looks at me and says, "That's a valid question."

I'd read about the class on the 5Rhythms website: on Friday afternoons from one o'clock to two-thirty, dancers were invited to join instructor Peter Fodera for a class taught to seniors with early to mid-stage Alzheimer's.

The potential neurological benefits of listening to music are fairly widely known, thanks to various scientific studies and to documentaries like *Alive Inside*, which follows a social worker named Dan Cohen as he administers music therapy to Alzheimer's patients.

The benefits of dancing, however, have been less heralded. They received dramatic support in 2003 when the *New England Journal of Medicine* published a twenty-one-year-long study of people over the age of seventy-five. Led by the Albert Einstein College of Medicine in New York City, and funded by the National Institute on Aging, the study looked at whether certain cognitive activities (e.g., reading, doing crossword puzzles, playing cards) and certain physical activities (e.g., bicycling, swimming, dancing) offered protection against dementia.

Surprisingly, the results suggested that, while reading reduced the risk of dementia by 35 percent and doing crossword puzzles at least four times a week reduced it by 47 percent, the only one of the physical activities studied to offer protection was dancing, which, if done frequently, reduced the risk by 76 percent.

Alas, the study didn't ask the obvious follow-up question—why is dancing at 76 percent while bicycling and swimming are at 0 percent? Activities that require a lot of rapid-fire decision-making help create the multiplicity of neural pathways that will help you at age ninety to remember the name of the actress who played opposite Tom Cruise in *Top Gun* or those bugs that plague the gardener in June. Surely, swimming and biking require a lot of split-second decision-making, so why does dancing score so much higher?

It's possible that it has something to do with dancing's integrative nature. Dancing can utilize several brain functions at once—emotional, logical, kinesthetic, musical—the combined forces of which may be especially potent.

In 2017, a six-month-long study published by researchers at the University of Illinois in Urbana made a similar discovery. Subjects in their sixties and seventies were asked to meet three times a week for an hour either to do a lot of brisk walking, stretching, or country dancing with choreography. While all the subjects showed some deterioration of their brains' white matter, only the dancers emerged with denser white matter in their fornix, a part of the brain connected to processing speed and memory.

So, if we're hoping to be neurally spectacular ninety-year-olds, maybe we should learn to simultaneously chew gum, jump rope, and cry to Beethoven's Fifth?

It's easier to take up dancing.

The first portion of our Friday afternoon dance parties saw us sitting around a makeshift conference table and chatting for ten or fifteen minutes. These bull sessions were led by Sandy, a sharp, energetic sixty-something liaison from the senior center who kept tabs on various members of the group, about twelve of whom would show up on any given Friday. Many of the seniors came to the class with a minder such as an aide, a sister, a spouse; I tended to be the only 5Rhythms dancer present, other than the three instructors, who took turns teaching.

For those who've not yet hung out with a group of our nation's 5.5 million Alzheimer's patients (one half of our nursing home residents), I would describe the experience thusly: it's a lot like spending time with teenagers. A typical Friday might start off as follows: while Sandy tries to engage us all in a conversation about, say, the subway, two of the seniors sitting at the conference table will be holding a private conversation about the coffee machine; two are dreamily staring out the window; one is getting up to retrieve something from her coat; and one thinks that we're talking about Subway, the factory outlet store of the sandwich industry.

As with teenagers, it's not difficult to get the group to rally around an opinion or to wax enthusiastic about a topic like, say, the color of Amanda's coat, or the restorative qualities of a well-cooked brisket. What's difficult is *maintaining* this enthusiasm. These folks' moods shift and dissipate like the weather in Ireland.

The conference-table conversations were a good way to glean information about the group—I learned early on that at least four of my fellow dancers had grown up in the Bronx; two were former lawyers, and one a former judge. One told me she had given up her therapy practice only a week ago: "I couldn't remember what their problems were," she told me.

One of the stars of the conversation portion of the session was a twinkly eyed, philosophical man, Bennett (I've changed the names of all the dancers in this section). At the first class, Bennett told me he was ninety-two, but by the second class he had demoted himself to ninety. I said to him, "I thought you were ninety-two. Last week you said you were ninety-two."

"I am," he admitted. "But ninety-two sounds vainglorious."

Bennett was always a good go-to when Sandy wanted to get a response from someone in the group. Once, for instance, while talking about courtship and marriage, Sandy handed the conversational baton to Bennett, who nimbly chimed in, "I've been married since 1944."

Sandy asked, "Is she the love of your life?"

"No, she's the essence of my life. There's a difference."

"What's the difference?"

"A love might be unrequited. Or it might be episodic. Essence is everyday."

I loved listening to Bennett. "The body is an interesting accumulation of events," he told me one day. At another class he opined, "We all walk around telling our stories, but with a piece missing that governs us. That piece is in our heart."

I tried not to be an elder-gawker. It was tempting, particularly during the bull sessions, to stare or diagnose or strap on a proverbial pith helmet. But I didn't want to get into that mindset. In the absence of any direction or specific guidelines from the 5Rhythms folks regarding what I was meant to do in the class other than move my body to music, I'd read a little about Alzheimer's before showing up the first time. The average life expectancy after diagnosis is eight to ten years. Short-term memory is lost in the early stage of the disease, and long-term memory in the moderate stage. Common moderate-stage symptoms include irritability, wandering, and an emotional incontinence that can lead to crying jags, unpremeditated aggression, and a resistance to caregiving.

In my first visits to the group, I saw very few of these moderate-stage symptoms. This would change.

* * *

But we came here to dance, no? So let's get up from the table and saunter over to the circle of chairs.

First we're going to sit and do some relaxation exercises to some gentle music like Ella Fitzgerald or Peggy Lee. Then we'll put some slightly more lively music on—hello, Mr. Presley, hello, shaggy Southern Californian brothers answering to Brian and Dennis—and start lifting our arms and legs into the air. Then we'll stand and dance—sometimes partnered, but mostly solo—in the fifteen-foot circle described by the chairs. Then we'll sit again, and play a follow-the-leader game in which someone initiates a gesture in time to the music and everyone duplicates it. Then we'll do a final relaxation exercise, possibly to classical music, or to something slow, like Nat King Cole singing "Smile."

With the exception of contact improv, this Stein Center dancing was probably the most intimate kind of dancing I've done. Our movements were confined to the fifteen-foot lagoon in the middle of the chairs; we were dancing during the day in a classroom, and engaging in a lot of eye contact; we'd all made some polite conversation and gotten to know each other a bit before busting out our moves. It would have been hard to hide.

Asked to reintroduce myself during the conversation portion of the third class, I told the group, "Hi, I'm Henry. You may remember my dazzling dance moves from the last two weeks." Sandy smiled and said, "You're already one of us."

The following week, Sandy greeted me with "Our dancer is back!" She looked around the table and continued, "You all remember Henry, whose comments about his dancing made us laugh. That's why we liked him—he laughed at himself. And the thing is, he's not a bad dancer."

Another interesting thing happened that day. The best male dancer in the group was the energetic, ruggedly handsome Tony G. Tony G. was also the person in the group with the most advanced Alzheimer's, sometimes requiring the ministrations of his wife, who sat on the sidelines of the dance floor with the other minders. He had nice, square shoulders and was given to wearing flannel shirts; he looked like the kind of grandfather who'd school you on fly-fishing and bourbon.

At one point that day, he started dancing toward me, throwing both his arms in front of himself vigorously as if batting smoke. Staring at me, he puffed out his cheeks—anger? mock anger?—and implored me, "Don't take my women away!"

It seemed too early to drop the gay bomb on him, so I opted instead to act as I'd seen Sandy and the three instructors act when faced with such outbursts: look at the dancer in the eyes and calmly inform him that, no, darling, we don't put the teakettle on the cat.

So I outstretched my hands and then shrugged my shoulders, sheepishly owning up to my powerlessness in the face of my devastating man-musk.

Two themes started to emerge. The first was my initial reluctance to initiate partnering. Though I was happy to let someone else grab my hand or to be included in any group-wide exercise that involved touching, I was initially reluctant, despite all my other dancing, to take anyone's hand or to encourage someone to get out of her chair if she was being a wallflower. It felt invasive to me, given all the mild dementia in the room. I was, for the more impaired members of the group, a total stranger each time I showed up. I didn't want to scare the horses.

But then I started to feel guilty about not taking more initiative. I'd decided early on that my role at these sessions was (a) to have fun and (b) to make an ass of myself so as to encourage anyone shy to come out of his or her shell. I'd also decided that I shouldn't do any dance steps that the seniors wouldn't be able to muster themselves, as that might seem show-offy.

But as for initiating partnering: I wanted to be that person, but

I was having trouble removing him from the packing crate. One thing that helped here was reading in *Dance Magazine*'s "Why I Dance" column about David Dorfman, the choreographer who is chairman of Connecticut College's dance department. His mother had MS. "I danced, at times frantically, to encourage her to take a step," Dorfman wrote. "Once after seeing me dance, she walked a few relatively pain-free paces before her body remembered she couldn't."

My failure was overcome in the fifth class. We were all seated, listening to some jazzy Tommy Dorsey while playing the pass-the-gesture game. The leadership had been passed to a gentleman who started gently punching the air, first with his right fist, then with his left.

Suddenly, the wiry and roiling Tony G., seated next to the air-puncher, jumped up and started dancing all alone in the circle. There were a few titters from the group—We're supposed to be in our chairs now, you could hear people thinking—when Tony G. abruptly turned toward me, grabbed my hand, and pulled me into the circle. We did about twenty seconds of shaking and shimmying at each other, at which point he grabbed my hands and lifted them up in the air as we both proceeded to twirl 360 degrees, as if jitterbugging.

There's a moment in any new dance endeavor when you finally let go. At first you're looking for the big, dry stones in the riverbed that will take your body weight and allow you to skitter to the other side; once you know where the rocks are, and are returning back to the riverbank, you can stop worrying about how icy cold that water is.

The second that Tony G. grabbed me and pulled me into the circle, I fully expected to feel the group's eyes bore into me and cause me to stumble. Tony G.'s confidence and verve and good looks—did I mention that he looks like someone who'd play Tony Goldwyn's father?—dissolved all that. He was driving the car, and it was a beauty.

At one point, Tony G. and I, hands held, started very gently rocking back and forth, and I could see relaxation pass over him like clouds on a TV weather map. Our mutual shoulders were lowered.

No wonder the Shakers had cribs in which to rock the elderly.

The other theme that emerged was the cultural dissonance to be found at the intersection of the earthy, occasionally wiseacre old-timers and the airy-fairy 5Rhythms folks.

One of the seniors, for instance, was a bit of a lech. One afternoon when Karen instructed us to "Let everything loose," the lech started unbuckling his belt. "Noooooo!" the group chorused in a slightly tired way that suggested they'd seen this action many a time.

At the end of another class, one of the seniors in the group asked a 5Rhythms guest—a jolly, zaftig, forty-something dance instructor from London interested in dance therapy—"Were we what you thought we were going to be?"

The guest smiled brightly and said, "You far exceeded it."

"How so?"

"Well, you're livelier, more passionate, more interesting, warmer, funnier, kinder . . ."

One of the men interrupted her with ". . . Dirtier?"

The guest blinked her eyes and said, "Well, I don't know about that." Tight smile. Giggles from onlookers.

Indeed, the seniors brought a lot of earthy realism to the table. In the first class held after New Year's of 2015, an instructor named Jason Goodman starting waxing cosmic about man's steadfastness in the face of time. He told the group, "Think of all the New Year's that you guys have lived through. [Bennett], you're just as handsome and smart and witty as you always were."

"Well," Bennett pointed out, "I changed my underwear."

Another time, Peter, the 5Rhythms instructor who'd started the Friday afternoon dancing at the senior center four years prior, instructed us, "Focus on your breath." Our movements slowed slightly as we all tried to home in on the passage of air in our lungs, imagining the fern-like tendrils of oxygen curling and uncurling in our inner sanctums. Meanwhile, Bennett counseled us, "If you're not breathing, lie down on the floor."

But my favorite interaction at the intersection of the two cultures occurred when Karen asked Leonard one day if he wanted to join in the pass-the-gesture game. Leonard was a tall, gaunt, Abraham Lincoln–ish man who, in the ten classes I'd seen him in, had not only never danced, but had spent most of the time staring sullenly at the floor. As with the other gentleman in the class who rarely participated, you got the sense that Leonard had been brought there at the insistence of an optimistic family member or doctor in the hope that social interaction might induce some alteration to his perma-funk. That Leonard's resting face was that of a scowl only underlined his remove from the outer world—while all the senior dancers seemed to be receiving radio waves from a station that the rest of humanity couldn't, Leonard also received these radio waves, but they only made him angry.

So, called upon by Karen, Leonard outstretched his arms in front of him and proceeded to swirl them in a gentle, octopoidal tangle that was so graceful and lovely and unexpected that several of us gasped.

After we'd watched this gorgeous swirl for a bit, Karen quietly urged him, "[Leonard], when you're ready, pass it along."

Leonard swiveled his head toward Karen and, while still smoothly gliding his arms in front of him and maintaining his gaze at her, slowly extended the middle finger of his right hand.

The woman sitting next to me let out a little moan; a few others tittered nervously. But Leonard kept his finger extended until he'd finished his contribution.

* * *

About five months into my visits, one of the men greeted me one day by arching his eyebrows and saying, "You weren't here last week!"

"You're right," I told him. "I promise I wasn't dancing with another senior center."

"Faithful is good, faithful is good."

The more I danced with the group, the more the emotional stakes were raised—because the more I was witness to dementia's inexorable march. One afternoon eight months in, we were all sitting at the conference table talking about snack foods. Bennett mentioned his mother, Florence. Sandy said, "Florence is your wife!"

"But also my mother."

"Two Florences? That seems like an awful lot."

"My mother was also Florence."

"No, if they were both named Florence, we would have heard about this by now."

Bennett looked down at the table, slightly embarrassed.

"You're right. My mother was Theresa."

But, obviously, the more I danced with the group, the more joyful moments I witnessed, too. At one class the final song was an acoustic version of "Over the Rainbow." I was sitting next to Erica, a newish recruit to the group who had a lot of restless energy. Erica had a difficult time following any direction or playing the pass-the-gesture game, preferring instead to snap her fingers; if you danced up to her on the floor, she'd look down at the carpet and keep on finger-snapping.

The music had a calming effect on her: her fidgeting subsided, and she stopped surveilling the corners of the room as if waiting for a friend to show up. As the song played on, her eyes started to well, and she sang along, as a few of us had started to do. When the music ended, she threw her arms around me and hugged me.

I'd had the hardest time coming here because I didn't want to feel pity for people who certainly wouldn't want that. With Erica's arms around me, however, I found myself enjoying the moment much more than I would have thought I could.

But it took me seven months with the group to see that I didn't keep returning to the class for this kind of moment. No, the moment that kept pulling me back was the one when dragged-into-duty Leonard had given Karen the finger. I couldn't shake that image from my consciousness—not because it was darkly comic and odd and I'd told all my friends about it, but because it seemed like a monument of something. A monument of having a fuck left to give.

The winter proved especially hard for the group, and the ranks temporarily thinned. A wonderful Caribbean woman we'd all loved dancing with had sustained a knee injury at home. Another dancer got an infection while traveling. Tony G. slipped on the ice and fell backward and hit his head.

We wondered if we'd see any of them again. The lessened energy in the room was palpable; it was hard, while shimmying to some burbling Frank Sinatra number, not to think about the missing members and wonder how they spent their Fridays now.

One Friday at the end of March, nine of us had just seated ourselves in the chairs on the dance floor at the beginning of class when I noticed two of the women smile and start rustling in their seats. I followed their line of vision and saw that Tony G. had finally returned after a few months' absence, his wife in tow. His senatorial good looks were still there, but now the bug-eyed expression that had been an occasional feature on the landscape of his face was a permanent one. Gone.

The music swelled, and we started dancing. All of Tony G's coiled energy was still in evidence, but he seemed to be looking through people rather than at them. At one point he wandered outside the circle of chairs, whereupon Jason, who was teaching that day, gently guided him back into the circle.

A few minutes later, Tony G. fell. He'd sat down for a spell during the dancing, and when he started to stand, he collapsed forward onto his knees and cried out, "I'm a baby!"

He wasn't hurt, but his wife flew over to him, and she and Jason nimbly helped him up while his eyes darted all around him as if in search of someone who might have pushed him.

Falling down was a very rare thing with the group—I'd only seen one person stumble, but not fall entirely. It took us all a song or two to regain our momentum.

Twenty minutes after his fall, Tony G., back in the fray on the dance floor, was wandering around the circle distractedly. When our gazes crossed, his eyes and nostrils flared.

I reached out and took both his hands. I ever so slowly lifted the fist sandwich of my right hand and his left hand up to the level of our shoulders; then, as we lowered these hands, we lifted our other ones at the same glacial pace.

Tony G. smiled wolfishly, so I decided to add legs: as we arched our arms up into the air, we'd accompany them with the corresponding leg, which we could both get to almost knee height.

I noticed a few of the other dancers staring at us admiringly.

After Tony G. and I had done six or seven arm-and-leg lifts, he let go of my left hand and proceeded to twirl 180 degrees. At the end of his twirl, I became aware of the fact that I was taking in the rear view of Tony's still-stylish haircut, and I remembered the Einstein quote about an infinitely powerful telescope showing the viewer the back of his own head.

Tony G. twirled around to face me and we continued our dance.

Maybe we should try to do slo-mo for the rest of the class, I thought. Maybe we can slow down time.

EPILOGUE

I WAS AT A GLITTERY MANHATTAN PARTY, THE KIND WHERE you find yourself thinking, So *that's* what a cable news anchor looks like when devouring an onion puff. Lurking among the hordes was a bright-eyed young balletomane acquaintance of mine, who, to greet me, elegantly stretched her neck to the left and right of my face like a cat smearing a branch with its scent glands.

She asked what I'd been up to, and I told her that I'd been doing a lot of contact improv and ecstatic dancing, and, indeed, had just finished writing a book about same.

She nodded her head. "Is the book . . ." she started to ask, a look of pained exhaustion passing over her face, as if we were talking about knee surgery, or about how so many male rock-and-roll vocalists, when singing, sound like they're trying to open a jar.

". . . *funny?*" she finished her question.

In the heat of the moment, I chalked up her air of disdain to her Yankee air of overly practical unflappability—Oh God, you're not going to try to do jokes, are you, how *unattractive.*

But on further reflection, it struck me that what had fueled her faint displeasure was less flintiness or snobbery than our friends, the

Functions. Were we able, in the manner of lab coat–wearing neuro-scientists, accurately to pinpoint and analyze what forces draw this woman to the world of ballet, I imagine we'd find that 70 percent of her MO is bound up in a quest for prestige. And why not? People in the ballet world are engaged in a five-hundred-plus-year-long struggle to maintain something exquisite and endangered, and if you can't feel a little proud about such a mission, then why live?

I'd attribute the other 30 percent of her interest in ballet to a desire to meet and mingle with VIPs and chic people. Again, totally legit and understandable—recently I walked through a crowded lobby of a ballet's intermission and enjoyed thinking, I bet Famous Actress over there is complaining to Famous Architect about the rapidly decaying patio he built her.

But neither of these quantities are ones that get me up to Lincoln Center these days—or to a jam or a Broadway show or the sticky and pockmarked nether regions of a grubby little dive bar in Baltimore.

As if the fact that the world of dance is composed of lots of little tribes weren't enough to subdivide all us dance lovers, here come those nasty functions to push us further into our own pens. Sure, ask a dancer or dance enthusiast about an idiom that is not his or her preferred one, and that person will blithely tell you "All movement is movement." But out on the street, you hear a different tune. The twerkers sometimes look askance at the bunheads; ain't nobody in the ballroom or hip-hop circuits gonna indulge me in my lamentations about the rigors of Zumba.

So, too, with the functions—a person drawn to dance as a form of rebellion might have very little truck with, or knowledge of, dance as a medium of religion or social entrée; people who like to watch feats of dancerly derring-do sometimes as dancers themselves radiate derring-don't.

On the bright side, however, the fact that dance serves so many gods—the fact that it is so eminently porous and adaptable—means that there are a million entry points for those of us drawn into its orbit. And who's to say that obsessing over the fantasy dance sequences on *My Crazy Ex-Girlfriend* is any more or any less valid than, say, driving your nephew's color guard squad to St. Louis, or devoting all your free hours to learning how to samba?

I hope my odyssey as recounted in these pages reflects this. Certainly it reflects the idea that what dance provides you, or what it means to you, is always shifting—if it helped me to ease into my sexual orientation in my twenties and to reduce work-related stress in my forties, for the past three years it's been my Saturday playdate. (I recently found myself telling an acquaintance, "I dance on the weekends. I'm a 'gentleman dancer'—which is not code for 'Edwardian male prostitute.'")

Now that I've written this book, dance is increasingly an excuse to travel, or to pause while traveling. Greg and I have thrilled to flamenco in Spain, tap dancing in western Massachusetts, and ballet in Miami. I've done ecstatic dancing or contact improv in Boulder, Seattle, Oberlin, Ohio, and Portland, Oregon; in a park under the Brooklyn Bridge, and in a parish hall three blocks from the Supreme Court. Am I turning into one of those perpetually tanned, artsy-fartsy women who wear six hundred silver bracelets and are always talking about their house in Santa Fe? Yes. By day. By night I am a wizened eighty-year-old shut-in who wants nothing more than to soak in a hot bath of Epsom salts and then put an ice pack all up in his "area."

Sometimes people ask me if I'm a better dancer as a result of all the dancing I've described in this book. It is both hilarious and ironic to me that, the last two times I did contact improv prior to sitting down to write this epilogue, I was given corrections by partners, a rarity among social dancers, particularly ones who aren't beginners. (One partner exhorted me to "Breathe!" and another said of my ham-handed attempts to lift her, "Less grabbing, please.") Apparently being a more confident dancer doesn't make you a better one, it just makes you a more vivid one.

In the end, maybe *how* we dance is just as important as *why*—how passionately, how often, how unguardedly. How, it seems, can topple why. Which takes me back to the beginning: three hours after I interviewed the Stanford dance historian Richard Powers about the benefits of social dancing, I went to watch him deejay a totally delightful weekly social dance called Friday Night Waltz. Held in the ballroom of the First United Methodist Church in downtown Palo Alto, Friday Night Waltz weekly draws hundreds of Bay Area folks for waltzes, polkas, and mazurkas. The crowd is diverse: I talked to shy Stanford students, charming Silicon Valley geeks, ebullient local longhairs, a cheery twelve-year-old girl wearing a lot of purple, an elderly Asian woman. One eighty-five-year-old participant—a former Hewlett-Packard engineer named Barry Lewis—had driven three hours for the event. When I asked him what attracts him to dancing, he explained, "It was either this or join a motorcycle gang."

The mood in the room was joyous; to see a gathering of people slough off the worries of the workweek is to witness a much lovelier and gentler version of the body-morphing segment of a superhero movie.

I thought that all the good vibes on display could not be beat. But, around 10:30 p.m., as I was saying my goodbyes, I saw something—or, actually three somethings—that delighted me even more than all the bonhomie swirling around the dance floor. I stumbled onto them by accident when, exiting the ballroom and moving into the vestibule, I turned my head to look down the hallway. They were there, leaning against the wall, nestled amid all the other accoutrements—bags, water bottles, knapsacks—that you'd expect to see at a dance.

Two pairs of crutches and a wheelchair.

ACKNOWLEDGMENTS

HUGE THANKS TO MY EDITOR, KARYN MARCUS, AND TO JON KARP and David McCormick. This book would not exist without you three.

Any mistakes or faults herein are my own, but thanks to people who commented on early drafts: Jess Taylor, Greg Villepique, Jenny Weisberg, Ann Earley.

Molto molto grazie, Laura Marmor, Stuart Emmrich, Aimee Bell, Robin Goldwasser, Stephen Williams at Noho Pilates, Rob Spillman, Norton Owen at Jacob's Pillow, Camilla Ha, JP Eltorai, Elisa Rivlin, and all the folks at Simon & Schuster, especially Anduriña Panezo, Rick Willett, Martha Schwartz, Julia Prosser, and Elizabeth Breeden.

I'm honored to have taken classes with, and danced with, Elise Knudson. And thanks to all my indulgent contact improv dance partners and colleagues, including Lucy Mahler, Tamar Kipnis, Gabrielle Revlock, and Emily Moore.

But my biggest thanks, of course, go to Greg. I literally couldn't have done it without you.

I lost two great ladies during the writing of this book. Rest in peace, Jocelyn Easton Alford and Susan Leroy Merrill. I miss you madly.

ABOUT THE AUTHOR

HENRY ALFORD has contributed to the *New York Times, Vanity Fair,* and the *New Yorker* for two decades. His books include *How to Live* and *Big Kiss,* which won a Thurber Prize for American Humor.